KEY STAGE TWO
SCOTTISH LEVELS C-E

# INFORMATION TECHNOLOGY

**ROB CROMPTON AND PHILIP MANN**

Published by Scholastic Ltd,
Villiers House,
Clarendon Avenue,
Leamington Spa,
Warwickshire CV32 5PR
Text © Philip Mann
© 1998 Scholastic Ltd
1 2 3 4 5 6 7 8 9 0   8 9 0 1 2 3 4 5 6 7

**AUTHOR**
PHILIP MANN

**EDITOR**
LORNA GILBERT

**ASSISTANT EDITOR**
JOEL LANE

**SERIES DESIGNER**
LYNNE JOESBURY

**DESIGNER**
ANNA OLIWA

**ILLUSTRATIONS**
PETER STEVENSON

**COVER ILLUSTRATION**
JONATHAN BENTLEY

**SCOTTISH 5–14 LINKS**
MARGARET SCOTT AND SUSAN GOW

Designed using Adobe Pagemaker

British Library Cataloguing-in-Publication Data
A catalogue record for this book is available from the
British Library.

ISBN 0-590-53783-0

# Contents

# Introduction

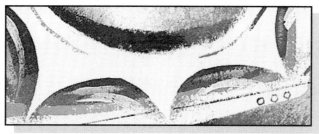

*Scholastic Curriculum Bank* is a series for all primary teachers, providing an essential planning tool for devising comprehensive schemes of work as well as an easily accessible and varied bank of practical, classroom-tested activities with photocopiable resources.

Designed to help planning for and implementation of progression, differentiation and assessment, *Scholastic Curriculum Bank* offers a structured range of stimulating activities with clearly stated learning objectives that reflect the programmes of study, and detailed lesson plans that allow busy teachers to put ideas into practice with the minimum amount of preparation time. The photocopiable sheets that accompany many of the activities provide ways of integrating purposeful application of knowledge and skills, differentiation, assessment and record-keeping.

Opportunities for formative assessment are highlighted within the activities where appropriate, while separate summative assessment activities give guidelines for analysis and subsequent action. Ways of using information technology for different purposes and in different contexts, as a tool for communicating and handling information and as a means of investigating, are integrated into the activities where appropriate, and more explicit guidance is provided at the end of the book.

The series covers all the primary curriculum subjects, with separate books for Key Stages 1 and 2 or Scottish Levels A–B and C–E. It can be used as a flexible resource with any scheme, to fulfil National Curriculum and Scottish 5–14 requirements and to provide children with a variety of different learning experiences that will lead to effective acquisition of skills and knowledge.

INFORMATION
TECHNOLOGY

## SCHOLASTIC CURRICULUM BANK: INFORMATION TECHNOLOGY

The *Scholastic Curriculum Bank: Information Technology* books help teachers to plan a comprehensive and structured coverage of the primary IT curriculum and help pupils to develop the required skills, knowledge and understanding through activities that are usually linked to other curriculum areas. There is one book for Key Stage 1/Scottish Levels A–B and one for Key Stage 2/Scottish Levels C–E.

### Bank of activities

Each book provides a range of activities that can be used in several different ways – to form a framework for a scheme of work; to add breadth and variety to an existing scheme or to supplement a particular subject activity. The activities are designed to be carried out in order, so that children develop IT skills progressively within a variety of curriculum contexts. The teaching of information technology is meant to support all curriculum subjects (apart from PE), and the majority of the activities have a strong subject context.

The IT skills developed in these activities will support work in a wide variety of subjects; cross-curricular links are outlined in the Overview Grid on pages 9–12. While children are using IT within the activities, they will be developing IT skills, knowledge and understanding. Some activities will develop their IT capability more efficiently than others. Teachers will need to be clear as to what particular IT skills can be developed through the various activities.

### Discussion and demonstration

Part of the development of children's IT capability is their understanding of how IT is used in the outside world. Most of these activities have larger-scale applications in commerce or industry, and children need to be aware of this. Increasingly, IT systems around us are becoming so much a normal part of life that often we need to awaken children to their existence (the bar-code reader at the supermarket checkout, for example). Teachers need to ensure that children are aware of how their particular use of IT reflects similar activities beyond the classroom.

### The nature of information technology

Through the wide range of activities that IT can be used for, children should realise how versatile a tool it is. IT can always offer quality output, although it may be some time before the children can achieve this. As with other curriculum areas, showing children examples of what can be achieved is helpful in the setting of standards. Children need to become skilled in the use of IT as a tool, and quality output will only follow the development of their IT skills.

Finally, children must come to realise that sometimes, technology will fail and let them down. This is bound to bring disappointment, but is part of the nature of the subject. We can learn to minimise the damage done by sudden failure (saving before printing, regular saving of files to back up our work), but we must never rely totally on this form of technology. There are many examples in the outside world where IT failure has caused undesirable results. This will also be reflected in your classroom from time to time!

### Health and safety

There are EC regulations and guidelines for those who work with computers. However, it is unlikely that your children will be sitting in front of a computer for very long periods of time. Within the classroom context, there are a number of health and safety points you should follow:
▲ metal computer trolleys must be earthed;
▲ a computer should not be linked to the mains through a four-way extension lead beyond the computer trolley;
▲ children should not be responsible for plugging in electrical equipment.
These following points are recommended:
▲ adequate seating for your children so that their eyes are at the same level as the top of the monitor and their hands reach the keyboard comfortably;
▲ the monitor is not facing a window or source of bright light so causing uncomfortable glare or reflections;
▲ adequate space available around the computer for uncluttered mouse movements;
▲ the use of a mouse mat;
▲ all equipment is cleaned regularly; static electricity attracts dust particles and the equipment can become dirty very quickly, especially the monitor screen.

### Lesson plans

Detailed lesson plans, under clear headings, are given for each activity and provide material for implementation in the classroom. The structure is as follows:
#### Activity title box
The information contained in the box at the beginning of each activity outlines the following key aspects:
▲ *Activity title and learning objective:* For each activity, a clearly-stated learning objective is given in bold italics. These learning objectives break down aspects of the programme of study into manageable teaching and learning chunks, and their purpose is to help teachers plan for progression. These objectives can be linked to the National Curriculum and Scottish 5–14 requirements by referring to the overview grid on pages 9–12. (The grid shows key areas of the PoS for each activity; but you will find that each activity covers numerous other aspects of the IT curriculum. Links to other subjects are also indicated.)
▲ *Class organisation/Likely duration:* the icons ♦♦ and ⏱ signpost the suggested group size for each activity and the approximate amount of time required to complete it. Time required at the computer is indicated separately to time

required for discussion/demonstration. Some activities are written to cover two or three sessions; you may also choose to extend other activities into more than one session.

### Previous skills/knowledge needed

This section indicates when it is necessary for the children to have acquired specific knowledge or skills prior to carrying out the activity. Other activities from the book that would provide suitable background experience are also suggested.

### Key background information

The information in this section is intended to help the teacher to understand the IT concepts and ideas covered in each activity. It generally goes beyond the level of understanding of most children, but will help to give the teacher confidence to ask and answer questions and to guide the children in their investigations.

### Vocabulary

This section gives the key IT vocabulary which occurs naturally in the context of an activity. It also includes vocabulary for other subjects where appropriate.

### Preparation

This section gives advice on any preparations needed for the activity. Details on setting up specific IT software or equipment are included as necessary.

### Resources needed

All of the materials needed to carry out the activity are listed so that the teacher, or the pupils, can gather them together before the beginning of the teaching session. For many of the activities, a colour printer is preferable; but where it is essential, it is indicated in this section.

### What to do

This section gives clear instructions, including suggestions for questions and discussion. It also highlights any problems that might arise and suggests how to solve them.

### Suggestions(s) for extension/support

This section suggests ways of providing differentiation within the activity. In all cases, suggestions are provided as to how each activity can be modified for the less able or extended for the more able.

### Assessment opportunities

Where appropriate, opportunities for formative assessment

of the children's work, either during or after a specific activity, are highlighted.

### Display ideas

Where appropriate, relevant and innovative display ideas are suggested and illustrated with examples.

### Reference to photocopiable sheets

Where activities include photocopiable activity sheets, small reproductions of these are included in the lesson plans, together with notes on how they should be used. In order to avoid unnecessary repetition, sheets which are intended for use with more than one activity are only shown once.

## Photocopiable sheets

Many of the activities are supported by photocopiable sheets for the teacher or children to use. Some of the sheets can be used with several activities.

## Software information

The software grid on pages 158-159 shows which particular software packages might be appropriate to use with each activity. The sources of these software packages are listed on page 160.

## INFORMATION TECHNOLOGY AT KEY STAGES 1 AND 2

### Expectations in IT

There is a sense in which IT is not a subject in its own right, although, of course, it is recognised as a separate subject within the National Curriculum. The challenge for schools is to identify the relationship between IT and the other subject areas. The activities suggested in this book should not be seen in isolation but should always be carried out in the context of a particular subject. There is a requirement in each of the National Curriculum orders, except in PE, that IT must support children's learning. In terms of management, therefore, IT is best planned through subjects and moderated and evaluated using the IT Programme of Study and Level Descriptions.

### The nature of IT

IT can be considered as a tool to support the development of knowledge and understanding of other subjects and, like any tool, it requires progressive acquisition of skills. Unlike other subjects with a long tradition in education, there is no generally accepted hierarchy of skill development within IT. However, some progression can be identified, and certain fundamental skills are recognised as a necessary base for further development. These ideas of progression have been incorporated into the sequence of activities in each chapter of this book. The activities should thus be undertaken in more or less the order in which they appear.

## Classroom organisation and management

Throughout this book, it is assumed that access to computers is one per class, and therefore the activities will normally be completed over a period of days rather than within a single lesson. This, of course, has implications for classroom management in terms of organising a rota and monitoring children's time on the computer. Many of the activities start with a teacher demonstration. Depending on the size of the computer monitor, these initial discussions may be with the whole class or with smaller groups. This initial introduction provides useful opportunities for the teaching of IT skills and is an efficient use of curriculum time. After the context has been established and the tasks have been set, the children will normally carry out the activity in pairs or small groups.

The nature of IT is such that children are usually focused on the task in hand, but within a busy classroom you may need to establish a formal system of monitoring to ensure that all children complete the task within the agreed time.

Inevitably, while children are involved in IT activities, they may be missing out on other aspects of the curriculum. This is unavoidable, but through careful organisation of the pupil rota these effects should be minimised. Strategies should be considered to increase children's time on the computer. For example, children may be able to use a computer in another classroom which is currently not in use – perhaps during a PE lesson or class visit. In addition to reducing the time for all children to complete the task, this provides opportunities for the development of independent learning skills.

An essential part of good classroom management is the provision of a well-ordered and clean computer workstation. Of course, the children can be involved in maintaining the computer area. Indeed, some teachers appoint 'IT consultants' who provide first-call practical support for simple technical problems and general help for the less confident children.

## Monitoring and assessment

It is important that all children have equal access to the variety of IT activities required by the programme of study. A useful way of monitoring in the classroom is to involve children in the process. For example, for each activity provide a sheet posted beside the workstation on which children enter the date and period of time spent on the computer. You may prefer to use a booklet for this purpose. At a glance, you can see which children have had access to the computer and for how long.

There is a wider level of monitoring, as seen in the school's yearly or termly curriculum overview. Within this there should be seen opportunities to offer children the full range of IT activities. You need to ensure that the activities you plan into your curriculum reflect the expectations laid out in the long-term planning.

Careful monitoring provides information for assessment. Many of the activities in this book identify opportunities for gathering this. Whereas the assessment of the children's finished product after an activity is relatively straightforward, assessing the process of making it is more complex.

If children maintain individual records of achievement, these provide a useful basis for focused discussion from which the level of their knowledge and understanding can be established. At appropriate points, the level descriptions for IT can then be used to judge the 'best fit' for each child. This process is essential in ensuring progression. Together with day-to-day informal assessment, this can feed into subsequent class and whole-school planning.

## IT at home

The pace of change in IT gives rise to particular challenges. Unlike other subjects in the National Curriculum, the rapid development of IT is having a huge impact on most aspects of everyday life. The increase in the number of home computers has important implications for education. Many children have a high level of technical skill, and sometimes teachers feel they are not able to capitalise on this. However, teachers have an important role in (a) making sure that children's knowledge and understanding is extended, and (b) exploiting such expertise for the benefit of other children.

The skills that children have are often highly software-specific, and it is important to ensure their range of expertise is extended. Where children are used as classroom 'IT consultants', they need careful induction into the role to ensure that the support they provide enables less confident children to develop their own independent skills.

## Resources

The activities within this book have been designed around the computers and software commonly found in schools. Most of them require only a basic hardware system. None of the activities are dependent on any specific computer system. In order to rationalise the management of IT across the curriculum, a small and carefully selected 'toolbox' of programs is recommended. This enables teachers to develop an in-depth knowledge of particular software and helps children to progress smoothly within a familiar software context.

Overview grid

| Learning objective | Title | PoS/AO | Subject links | Content/type of activity | Page |
|---|---|---|---|---|---|
| **Chapter 1: Communicating information** | | | | | |
| To learn and practise using the deletion and insertion facilities in word processing software. | Add an adjective | 1.1a; 1.2a/ Level A, B | English 3.1a; 3.2a. Reading 2.2b. | Pairs insert appropriate adjectives in a piece of preloaded descriptive work. | 14 |
| To practise the insertion and deletion of text on screen and become familiar with the use of shift key(s) by correcting pre-loaded text. To use a computer for a real purpose. To print out corrected text. | Spot the mistakes! | 1.1a; 1.2a/ Level B, C | English 3.1a; 3.2a. | Pairs work on a piece of preloaded text, correcting errors within the text. | 15 |
| To practise altering text on screen using deletion and insertion and re-drafting text. | Editing challenge | 1.1a; 1.2a/ Level C | English 3.1b; 3.1c; 3.2b. | Through an awareness of repetition and redundancy within text, pairs redraft text down to a given number of words. | 16 |
| To become familiar with the functions of the delete and return keys, and with saving and printing using word processing software. To introduce the layout facilities available in word processing. | Acrostics | 1.1a; 1/2a/ Level B, C, D | English 3.1a, b, c; 3.2a, b, c, d; 3.3a. | Pairs write and lay out an acrostic poem, using a word processor and printer. | 18 |
| To become familiar with the formatting functions in word processing software. To lay out text in appropriate ways, for example by centring or justifying. To practise saving to disk and printing out. | Shape poems | 1.1a; 1.2a/ Level C, D | English 3.1a, b, c; 3.2a, b, c, d; 3.3a. | Pairs create a shaped poem, using the formatting facilities. | 19 |
| To practise layout and format, choosing appropriate font size and style. To use the computer for a real purpose. To practise saving and printing. | Dear Sir or Madam | 1.1a, b; 1.2a/Level C, D | English 3.1a; 3.2a, b, c, d; 3.3a. | Pairs compose, lay out and print a letter to the editor of a local paper. | 21 |
| To produce quality text within a book format, using a variety of suitable font styles and sizes in different colours. | My version | 1.1a; 1.2a/ Level C, D | English 3.1a, b; 3.2a, b, c, d; 3.3a. | Pairs rewrite nursery rhymes in their own words and present them for a younger audience. | 22 |
| To use a computer to produce a classroom resource. To offer IT opportunities to experiment with layout for a particular purpose and content. | Making data collection sheets | 1.1a, c; 1.2a, b, c/ Level C, D | Cross-curricular. | Group work to produce data collection sheets for any aspect of class work. | 24 |
| To use word processing software to redraft text. | In the news | 1.1a; 1.2a/ Level C, D | English 3.1a; 3.2a, b, c, d; 3.3a. | Pairs rewrite and present a news story appropriate for a younger audience. | 26 |
| To use word processing software to communicate in writing with others, perhaps using transmission by e-mail (optional). | Pen portraits | 1.1a; 1.2a/ Level C, D | English 3.1a, b; 3.2a, b, c, d; 3.3a. | Pairs write a short description of themselves which would be appropriate for an e-mail communication to a distant pen-pal. | 27 |
| To design and format text for a wider audience. To provide opportunities for using the graphic facility within a desktop publishing program. | Our school | 1.1a, b; 1.2a/Level C, D | English 3.1a, b; 3.2a, b, c, d; 3.3a. | Pairs write and design a 'pupils' prospectus of the school'. | 28 |
| To introduce DTP format facilities. To use clip art to enhance a product. | Designing a poster | 1.1a; 1.2a; 1.2b/Level C, D | English 3.1a, b, c; 3.2a, b, c, d. Art 1; 2b, c; 4a, b; 7a, d; 8a, d, f; 9b, d. | Pairs use desktop publishing to produce a poster for a school event. | 29 |
| To use DTP software to create a design for a special purpose. To use a variety of fonts, including rotated fonts, and clip art or graphic files produced in an art application. | Designing a cover | 1.1a; 1.2a; 1.2b/Level C, D | English 3.1a, b, c; 3.2a, b, c, d. Art 1; 2b, c; 4a, b; 7a, d; 8a, d, f; 9b, d. | Individual or paired activity to create an appropriate relevant design for a CD or cassette cover. | 31 |
| To search a CD-ROM and select images and text for saving and downloading into word processing software. | Famous people | 1.1a, b; 1.2a; 1.2b/ Level C, D, E | English 3.1a, b, c; 3.2a, b. | Group activity with a range of choice across the class: to make biographical pages of five famous people – including a portrait and information. | 33 |
| To have the opportunity to select, write and illustrate within a context, using IT. To provide the opportunity to edit, cut and paste and write in a variety of styles using IT. | The class newspaper | 1.1a, b; 1.2a/Level C, D | English 3.1a, b, c; 3.2a, b. Art 1.1a, b, c; 1.2a, b. | Whole-class activity directed by the teacher: to produce a class newspaper. | 35 |
| To use flood fill techniques with accuracy. | Four-colour exercise | 1.1a; 1.2a/ Level B, C | Art 1; 2c; 4b, d. | Pairs producing individual work making a pattern, so that no two boundaries are bordering the same colour. | 37 |

9

INFORMATION TECHNOLOGY

| Learning objective | Title | PoS/AO | Subject links | Content/type of activity | Page |
|---|---|---|---|---|---|
| To become familiar with line, draw and flood fill facilities. To understand that simple line and shape may produce simple results. To appreciate that background colours other than white can be used. | Kandinsky prints | 1.1a; 1.2a/ Level B, C, D | Art 1; 2c; 4b, d; 7e, 9b, d. | Pairs producing individual work from a stimulus of Kandinsky prints. | 39 |
| To experiment with a variety of graphic tools to achieve a specific outcome. | Mood pictures | 1.1a; 1.2a/ Level B, C | Art 1; 2a, c; 3; 4b, d; 7e, f; 9b, d. | Pairs producing individual work. Teacher uses appropriate mood pictures as stimulus for children to produce a 'happy' pattern. | 40 |
| To become familiar with colour palette changes. To use a variety of tones of the same colour to produce a picture within a relevant context. To learn to use the subtleties of shade or tone within a single colour. | Monocolour pictures | 1.1a; 1.2a/ Level C, D | Art 1; 2c; 4b, c, d; 7e, f; 9b, d. | Pairs producing individual work. Teacher uses appropriate monotone pictures as stimulus. | 42 |
| To use the paint spray tool within a graphics program. | Design a tag | 1.1a; 1.2a/ Level C, D | Art 1; 2c; 4b, d; 7e; 9b, d. | Individual work, with the teacher providing examples of street graffiti. | 43 |
| To provide further practise in using the paint spray tool to imitate a specific style of art. | Impressionist style | 1.1a; 1.2a/ Level C, D | Art 1; 2c; 4b, d; 7e, f; 9b, d. | Individual work, with the teacher providing a good range of examples of impressionist art. Children emulate Impressionist paintings. | 45 |
| To use a variety of IT tools for a purpose. To learn that bold, clear images communicate meaning more effectively. | Picture the rules | 1.1a; 1.2a/ Level C, D | Art 1; 2c; 4b, d; 7a; 9b, d. | Paired working, producing a display of school rules with some examples of icons to stimulate their ideas. | 47 |
| To use the fine brush tool in a graphics program to produce detailed results. | Sweet wrappers | 1.1a; 1.2a/ Level C, D | Art 1; 2c; 4b, d; 7a; 9b, d. | Paired working with observational activity, to design a sweet wrapper. | 49 |
| To use the existing patterns available or to create patterns from the colour palette within a graphics program. | Fashion show | 1.1a; 1.2a/ Level C, D | Art 1; 2a, c; 4a, b, c, d; 7a; 9b, d. DT 1.1a, b, c,; 1.2e. | Paired activity with examples to stimulate ideas. Children produce colour combinations for clothing. | 50 |
| To use the cut and paste facility to produce repeat patterns in graphic software. | Repeat patterns | 1.1a; 1.2a/ Level C, D | Art 1; 2c; 4a, b, d; 7e; 9b, d. | Paired activity with teacher choosing the context. To produce repeat patterns of a simple motif. | 52 |
| To use a hand-held scanner to produce an image. | Scan a leaf | 1.1a; 1.2a/ Level D | Art 1; 2c; 4a, b, c, d; 9b, d. DT 1.1a, b, c; 1.2e; 1.5g. | Individual scanning task; group use of scanned images of a leaf for design. | 54 |
| To insert a scanned image into a graphics application for ubsequent artistic manipulation. | Growing old gracefully | 1.1a; 1.2a/ Level D | Art 1; 2c; 4a, d; 7c, e; 8d, e; 9b, d. | Individual task, probably requiring some time to complete: manipulating a scanned image of a face by adding glasses, a beard etc. | 55 |
| To provide opportunity to use music composition software for a definite purpose. | Musical illustration | 1.1a; 1.2a/ Level C, D | Music 1a, b; 2a, b, d, g; 5b, f, h. | Group activity with individuals using the software to compose for a particular theme, matching the content of a poem, picture or historical event to a musical style and atmosphere. | 57 |
| To use IT to compose a tune with an appropriate tempo and structure to accompany a short dance sequence. | Let's dance! | 1.1a; 1.2a/ Level C, D | Music 1a, b; 2a, b, d, g; 4b; 5b, d, f, h. | Paired or group activity. Fast and slow dances produced for class appreciation. | 59 |
| To use software using standard notation to compose. | Recognise this one? | 1.1a; 1.2a/ Level C, D | Music 1a; 2a, b, d, g; 5b, f, h. | Individual task or group activity. Children compose familiar tunes, for example nursery rhymes. | 61 |
| To create a multimedia presentation and use standard notation software to compose some appropriate music. | Multimedia music | 1.1a; 1.2a/ Level D | Music 1a, b; 2a, b, d, g; 4a, b; 5b, f, h | Group or individual activity, probably requiring teacher support. Pupils compose suitable tunes to add to a multimedia presentation. | 62 |
| To use the Roamer's music facilities to play tunes. | Wherever I may roam | 1.1a; 1.2a/ Level C, D | Music 1a, b; 2a, b, d, g; 4a, b; 5b, f. | Paired activity with opportunity to demonstrate findings. Pairs asked to compose recognisable tunes such as a nursery rhyme. | 63 |

## Chapter 2: Information handling

| | | | | | |
|---|---|---|---|---|---|
| To collect accurate information and enter it into a computer database. To use the database to produce graphical illustrations. | Looking at us | 1.1a, b; 1.2a, b, c, d/Level B, C, D | Maths 1.3b, c; 1.4b, c, d; 3.4b; 4.2a, b, d Science 0.1d; 0.4c; 1.2a, b, c; 1.3a, b, c, d, e. | Whole-class activity, with pairs accessing the computer in turn to enter data about a variety of physical aspects of pupils in the class. | 66 |

INFORMATION TECHNOLOGY

| Learning objective | Title | PoS/AO | Subject links | Content/type of activity | Page |
|---|---|---|---|---|---|
| To enter data into a database and interpret graphical information. | Watching it grow | 1.1a, b; 1.2a, b, c, d/Level B, C, D | Maths 1.3b, c; 1.4b, c, d; 3.4b; 4.2a, b, d. Science 0.1d; 0.4c; 1.2a, b, c; 1.3a, b, c, d, e; 1.2b, c; 2.1b; 2.3a. | Long-term activity with weekly measurements. Pairs take turns to measure and enter data monitoring the weight (or height) of a pet (or plant) over time. | 69 |
| To gather data using collection sheets. To enter the data into a database and then plot graphs to draw conclusions. | Traffic patterns | 1.1a, b; 1.2a, b, c, d/Level C, D | Maths 1.3b, c; 1.4b, c, d; 3.4b; 4.2a, b, d. Geography 1c; 2b, c; 3f; 5c; 10a. | Paired collections at particular times of the day. Class activity once data is entered: to compare the daily variations of traffic flow and reach conclusions. | 71 |
| To devise a questionnaire using appropriate software. To reach conclusions by analysing the results. | What's on the menu? | 1.1a, b; 1.2a, b, c, d/Level C, D | Maths 1.3b, c; 1.4b, c, d; 3.4b; 4.2a, b, d. Science 1.2b; 1.3a, b; 2.2b. | Small group to devise questionnaire, whole-class extended exercise once data becomes available. To investigate likes and dislikes of particular foods. | 72 |
| To use a database that has a keyword facility. To become familiar with the keyword option. | Book reviews | 1.1a, b; 1.2a, b, c, d/Level B, C, D | English 1.1a; 1.2b; 2.1a, b, c; 2.2a, b, c. Maths 4.2a, b, d. | Teacher-led activity establishing keywords. Group work entering weather data on a daily basis in order to compare weather in different months. | 74 |
| To use an appropriate database within which data may be stored for comparison. | Whatever the weather | 1.1a, b; 1.2a, b, c, d; 1.3b/ Level C, D | Maths 1.3b, c; 1.4b, c, d; 3.4b; 4.2a, b, d. Geography 3f; 8a, b. | Whole-class activity, with pairs taking turns to collect weather data on a daily basis in order to compare different months. | 76 |
| To search a database to find out facts which allow conclusions to be drawn. To become familiar with search routines. | Finding the facts | 1.1a, b; 1.2a, b, c; 1.3b/Level C, D | Maths 4.1b, c; 4.2a, d. Cross-curricular. | Paired task from pre-prepared database (eg on British Birds or Volcanoes). Teacher provides question sheet for pupils, requesting facts and conclusions (to be drawn from the information discovered). | 78 |
| To search the information held on a CD-ROM encyclopaedia for specific facts from which to draw conclusions. | CD-ROM search | 1.2a, b, c; 1.3b/Level C, D | Maths 4.1b, c; 4.2a, d. Cross-curricular. | Paired task with pre-prepared question sheet concerning aspects of the information held on a CD-ROM. Pupils use the search routines to access information and draw conclusions. | 80 |
| To use a spreadsheet to store information. To use spreadsheet facilities such as total, average, sort and graph to illustrate their findings. | Looking at spreadsheets | 1.1a, b; 1.2a, b, c; 1.3b/Level C, D | Maths 1.3b, c; 1.4b, c, d; 3.4b; 4.2a, b, c, d. Science 0.1d; 0.4c; 1.2a, b, c; 1.3a, b, c, d, e; 1.2b; 1.3a, b, c, d. | Group activity: collecting data and entering it into a spreadsheet. Whole-class work on interpreting and drawing conclusions from data on the physical dimensions and attributes of class members. | 82 |
| To collect data and practise inputting into a spreadsheet. To use the sort facility to draw conclusions. | What are we eating? | 1.1a, b; 1.2a, b, c; 1.3b/Level D | Maths 1.3b, c; 1.4b, c, d; 3.4b; 4.2a, b, c, d. Science 2.2b. | Individual data collection. Group entering data from food packets and entering agreed values into spreadsheet. Class interrogation of findings. | 85 |
| To use a spreadsheet to model the running of a small business. To be able to ask 'What if...?' and make decisions from conclusions drawn. | Business plans | 1.1a, b; 1.2a, b, c; 1.3b/Level D | Maths 1.3b, c; 1.4b, c, d; 3.4b; 4.2a, b, d. | Group activity with teacher-led enquiries (perhaps in the form of a worksheet) requesting the What if? line of enquiry in relation to numerical data about a tuck shop or car wash business. | 87 |

## Chapter 3: Controlling, monitoring and modelling

| Learning objective | Title | PoS/AO | Subject links | Content/type of activity | Page |
|---|---|---|---|---|---|
| To use a Logo program to build a procedure using the 'REPEAT' facility. | Squares all over | 1.1a; 1.3c, d/Level C, D | Maths 1.4b; 3.1b; 3.3a, c. | Pairs at the computer, following a teacher-led demonstration, drawing a square and then creating a pattern consisting of squares of different colours, sizes and orientations. | 90 |
| To use simple formulas to enter information into a spreadsheet. To see the immediate result of any changes to the information. | Party time | 1.1a; 1.3c, d/Level D | Maths 1.2b, d; 1.3c; 1.4b; 3.1b; 3.3a, c. | Paired activity, following teacher-led demonstration with question sheet to direct possible strategies, entering the costings of a class party into a spreadsheet, then changing the costings to see the immediate change in the total spent. | 92 |
| To become familiar with the control box. To switch outputs on and off in a predetermined way. | ON/OFF – Controlling outputs | 1.1a, d; 1.3a, b/ Level C, D | DT 1.5d, f, i, k. Science 4.1b. | Teacher input to class, followed by paired activity. Demonstration of connection of outputs. Teacher-led demonstration of outputs. Pupils then connect up appropriate components to the control box and use the control software to turn outputs on and off. | 94 |

| Learning objective | Title | PoS/AO | Subject links | Content/type of activity | Page |
|---|---|---|---|---|---|
| To emulate a traffic light sequence using a control box. To write a 'LIGHTS' procedure. | Traffic lights | 1.1a, d; 1.3a, c/ *Level C, D* | DT 1.3a, b, c, d, e, g; 1.5d, f, l, k. Science 4.1b. Maths 1.4b. | Paired activity. Three lights are programmed to emulate traffic lights. The sequence is put into a procedure called 'Lights'. | 96 |
| To use one input, such as a switch, and a variety of outputs. To control several outputs by activating one input. | Press me and watch! | 1.1a, d; 1.3a, b/ *Level C, D* | DT 1.5d, f, i, k. Science 4.1b. Maths 1.4b. | Paired activity, with challenges set for subsequent pairs. Pupils connect up one switch as a single input. They write a series of commands which will turn on several outputs when the switch is activated. | 98 |
| To use the control box as a security alarm. | Jewel security | 1.1a, d; 1.3a, b/ *Level C, D* | DT 1.3a, b, c, d, e, g; 1.5d, f, i, k. Science 4.1b. Maths 1.4b. | Paired activity, with challenges set for other contexts. Pupils connect a vibration sensor as an input and arrange a simple alarm system, using a buzzer as a single output. | 101 |
| To become familiar with using a temperature probe. | Hot spots | 1.1a; 1.1d; 1.3b/*Level D* | Science 0.1a, b, d; 0.4c; 1.2a, b, c; 1.3a, b, c, d, e. | Class exercise, with pairs carrying out the practical activity. Pupils investigate where the warmest place is in the classroom. | 103 |
| To monitor environmental conditions over a 24-hour period using data logging equipment. | 24 hours in class | 1.1a; 1.1d; 1.3b/*Level D* | Science 0.1a, b, d; 0.4c; 1.2a, b, c; 1.3a, b, c, d, e. | Groups of three set up equipment. Then the whole class interpret the findings through the use of a questionnaire. | 105 |
| To link a variety of sensors together to gather information. | Hamster watch | 1.1a; 1.1d; 1.3b/*Level D* | Science 0.1a, b, d; 0.4c; 1.2a, b, c; 1.3a, b, c, d, e. | Group exercise, with class involvement in the interpretation of findings. Pupils link sensors (sound, vibration) to a hamster cage, so that nocturnal activity can be monitored. | 107 |
| To enter a sequence of commands that guides a floor robot. | Twist and turn | 1.1a; 1.3a, d/*Level B, C, D* | Maths 3.1b; 3.3a, c. | Paired activity with demonstrations given and further challenges set by pupils, guiding a robot around a slalom course of variable difficulty. | 108 |
| To enter a longer sequence of commands. To write sequences for making two robots 'interact' with each other. | Robot rumba | 1.1a; 1.3a, d/*Level C, D* | Maths 3.1b; 3.3a, c. | Pairs working together, programming a robot to dance. With two robots, there are more possibilities! | 110 |
| To command the robot by using a variety of longer sequences. | Robot sheep dog | 1.1a; 1.3a, d/*Level C, D* | Maths 3.1b; 3.3a, c. | Paired activity with shared demonstrations and further challenges set: to program a robot to round up lost sheep and guide them into a fold. | 111 |
| To create a procedure that will draw a specified design. | Pattern repeated | 1.1a; 1.3a, d/*Level C, D, E* | Maths 3.1b; 3.2a, b, c; 3.a, c. | Paired activity with shared outcomes, producing further challenges. Drawing a series of squares to produce a multiple pattern. | 112 |
| To use Logo to draw on the screen and to print out the results. | Letters and numbers | 1.1a; 1.3a/ *Level C, D* | Maths 3.1b, c; 3.2a, b, c. | Paired activity at the computer. Pupils program the screen turtle to draw out letters and numbers. | 114 |
| To become familiar with Logo commands. | Through the maze | 1.1a; 1.3a/ *Level C* | Maths 3.1b, c; 3.3c. | Teacher prepares several mazes on acetate sheets stuck to the computer monitor. Paired or individual activity to meet the challenge of completing the maze. | 115 |
| To use Logo to produce a design for a purpose. | Logo bookmark | 1.1a; 1.3a, d/*Level C* | Maths 3.1b, c; 3.3c. DT 1.1a; 1.3c; 1.4f, g. Art 1; 2c; 4a, b, c, d; 7c. | Paired activity following teacher demonstration: to produce a bookmark design. | 116 |
| To use Logo procedures to draw a series of specified shapes. | Geometric shapes | 1.1a; 1.3a, d/*Level C* | Maths 3.1b, c; 3.2a, b, c; 3.3c. | Paired activity, with pupil feedback to raise further challenge for subsequent pairs. The task is to draw a number of different polygons, then produce a pattern consisting of polygons of different sizes, colours and orientations. | 118 |

Entries given in italics refer to the Scottish 5–14 Guidelines for Information Technology within Environmental Studies.

**INFORMATION TECHNOLOGY**

# Communicating information

The activities in this section of the book give the children opportunities to explore the many facilities that IT offers in the area of communicating information. Information takes several forms, chiefly as text, sound and images. Software that manipulates text – word processors and desktop publishers – are commonplace in schools and offer the children a cross-curricular resource so that they can use text to communicate any aspect of their school experience. It is important that the children make use of IT's flexibility by composing text on the screen rather than copying previously written material.

Communicating by sound usually takes the form of music composition and performance on the computer. The computer could be linked to an electronic music keyboard for either music input or playback. Music software can offer remarkable facilities, such as transposing into any key or playing a piece backwards. Activities here include the use of both non-standard and standard music notation software.

Communication by pictures or graphics is a powerful IT facility. Computer-generated images are often of the highest quality, and IT even allows us to see what things will look like before they are made. Again, the children can use graphics software to enhance and illustrate any aspect of their school work.

INFORMATION
TECHNOLOGY

# ADD AN ADJECTIVE

***To learn and practise using the deletion and insertion facilities in word processing software.***

†† *Individuals or pairs.*

⏲ *20 minutes at the computer; 10 minutes demonstration.*

## Previous skills/knowledge needed

The children need to have experience in using a mouse and/or the cursor keys to place the cursor appropriately within a text. They should be aware of how to achieve correct spacing using the space bar. Some previous work on adjectives is also necessary so that the children understand what an adjective is.

## Key background information

Inserting or deleting text on screen is easy when using word processing software. The following activity gives the children practice in using the cursor keys or mouse pointer to select the correct place for entering a chosen word to complete a sentence.

## Vocabulary

Insert, delete, cursor, caret (omission mark), space bar, format.

## Preparation

Make one copy of photocopiable page 122 for each child.

Find several different passages of text to match the range of levels within your class. Enter this text on screen, omitting all of the adjectives but leaving gaps to show the

children where to enter their choice of word, then save to disk. The passages could relate to other curriculum areas such as geography, history, science, maths or RE. Offering open-ended possibilities allows the children to be creative and use their knowledge of adjectives imaginatively. However, it may also be helpful to prepare flash cards with the appropriate adjectives to choose from, particularly for less confident children. (Keep the cards in separate sets to match the different texts.)

Display a list of the children's names organised into pairs to show them the running order for computer access.

## Resources needed

A computer, word processing software, a printer (preferably colour but not essential), paper, different texts specially prepared and pre-loaded onto a computer (see Preparation), flash cards showing the adjectives to choose from (for those children requiring support), photocopiable page 122.

## What to do

Give each child a copy of photocopiable page 122. The aim of the task is to fill in the missing adjectives from the list provided on the sheet. Remind the children what an adjective is and allow them time to complete the photocopiable activity. Explain that they are now going to do a similar activity using the computer, inserting adjectives into some existing text on screen. Before they start the IT task, however, give a whole class or large group demonstration of how to insert and delete text on the computer. Show them the flash cards which accompany the task, if appropriate, and encourage any relevant questions. Point out the list of names showing the order in which each pair of children will have access to the computer. The children can also use this list to ask for help from those who have already completed the activity if necessary. Encourage each pair to take their turn in completing the activity on screen.

You can adapt this activity to help develop the children's familiarity with other parts of speech such as nouns and verbs.

**INFORMATION TECHNOLOGY**

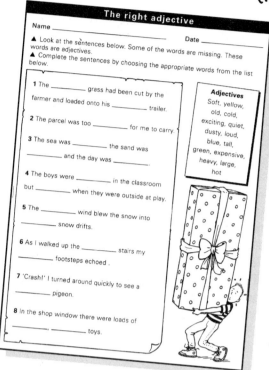

**The right adjective**

Name _____ Date _____

▲ Look at the sentences below. Some of the words are missing. These words are adjectives.
▲ Complete the sentences by choosing the appropriate words from the list below.

1 The _____ grass had been cut by the farmer and loaded onto his _____ trailer.

2 The parcel was too _____ for me to carry.

3 The sea was _____ the sand was _____ and the day was _____.

4 The boys were _____ in the classroom but _____ when they were outside at play.

5 The _____ wind blew the snow into _____ snow drifts.

6 As I walked up the _____ stairs my _____ footsteps echoed.

7 'Crash!' I turned around quickly to see a _____ pigeon.

8 In the shop window there were loads of _____ toys.

**Adjectives**
Soft, yellow, old, cold, exciting, quiet, dusty, loud, blue, tall, green, expensive, heavy, large, hot

## Suggestion(s) for extension

Include gaps within the text that require several words for completion, increasing this to longer amounts of text as appropriate. Ask the children to rewrite each sentence in their own words as a further extension. Including saving and printing as part of the task will help to extend the children's IT capability.

## Suggestion(s) for support

Some children may benefit from having flash cards with a selection of words for insertion into the text. Additional support in the form of an adult working alongside them may be needed initially to ensure that they are confident with the task.

## Assessment opportunities

This activity will enable you to assess the children's use of IT to insert and amend text. Specifically, look for the insertion of appropriate words into sentences to convey information appropriate to the purpose. There are also opportunities to make assessments in English, such as accuracy in writing and spelling.

## Display ideas

Display the children's work under a title such as 'Our describing words'. The children could highlight their inserted words by using different colours or fonts to enhance the display.

## Reference to photocopiable sheet

Photocopiable page 122 shows several sentences in which the adjectives are missing. Children should choose the most appropriate words from the lists provided on the sheet.

# SPOT THE MISTAKES!

*To practise the insertion and deletion of text on screen and become familiar with the use and function of the shift key(s) by correcting pre-loaded text. To use the computer for a real purpose. To print out corrected texts.*

†† *Individuals or pairs.*

⏰ *20 minutes at the computer; 10 minutes demonstration.*

## Previous skills/knowledge needed

Children will need some familiarity with the basics of word processing, including the ability to delete and insert text, and to use the shift keys.

## Key background information

Commercial word processing software includes 'spell checkers' which are normally used to make corrections in a single session once the document is completed. This may not be practical in the classroom as the children will want to correct as they go along. Correcting errors on screen is simple and, unlike pencil and paper corrections, leaves no traces, a point that appeals to children. The activity below challenges the children to recognise any errors and to rectify them using basic word processing functions. It can also be used to challenge the children's spelling and punctuation skills and their factual knowledge. Offering them a misleading or inaccurate text within a historical or scientific context, for example, will give them a chance to seek out the correct information, providing a valuable cross-curricular dimension.

## Vocabulary

Error, detection, delete, insert, shift key, capital letters, punctuation.

## Preparation

Make one copy of photocopiable page 123 for each child planning to work at the computer. Type on screen some text containing errors that are recognisable and appropriate for the children in your class, then save to disk. You could include errors in spelling, punctuation, formatting or content (factual errors). Omitting capital letters will give the children practice in using the shift keys.

## Resources needed

A computer, word processing software, a printer, paper, some teacher-typed text containing deliberate errors (see above), photocopiable page 123, pens/pencils.

## What to do

Provide a copy of photocopiable page 123 to those children who are just about to use the computer for this activity.

Use the sheet to familiarise them with the task of spotting as many errors as they can. Ask them to correct these using a pen/pencil. This should increase their awareness of the variety of errors that can occur such as spelling, punctuation or formatting. Moving on to use the computer will help the children to appreciate how much easier it is to edit out mistakes on screen than on paper.

First, however, provide a whole class or group introduction to the task. Call up the pre-loaded text and tell the children that you typed it when you were very tired, so you have made lots of mistakes which you would like them to correct. Run through the main keys or functions that the children will need to use, such as the shift and cursor keys. If appropriate, show them how to print out text. Then allow the children access to the computer to complete the activity. A limited time allocation can be used to increase the challenge if appropriate. The children could print out their corrected versions for you to check.

## Suggestion(s) for extension

Prepare a sequence of erroneous texts offering increasing challenge. The errors could start as spelling only, then progress to punctuation only and finally to a mixture of both. Include factual errors if appropriate. The children may also like to devise their own error-riddled texts for their friends or for the whole class/teacher to correct. This would require them to create text containing errors, saving it and perhaps reloading it ready for the next child. They could also print out a corrected version to act as an answer sheet.

## Suggestion(s) for support

Initial support for those children who lack confidence is important; appointing a more knowledgeable child as a

guide may help. Choose the content of the text carefully matching the level of errors to the understanding and ability of the children.

## Assessment opportunities

This activity will enable you to assess the children's ability to use IT to amend information in textual form for a particular purpose. You will be able to see how confident they are at making corrections using the deletion and insertion facilities. There are also good opportunities to assess spelling and punctuation as many of the errors will fall within these areas.

## Display ideas

The children may like to display the uncorrected text alongside their corrected versions.

## Reference to photocopiable sheet

Photocopiable page 123 includes several pieces of text such as posters, flyers and lists, that have a variety of punctuation and spelling errors. The children must correct these using pen/pencil.

## EDITING CHALLENGE

***To practise altering text on screen using deletion and insertion and redrafting text. To use a computer for a real purpose.***

†† *Individuals or pairs.*

🕐 *20–30 minutes at the computer; 15 minutes demonstration/discussion.*

## Previous skills/knowledge needed

Children will need a basic ability to use word processing software and should also be at approximately Level 3, or beyond, in writing.

## Key background information

Creating factual texts that are clear, brief and to the point is an important skill. The ability to edit text either by padding it out or précising it, depending on the need, is made easier through the use of a word processor. Word processing software allows us complete freedom in manipulating words. Unlike handwritten text on the page, text in a computer can be easily amended right up to the moment before it is printed out. This flexibility with words is what makes computers such powerful tools. To edit a piece of text on paper is difficult. On the computer, the task is made much easier through the use of deletion and insertion facilities.

In the activity below, the children are given a piece of text of a certain length, which they must then edit down to a given number of words without changing the meaning. This will provide good opportunities for redrafting text.

## Preparation

Make one copy of photocopiable page 124 for each child. You will also need to prepare and save to disk several different texts at appropriate levels for the children to work on. These texts should contain clear examples of repetition and redundancy which the children can edit out. You can use texts relevant to any curriculum area to help support the children's knowledge and understanding as well as developing their IT skills.

## Vocabulary

Précis, edit, repetition, redundant, highlight, delete, word count.

## Resources needed

A computer, word processing software, a printer, paper, various texts specially prepared and pre-loaded by the teacher for editing (see above), photocopiable page 124.

## What to do

The aim of the task is for the children to practise their IT skills by reducing the length of a given text on screen, without changing its meaning. Start by discussing with the children those occasions when it is important to be clear but brief in writing something, for example a report, an urgent message, a newspaper advert, a letter of complaint, and so on. Then use photocopiable page 124 to introduce the editing exercise to the children. Doing this task on paper first will help them to appreciate how much easier it becomes when using a computer.

Once the children have completed the photocopiable activity, provide a whole class or large group demonstration to explain the IT task. Show them an original text and an amended version where the number of words has been reduced. Ask them to spot the differences between the two texts on screen. Then show them the main computer functions that they will need to use for this exercise, such as moving from line to line, inserting and deleting text, saving and printing out. Emphasise that you want them to edit the text on screen and not just copy their shortened version below the original. (The length of the original text and the final number of words to which it can be edited will obviously depend on the children's language ability.) Then let the children take turns to use the computer to complete the activity, making sure that they are clear as to the number of words that they must edit down to. If they are unable to finish, they can save the text and return to it at a later date. They may have the opportunity to produce several drafts, and word processing software is an excellent tool for doing this. Each draft may be saved and printed out so that the children gain more insight into the process of arriving at their final goal.

Attempting to do the task in reverse by expanding text and embroidering the content is also an interesting activity as it offers opportunity for focused creative writing.

## Suggestion(s) for extension

The more confident children can be set an exact target figure of words to edit down to, depending on the number of words in the original text. To achieve an exact target will demand greater editing skills. The content of the text will affect their ability to edit – long descriptive pieces will be more difficult. Texts with important hidden messages, where certain words are crucial to the meaning, will offer further challenge.

## Suggestion(s) for support

For children with less confidence, make the task simpler by setting a target range for editing a piece of text down to, for example, 'between 15 and 25 words' or 'less than 20 words', rather than a set number. Reading through the text with the children beforehand will offer opportunities to discuss where the relevant or irrelevant parts are. Discussion about what they think the meaning of the passage is will also be helpful.

## Assessment opportunities

This activity will enable you to assess how well your children use IT to amend and edit text for a real purpose. Look at how the children are deleting words and replacing/inserting them with their own text, and at how confident they are in finding their way around the text with the cursor keys. There are also opportunities to assess writing, especially organisation, grammar, spelling and punctuation.

**INFORMATION TECHNOLOGY**

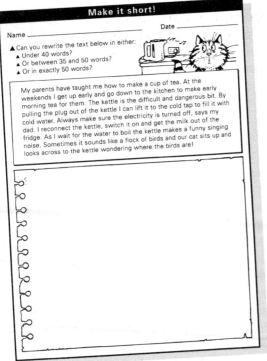

**Make it short!**

Name _____  Date _____

▲ Can you rewrite the text below in either:
  ▲ Under 40 words?
  ▲ Or between 35 and 50 words?
  ▲ Or in exactly 50 words?

My parents have taught me how to make a cup of tea. At the weekends I get up early and go down to the kitchen to make early morning tea for them. The kettle is the difficult and dangerous bit. By pulling the plug out of the kettle I can lift it to the cold tap to fill it with cold water. Always make sure the electricity is turned off, says my dad. I reconnect the kettle, switch it on and get the milk out of the fridge. As I wait for the water to boil the kettle makes a funny singing noise. Sometimes it sounds like a flock of birds and our cat sits up and looks across to the kettle wondering where the birds are!

## Display ideas

Put up a 'Before and after' display showing how, from the same starting point, a piece of text has been reduced in a variety of ways.

## Reference to photocopiable sheet

Photocopiable page 124 provides a passage of simple factual text for the children to edit down. They can choose their 'target length' from the list of options provided.

# ACROSTICS

*To become familiar with the functions of the delete and return keys, and with saving and printing using word processing software. To introduce the layout facilities available in word processing.*

🕐 *Individuals or pairs.*

†† *30 minutes at computer; 10 minutes demonstration.*

## Previous skills/knowledge needed

Children will need to have a basic familiarity with word processing software.

## Key background information

The ability to place text anywhere on screen and to amend it easily by deletion and insertion offers children a liberated approach to their written work. Early writers are hampered by the physical process of getting letters and words in the right place on the paper, correctly spelled and with acceptable punctuation. Using a computer frees them from many of the physical difficulties.

Using the acrostic form for simple creative writing activities can be most rewarding. By using word processing software to write their own acrostics, the children can produce work of quality, having had the opportunity to change and hone their words. It is important that the children write at the screen and not copy out previously written material. Such copy-typing detracts from the computer's power to offer freedom and flexibility in the positioning of text.

## Vocabulary

Acrostic poem, rhyme, layout, delete, insert, format, capital letter.

## Preparation

Make a copy of photocopiable page 125 to show the class. Collect some further examples of acrostic poems, if possible, to provide a good variety.

## Resources needed

A computer, word processing software, a printer, paper, photocopiable page 125, other examples of acrostic poems (optional).

## What to do

This is a popular language activity which the children may well have done before on paper. Show them the examples of acrostic poems on photocopiable page 125 and any other examples to make sure they understand how such poems are structured. Now tell them that they are going to write their own poems using the computer. You can suggest particular themes for them to write about, perhaps linking in with current class topics, or allow them to choose their own.

Start with a whole class or large group demonstration of how to set out an acrostic poem on the screen. Show the children how text can be added to any line in any order, and how words are inserted and deleted. If appropriate,

demonstrate saving to disk and printing out. Then give the children access to the computer to write their poems.

## Suggestion(s) for extension
To extend their IT skills, children could highlight initial letters in a different size, colour and/or font. Children who are more able writers may be challenged to find longer words/more letters with which to start each sentence. A further challenge is to also have the final letter of each sentence as a second acrostic!

## Suggestion(s) for support
Ask an adult to sit with less confident children to help them with the language work and/or initial involvement with the computer.

## Assessment opportunities
This activity will enable you to assess how the children are using IT to create, lay out and edit text to a given format. Watch carefully to see how confident the children are at placing the text in the correct position. You can also assess the content and variety of their writing and understanding of the acrostic poem format.

## Display ideas
Create a classroom wall or corridor display of the children's acrostic poems, or collect the poems together for mounting into a class-designed anthology. Put the anthology in the book corner for the children to read.

## Reference to photocopiable sheet
Photocopiable page 125 shows several examples of acrostics which can be used as a prompt for the activity.

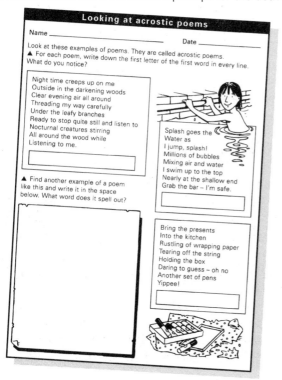

# SHAPE POEMS

*To become familiar with the formatting functions in word processing software. To lay out text in appropriate ways, for example by centring or justifying. To practise saving to disk and printing out.*

†† *Individuals or pairs.*

🕑 *30 minutes at the computer; 15 minutes demonstration.*

## Previous skills/knowledge needed
Children will need to be at Levels 2/3 or above in writing, and to know what centred text looks like. They should have a working knowledge of word processing.

## Key background information
A solid block of text is difficult to read. Using paragraphs and spacing on the printed page allows the eye to absorb the text much more easily. In the printing trade, people who lay out pages refer to 'rivers of white', meaning the blank areas of the printed page which they consider to be as important as those areas with text!

The task below allows the children to experiment with the layout facilities of word processing software, with the aim of producing a text layout that is appropriate to the content – for example, a snow poem in the shape of a snowman, a description of a desert scene in a pyramid shape, a firework poem in the shape of a rocket.

Symmetrically shaped poems can be formatted easily by using the 'centre text' option. A shapeless piece of text can often be made to look more interesting by centring it. Children will enjoy discovering that verses of their poems immediately look more like 'real' poetry when they are centred. Texts shaped in a non-symmetrical way are more challenging to produce; but with careful manipulation of the 'enter' and 'space' keys, visually effective results can be achieved.

Using the computer enables the children to experiment freely on screen before printing out their final versions. It allows them to achieve a strong visual impact in their work, with the text brought to life by being placed within a particular shape. Often, the children's ideas for laying out text on the computer will spread to their writing done on paper.

## Vocabulary
Justifying, centring, format, font size, layout.

## Preparation
Make one copy of photocopiable page 126 to show the class, or copy several for smaller groups of children. Find some examples of other texts presented in an interesting way using computer formatting.

### Resources needed

A computer, word processing software, a printer (preferably colour), adhesive, scissors, coloured paper and card, photocopiable page 126.

### What to do

Providing a whole class or large group demonstration is a good starting point for this activity. Show the children the examples of shape poems provided on photocopiable page 126 and any other texts that have been printed in an interesting way to help stimulate their ideas. Explain that computers can be used to present text in more interesting ways, and demonstrate on screen some simple techniques such as centring and justifying. Make sure that the children are familiar with the correct formatting keys and with saving and printing. Then explain that you want them to write their own shape poems on the computer, laying them out in an appropriate way. You may wish to specify a general topic for the poems, perhaps related to current work, or let the children choose a theme for themselves.

It is essential that the children write straight onto screen without an initial dummy run on paper. Encourage them to use the flexibility offered by the word processing software, allowing them to place their words anywhere initially, rather than coming to the computer with preconceived ideas. Point out that care should be taken in changing the font size as this will instantly disturb the shape of their layout. It is best to choose the font size required in the finished product at the outset of the task. The children should use the 'centre text' facility to produce a symmetrical layout of their text around a central vertical line.

Shaping words

Once the poems have been saved and printed out, the children can draw carefully around the text to emphasise the shape or cut it out and stick it onto coloured paper or card.

### Suggestion(s) for extension

Word processing software offers a variety of formatting options. Children may like to use different fonts and highlight words by using bold, italics or underlining and varying the colour.

### Suggestion(s) for support

Children should experiment on screen by writing a sentence or two first, and then seeing how the text can be moved around and shaped before embarking on writing more.

### Assessment opportunities

This activity will help you to assess how well your children use IT to create, edit and format text for a specific purpose. Watch how the children set out their text and with what degree of confidence they can place the text appropriately. There is also the opportunity to assess the children's ability to convey appropriate information through a specific poetic format, and to make assessments in English through the content, variety and interest of their poems.

### Display ideas

Wall mount the children's poems, giving additional impact by cutting around the shapes on coloured paper to produce double or triple mounting.

### Reference to photocopiable sheet

Photocopiable page 126 shows some examples of shape poems in different layouts and formats to stimulate the children's ideas.

# DEAR SIR OR MADAM

*To practise layout and format, choosing appropriate font size and style. To use the computer for a real purpose. To practise saving and printing.*

**††** *Individuals or pairs.*

🕒 *30 minutes at the computer; 10 minutes demonstration.*

## Previous skills/knowledge needed

Children should be writing at Levels 3/4 or above, and should have a basic familiarity with word processing software.

## Key background information

Desktop computers worldwide are used mainly for writing letters. Children need to develop letter writing skills, both conventionally using pen and paper and also by using IT.

Word processing software is often fairly sophisticated, offering facilities for checking spelling and providing 'dictionaries', besides many other useful features. Using a computer for writing letters should therefore result in quality work.

## Vocabulary

Layout, formatting, paragraph, justification, font, point size, e-mail (if appropriate).

## Preparation

Finding genuine opportunities for the children to write letters will allow them to use IT for a real purpose. This could be arranged with an outsider, with children from another school, an ex-pupil, a local business and so on. Corresponding with pupils overseas offers excellent cross-curricular opportunities, and access to e-mail would extend such possibilities.

Alternatively, make copies of photocopiable page 127 for children working individually or in pairs. This sheet

provides several different situations for lette[r] give the children meaningful contexts within [w] IT. Other contexts could include letters requesti[ng] [p]articular information, a special thank-you letter or a letter of praise/complaint to a television channel.

## Resources needed

A computer, word processing software, a printer, paper, an imaginative or real context for letters to be written, an e-mail facility (optional), photocopiable page 127.

## What to do

Explain to the children that they are going to use the computer to write some letters. Begin with a group demonstration of the correct way to set out a letter on the page. (A first draft on paper is useful here, to help the children concentrate on the correct format of a letter rather

than on content.) Talk about the importance of using appropriate font styles and sizes for when the children come to write their letters on the computer. Show them how easy it is to change the style and size of fonts, and remind them of useful formatting keys such as those for centring and justifying text. Make sure they are familiar with how to save and print text.

Now introduce the context for the children to write their letters, either presenting a real situation that you have helped to set up (see 'Preparation') or using photocopiable page 127 as a stimulus. If the children have real opportunities to write to their counterparts in other areas of the country or overseas (perhaps using e-mail), they can exchange details such as what they do at playtimes, what they eat for lunch, games they play after school and so on. This will help to widen their horizons, especially if the school is on the other side of the world!

While the context and content of the letters are important, keep the focus firmly on the development of IT skills throughout the activity.

## Suggestion(s) for extension

Changing the context of the letter can be used to offer greater challenge. Write a letter to Guy Fawkes, King Alfred or the Prime Minister, for example. You might also suggest that children work in pairs, writing to their partner, then exchanging letters and writing replies. IT skills may be further extended through the design of a particular address format appropriate to the sender, for example from a firm of rope makers, bridge builders or free-fall parachutists.

## Suggestion(s) for support

Keeping the letter content short will help less confident children by allowing them to concentrate more closely on format issues. Writing out the first draft with a more able partner will also help them to concentrate on the word processing features.

## Assessment opportunities

This activity gives you the opportunity to assess children's understanding of the letter format and how well they use IT to convey information within this. In English, assessments of both writing and spelling may be made as well as literary style.

## Display ideas

Displaying the letters, colourfully mounted and perhaps with accompanying illustrations, will enliven the children's working area.

## Reference to photocopiable sheet

Photocopiable page 127 contains several situations for the children to choose from to write an appropriate letter.

## MY VERSION

*To produce quality text within a book format, using a variety of suitable font styles and sizes in different colours.*

†† *Pairs.*

🕐 *30–40 minutes at the computer; 15 minutes discussion/demonstration.*

## Previous skills/knowledge needed

Children need to be writing at Levels 2/3 or above and have a basic familiarity with word processing software. They should also be able to recall some nursery rhymes.

## Key background information

Word processing offers great freedom in writing text. Mistakes are quickly rectified without trace and words can be rearranged easily. Subsequent drafts incorporating changes can be made and printed out. Although this activity can be done with pen and paper, IT offers much greater flexibility and the advantages of a range of layout and formatting options.

## Vocabulary

Redraft, reorganise, version, font, point size.

## Preparation

Gather together various books containing nursery rhymes as a stimulus for the children's work. Preparing a printed

**INFORMATION TECHNOLOGY**

sheet with a list of sentences in different font styles and sizes may be useful to help the children see the range available.

## Resources needed
A computer, word processing software, a printer (preferably colour), paper, books of nursery rhymes.

## What to do
Show the children some books containing nursery rhymes and hold a whole class or group discussion. Explain that nursery rhymes are part of an oral tradition, passed down originally by being told and sung. They were not written down until much later, by which time different versions probably resulted. Now make a list of the children's favourite rhymes, and ask the children to think of alternative endings to some of these.

Tell the children that they are now going to work in pairs using the word processing software to write their own versions of well-known nursery rhymes. (Asking the whole class to produce their text in longhand first will ease the problem of limited access to the computer.) Each child must pick their favourite rhyme and re-tell it in their own words, adding their own ending. Explain that their revamped versions will be collected together to produce an attractive, quality book for younger pupils to read, so they will need to think carefully about the audience they are writing for.

Point out that using the computer will help to give the children's rhymes a professional finish. Tell them that using a variety of font styles and sizes will add interest to their completed rhymes. Discuss how some fonts are easier to read than others. Italic fonts lean forwards and appear to be in a hurry. Other fonts have characteristics that are bold, thin, flowery, fancy or sometimes funny. Demonstrate how easy it is to manipulate fonts, then let the children

experiment and choose whichever ones they are happy with. They may choose to pick out individual words in a different font style or size, but explain that it is not good practice to use many different font styles within the same piece of text! You could set up an 'editing team' who take on the responsibility of organising the different rhymes within the final book version. Print out the rhymes individually and paste them into a simple book. This could have a hard front and back, suitably decorated with a tape hinge, and containing folded double sheets. Secure the sheets with a ribbon or wool thread.

The children will need to produce several drafts before all the rhymes are ready to be collated, so there will be plenty of opportunities to practise saving to disk and printing out. Illustrations to accompany their rhymes could be included to add to the book's appeal.

## Suggestion(s) for extension
Producing appropriate illustrations for the class book of rhymes using a graphics program will extend the children's IT capability. More advanced writers may also like to seek out some less well-known rhymes and write up their own versions.

## Suggestion(s) for support
Less confident writers will need more time at the keyboard. Ensuring that they choose a straightforward nursery rhyme will also simplify the task and enable them to focus more on developing their IT skills.

## Assessment opportunities
This activity offers opportunities to assess the children's use of IT to convey information in textual form, and to assess their ability to choose different fonts and alter font size appropriately. There are also opportunities to assess

**INFORMATION TECHNOLOGY**

writing in the form of their 'literary style' and their use of connectives and subordinate clauses.

### Display ideas

The children will have been aiming to produce a book for younger pupils which looks good, has quality text and is fun to read. The proof of the pudding is in the reading, so make sure you give the book to younger pupils to read and comment on! Encourage them to provide feedback to your class, saying which rhymes were their favourites and how much they enjoyed reading them.

# MAKING DATA COLLECTION SHEETS

*To use a computer to produce a classroom resource. To offer IT opportunities to experiment with layout for a particular purpose and content.*

†† *Individuals or pairs.*

🕐 *30–40 minutes at the computer; 15 minutes discussion.*

### Previous skills/knowledge needed

Children will need the ability to write at Levels 2/3 or beyond, and will require some basic knowledge of word processing.

### Key background information

The questionnaire is a popular and useful tool for gathering a variety of data. The data is usually fed straight into a computer which then analyses and processes the results.

This activity encourages the children to use IT for the specific purpose of producing their own professional-looking data collection sheets. These sheets can then be used in a wide variety of curriculum contexts to collect data.

### Vocabulary

Spacing, insertion, data, information, tally, field, heading, units.

### Preparation

Make enough copies of photocopiable page 128 for children to have one each, whether working individually or in pairs. Find a variety of examples of data collection sheets to show the children, for example from maths, science or geographical work books. Set up one or more real contexts for gathering data, such as school visits to museums, local factories or businesses, science experiments, investigational maths activities and so on. Linking the activity below to real situations like these will help to increase the status of the finished results. However, other sources of data can be used, such as information collected from CD-ROM or from pages on the Internet.

### Resources needed

A computer, word processing software, a printer, paper, examples of data collection sheets, a real context for data collection, sources of data such as CD-ROMs or pages from the Internet, coloured paper, pencils/pens, photocopiable page 128.

### What to do

Start with a whole class introduction, talking to the children about why we need to gather information. Use

photocopiable page 128 as an introduction to the process of data collection. The photocopiable activity involves designing a sheet which a new parent visiting your school for the first time could use to collect useful information. Discuss the importance of a clear layout for the data sheet, and in what form the information is required – will there be 'yes/no', multiple choice or open-ended responses? Talk about the purpose of the information and what makes it relevant and useful. Can the children think of any other facts that would be useful to include? Now ask them to design their own version of this data collection sheet on the photocopiable sheet. Alternatively, encourage them to provide you with layout and content suggestions and use these to create a single data collection sheet to demonstrate the process for the whole class. (Doing a pen and paper exercise first will help the children to appreciate the advantages of using IT.)

Next, tell the children that they are going to design their own data-collection sheets on the computer. Show them some of the other examples you have gathered together. Introduce the terminology of 'data', 'tally', 'field' (an alternative word for heading/label), 'heading' and 'information'. Depending on your classroom situation, you may choose to have all the children working within one context, or several groups working within a variety of contexts, designing sheets for different purposes. If it is not possible for children to use real contexts to gather data, provide suitable alternative sources of information such as CD-ROMs and Internet pages.

What is this school like?

Imagine that some parents are visiting your school to find out more about it. Below are some questions that they need to write down answers to.

Name and address of school

When did the school open?

Names of teaching staff

Names of support staff

How many pupils, girls/ boys?

How many classrooms?

How many subjects taught?

Age ranges of pupils

What sports are played?

What clubs are there after school?

How many computers are there in school?

How many pupils are there to one computer on average?

List the software that pupils use in the school

▲ Can you design and lay out a data collection sheet to enable the parents to gather the information below? You will need to think carefully about leaving enough space for them to write in the answers. Consider the type of responses – will they be 'yes/no' or open-ended? What other things will you need to think about carefully?

Explain to the children that they must think carefully as to what information needs collecting and in what form – will it be in words or numbers? If numbers, are there any units? The content depends on the context, but their sheet is likely to include numbered questions and extra space for additional comments or an illustration of some sort. Emphasise that the children should concentrate on features such as spacing, clarity, where answers are to be inserted, spacing for individual names, headings and subheadings. (It may be helpful to provide demonstrations of these formatting techniques on screen for them.) Although the children will use the computer to produce their final version, this is one of the rare occasions when producing a paper and pencil mock-up first is helpful.

The children can test their completed data collection sheets by using them for the purpose for which they were originally designed. They may use them individually or a group, discussing how useful the sheets proved to be. Th activity should include evaluation and suggestions for changes to improve the effectiveness of the data collection sheets.

### Suggestion(s) for extension
If a desktop publishing (DTP) application is available, even more professional results may be obtained. Children who need challenging can use the frames and other formatting facilities provided in DTP software to produce these high standards.

### Suggestion(s) for support
Producing a handwritten first draft is a good start and will guide less confident children. Working in pairs will provide mutual support for these children.

### Assessment opportunities
This activity allows you to assess how well the children use IT to convey information using text in the form of data collection sheets designed for a specific purpose. Look out for accurately placed labels, appropriate font sizes, and clarity in the layout. Some limited additional opportunities for assessments of the children's writing are also possible in the form of punctuation and spelling.

### Display ideas
The display of data needs careful consideration, and requires good creative management to produce effective results. Encouraging the children to present data on professional-looking sheets, using coloured fonts and interesting layouts, will help to enhance the display. Printing the collection sheets on coloured paper is another way of making a display more lively. Producing graphs to show patterns in the data, and using captions to link these to the data itself, will also raise visual interest. For any visual display of data, labelling is essential: it allows the onlooker to see at a glance what the information is all about. Using large headings such as, 'Did you know that...?', and 'Can you guess what we found...?' will attract attention.

### Reference to photocopiable sheet
Photocopiable page 128 involves designing a data collection sheet that would be useful for a new parent visiting your school for the first time.

...cessing software to redraft text.

...minutes at computer; 15 minutes discussion.

### Previous skills/knowledge needed
Children should have the ability to write at Levels 3/4 and confidence in using word processing software. Experience in writing examples of précis would also be helpful.

### Key background information
This activity would be particularly appropriate during a project on newspapers or communication. Newspaper journalists often obtain stories from news agencies or other sources which have to be completely rewritten (as 'copy') for their own particular newspaper style and readership. This activity gives children the opportunity to rewrite a newspaper piece or other story for an audience different from that for which it was originally written.

### Vocabulary
Copy (as in newspaper text), text, style, audience, redraft, journalist, editor, deadline.

### Preparation
Make one copy of photocopiable page 129 for each child. Collect a variety of different newspapers – national, local, daily and weekly. Try to find a story that appears in several different newspapers so that the children can compare them.

### Resources needed
A computer, word processing software, a printer, a variety of newspapers, pens, paper, photocopiable page 129.

### What to do
Give the children copies of the news story on photocopiable page 129 or provide them with stories from real newspapers. Explain that you want them to rewrite the story for a different audience, for example very young children, teenagers or grandparents. Let the children use pen and paper to begin with. This will help them to appreciate how much easier the task is when they can use the computer.

Now show the children a variety of newspapers. Ask them to look particularly at the different styles of writing in each. Show them the same news story printed in various newspapers and discuss the similarities and differences in style, vocabulary and so on. Tell them to choose a story that particularly interests them and, using a computer, redraft the story to make it appropriate for a younger audience.

### Suggestion(s) for extension
Ask the children to rewrite the text for a second particular audience – for example, grandparents, eccentric scientists, aliens from another galaxy or people from a past civilisation. You could ask them to redraft their stories, increasing or reducing the number of words. This will require them to show further IT editing skills.

### Suggestion(s) for support
Go over the original story with less confident children to help them pick out the major points. Additional support could be provided by using a highlighter pen to mark the appropriate text, and asking them to present two or three sentences for you to check before continuing.

### Assessment opportunities
This activity will enable you to make assessments of how well the children are using IT to convey information in the form of text, in the context of writing newspaper stories for a particular audience. Look out for the children's degree of confidence in using the word processing software, how they carry out edits on the screen (when they change their minds concerning some text), and the ease with which they save and print out text. There are also opportunities to make assessments in English, especially in the form of organisation and clarity. Further assessments of spelling and punctuation are possible.

### Display ideas
This work can provide wonderful opportunities for display, perhaps with a heading such as 'Our class newspaper – stories straight from our own correspondents!' Enlarged photocopies of the children's stories alongside the originals, perhaps with accompanying photographs, will create an interesting class or school display.

INFORMATION TECHNOLOGY

**Making the headlines**

▲ Below is a news story which needs to be redrafted so that it is appropriate for your newspaper's readers. Think carefully about your audience before rewriting this on paper or typing it into the computer for redrafting.

A light aircraft made a forced landing onto a motorway. Traffic swerved to avoid the plane. The plane landed in the direction of the traffic flow. There were two people on board the plane. The plane had flown into a flock of Canada geese and one of them had hit the propeller, breaking it. The plane stopped and pulled into the hard shoulder of the motorway. The pilot's name was Jim Fraser and it was the second time he has made a forced landing. The plane had to be taken apart to get it off the motorway. There was a 24 mile traffic queue while the plane was removed. The passenger in the plane was Mr Fraser's twelve-year-old daughter Catherine. Catherine said it was a great adventure and she wouldn't have missed it for the world.

### Reference to photocopiable sheet
Photocopiable page 129 displays a short 'typical' news story which the children have to redraft in a style appropriate for a particular audience. It can be used as an onscreen exercise, or as a pen and paper exercise to introduce the IT task above.

## PEN PORTRAITS

*To use word processing software to communicate in writing with others, perhaps including transmission by e-mail (optional).*

†† *Individuals or pairs.*

🕐 *20 minutes at computer; 10 minutes discussion.*

### Previous skills/knowledge needed
Children should be confident in using word processing software.

### Key background information
Children often find writing about themselves easier than writing about other subjects. The aim of this activity is for them to use IT to communicate, perhaps through e-mail, with an unknown person and to include as many interesting facts about themselves as possible.

E-mail is the communication medium of the future, being fast, cheap and direct. Schools all over the world are able to communicate easily through this medium with excellent curriculum benefits. Although access to e-mail is not essential for this activity, it opens up many possibilities if your school has an Internet link. Children are able to exchange information about what they do at school, what

they eat for lunch, games t[...] descriptions of local places [...] Often, pupils will pair up [...] correspond with. At som[...] exchange descriptions of t[...] more personal, and this a[...] these.

If e-mail facilities are not available, you can use [...] personal descriptions with the whole class or groups, perhaps playing a guessing game to find out which child each description applies to.

### Vocabulary
E-mail, electronic mail, modem, on-line, log on, Internet, Internet provider, World Wide Web.

### Preparation
If you have an e-mail facility, set up a suitable link, such as with another school in a different part of the country or overseas, to enable the children to transmit their descriptions to.

### Resources
Computer, printer, paper, e-mail facility (optional).

### What to do
Even without an e-mail context, writing personal descriptions or 'pen portraits' is a useful exercise for the children, offering opportunities to appreciate similarities and differences between people in a positive way. Start by discussing with the children what kind of information would

**INFORMATION TECHNOLOGY**

...nd interesting for a distant pen pal or someone ...ho not know them. Then allow them access to the ...puter in pairs, or individually, to enter their descriptions. ...ncourage the children to print out their finished ...escriptions and perhaps to draw illustrations of themselves to accompany their work. If an e-mail contact is possible, several personal descriptions may be sent out to a distant contact. Hopefully, this will produce individual replies enabling the children to match up with a distant pen pal. If an e-mail facility is not available, the children could play a game where they choose a description at random (cover up or omit the name first!) and see whether they can recognise the child it relates to.

### Suggestion(s) for extension

This task could also provide an information handling exercise. The children could create a class database in which they group themselves according to their various attributes. As well as self-written portraits, the children could write portraits about their friends. This would produce some interesting results – which were the most accurate and why? Alternatively, the children could reduce their descriptions to a shorter length or produce a description which consists of their own ideas, plus those suggested by a friend.

### Suggestion(s) for support

For less confident children, provide a list of specific characteristics for them to describe. Focusing on physical characteristics such as hair and eye colour, shoe size and so on, will help them.

### Assessment opportunities

The activity provides opportunities to assess the children's IT capability in communicating information, and in their ability to compose and redraft using word processing software. Similarly, in English there are opportunities to assess organisation, imagination and clarity within their personal descriptions. Assessment of grammatical construction, punctuation and spelling are also possible.

### Display ideas

The children's descriptions can be used to create an interesting display. Adding old or current photographs of the children, and drawings which they have created using a variety of media, can add to the appeal. Such a display offers good opportunities to raise the children's self-esteem and to discuss cultural similarities and differences.

## OUR SCHOOL

*To design and format text for a wider audience. To provide opportunities for using the graphic frame facility within a desktop publishing program.*

†† *Whole class working in pairs.*

🕐 *40 minutes at the computer; 20 minutes discussion.*

### Previous skills/knowledge needed

Children must be confident in using a word processing or DTP application. They should also have looked in detail at the existing school prospectus.

### Key background information

In the world of marketing and selling, quality presentation is increasingly important. High standards of communication, efficiency in telling people what they want to know, and making access to this information as enjoyable as possible is all part of the marketing process. Competition is a driving

force and children need to be aware of its benefits and pitfalls. A school prospectus is not only a marketing tool but also an opportunity to tell parents what they want to know. The better the quality of the prospectus, the more impressed parents will be. In this task, the children use their school prospectus as a model to enable them to create their own 'Pupils' Prospectus' on the computer, making it look as professional as possible.

## Vocabulary
Format, style, content, section, chapter, paragraph, frame, flat plan.

## Preparation
Collect several copies of the school prospectus for the children to look at.

## Resources needed
A computer, word processing software, desktop publishing software (optional), printer (preferably colour), paper, copies of the school prospectus.

## What to do
Let the children examine copies of your school prospectus. Discuss with them the purpose of a school prospectus and its organisation, layout, style and content. Explain that they are going to write their own prospectus, but it will be aimed at pupils rather than parents. It will be written from their own point of view, to give new children coming to the school an idea of what it is like and perhaps to persuade other children to attend their school. Consider how the children can market or 'sell' their school to the best advantage.

Ask the children to work in pairs and assign each pair a different area to write about, or let the children choose for themselves. Decide as a group on the contents of the prospectus and the number of pages, then draw up a 'flat plan' – a plan of what goes on each page. Remember to include the cover. Ask the children to keep their entries short and emphasise the need for factual information rather than anecdotal content, although a certain amount of this could add to the style. If a DTP application is available, encourage the children to place text within the graphic frames facility to achieve a high quality of presentation. You may need to demonstrate how to do this by accessing the frame tool and placing a graphic onto the page. Further enhancements may be made by giving the frames particular borders.

Once the children are happy with their individual entries, ask them to print these out so that they can be collated. IT graphics or hand-drawn pictures could be used to illustrate the covers and inside pages of the prospectus. (Page 31 provides an activity on designing covers.)

## Suggestion(s) for extension
Children might like to insert computer generated graphics into appropriate sections. These may take the form of scanned images, video images or pictures drawn in a graphics application.

## Suggestion(s) for support
Children with less confidence will find it easier to write about what they know well such as the school uniform, the games facilities, school rules, school visits and trips. Talk to them to clarify the content of their writing.

## Assessment opportunities
This activity will enable you to make assessments in IT capability at Levels 3 and 4. Focus on the children's ability to combine text and graphics and to use appropriate fonts and formats relevant to the audience, as well as to redraft and work more independently.

## Display ideas
Pages from the children's 'prospectus' could be displayed in the school entrance to provide an entertaining and informative account of school life.

## DESIGNING A POSTER

*To introduce DTP format facilities. To use clip art to enhance a product.*

†† *Whole class working in pairs and larger groups.*

🕐 *45 minutes at computer; 15 minutes discussion.*

## Previous skills/knowledge needed
Children should have the ability to use a variety of fonts and to vary the font size and colour. An understanding of how to use computerised 'clip art' illustrations to enhance their work would be helpful. They should also have seen a selection of posters to appreciate the type of information that these can convey.

INFORMATION
TECHNOLOGY

## Key background information

IT provides an efficient and flexible tool for poster design and production. Designing onscreen allows ideas to be tried out, formatting changed, particular words emphasised and illustrations added to enhance and embellish. Some software includes templates for poster production and, although this takes most of the creativity out of the process, it allows the children to complete their task quickly, easing the burden of access to the computer. The final printout can be of excellent quality and can be photocopied to produce high-quality posters or flyers for school events, whether for a larger audience or simply for other pupils.

## Vocabulary

Heading, emphasis, font size, centring, visual impact, laser printer, print run, flyer, graphic, clip art.

## Preparation

Gather together a collection of different posters and flyers as a stimulus for the children's own work. Make several copies of photocopiable page 130 for small groups of children or enlarge it for larger groups or the whole class. Try to link this activity with a real context for the children to produce posters or flyers, such as a school fair or sports day. Alternatively, devise an imaginary context for them along similar lines.

## Resources needed

A computer with desktop publishing software, a printer, paper, examples of posters and flyers, a collection of relevant clip art, conventional art materials (felt-tipped pens, paint and so on), photocopiable page 130.

## What to do

Show a variety of different posters and flyers to the class or a large group and discuss the purposes of posters and what makes them effective. Who do the children think the posters are aimed at and how can they tell? Ask them to pick out examples that they think work particularly well. Can they explain why this is? The children may start to see that often the more simple a poster is the more effective it is in conveying its message. Use photocopiable page 130 to encourage them to look at a poster more critically and to make suggestions for improvement.

Now tell the children that they are going to design their own posters for a special school event – whether this is a real or imaginary event will obviously depend on the situation. Explain that it is good marketing to advertise the same event in different ways, so you want groups of children to produce different styles of posters and flyers. Discuss important information that the posters must include such as date, time, place and cost, and encourage them to think carefully about who the posters are aimed at. The children could embellish their work with clip art, but they may be tempted to overfill their poster. Emphasise the importance of leaving some empty space to allow the eye to rest.

Divide the children into small groups and ask them to decide on the type of poster or flyer they wish to produce. Some children will use the computer and others will do this task using conventional art materials. Individual tasks could be allocated within those groups using IT to allow the children to work in pairs on the computer. These tasks could match the children's individual strengths such as language ability, design or layout skills.

When the children's different versions of posters and flyers are completed, hold a whole class session in which the children judge the examples. This will allow a true comparison between IT and conventional art techniques and the children should be encouraged to discuss the advantages and disadvantages of both processes.

The children may like to follow up this activity by designing a ticket or brochure for an event such as a mission to Mars trip, a tea clipper to India journey, a Polar expedition and so on. Again, the necessity of clarifying the purpose, style, content and audience is important.

### Suggestion(s) for extension
More able children could produce posters to illustrate historical rather than current events, for example: 'Grand opening of the Pyramid of Cheops', 'Volunteers wanted to build Stonehenge' – the opportunities are endless! They should use appropriate fonts and search out relevant clip art for these extension activities.

### Suggestion(s) for support
Keep the content simple for less confident children. Having entered their text and centred it, it may be sufficient as they can enhance it afterwards with hand-drawn or cut-out illustrations rather than IT graphics.

### Assessment opportunities
Opportunities are available in this activity to assess IT capability at Level 4. Focus on the children's ability to combine text and graphics and to write for a variety of audiences. There are also opportunities to make assessments in art.

**Poster mix-up**

The poster on the right is full of mistakes including ambiguous information, impossible times, too many fonts, spelling errors and irrelevant pictures.

parents join the pta
come and spend
**entrance 50**
an enjoyable
morning
*■ ▼** ▲**□● *●●●
Friday evening
in the school hall
bring a freind
*the* family *bring*
beetle drive

▲ How many mistakes can you spot? Could you design a better poster? What could you do to improve it?

### Display ideas
A noticeboard or corridor with an eye-catching display of posters can be most attractive. If large fonts are used, the children's work can be displayed higher up or at a greater distance from onlookers. Pinning posters at angles or using the ceiling for a display can enhance the effect.

### Reference to photocopiable sheet
Photocopiable page 130 shows an example of a poster containing many mistakes including ambiguous information, impossible times, too many fonts, spelling errors, irrelevant graphics and so on. How many mistakes can the children spot? Could they design a better one?

YOUR
**PHARAOH**
NEEDS
**YOU**

## DESIGNING A COVER

*To use DTP software to create a design for a special purpose. To use a variety of fonts, including rotated fonts, and clip art or graphic files produced in an art application.*

†† *Pairs.*

🕐 *45 minutes at the computer; 10 minutes discussion.*

### Previous skills/knowledge needed
Familiarity with DTP software will help the children in this task, together with knowledge/experience of mixing graphics with text.

### Key background information
The technological revolution has had a huge impact on the design and printing world. The facility to use IT in the

classroom to produce the high standards possible today was unimaginable until relatively recently. The computer in your classroom can probably be used to produce professional quality labels, covers and simple designs. Children are enthusiastic about their favourite books and music, and so designing a cassette case insert, a CD cover or a book cover gives them an opportunity to combine IT tools and their imagination to good effect. The use of DTP tools, especially font manipulation, rotation and shadowing, provides visually exciting results well within the children's reach.

### Preparation
Make a collection of a variety of attractive book covers and CD and cassette inlay cards.

### Resources needed
A computer with a desktop publishing package, a hand-held scanner (optional), a printer, paper, pencils, conventional art materials (felt-tipped pens and paint), examples of book covers, CD/cassette inlay cards.

### What to do
Begin this activity by showing the children examples of the various book covers and inlay cards that you have collected. Draw their attention to the importance of clarity of design, especially with reference to the title and author, and how pictures or graphics enhance the product. Some modern designs leave much to the imagination by being unclear in the title, especially some pop music material which relies more on images. Consider the audience each

cover or inlay is aimed at, and encourage the children to comment on how clear the titles are. Look at other information such as the publisher, cost and contents.

Tell the children that they are going to design their own book covers or CD/cassette inlay cards. Ask them to think about their 'product' and, in pairs, allow them to rough out their ideas using pencil and paper. Then give them access to the computer in pairs. They may want to rotate fonts and you will need to demonstrate how to do this. However, it is best for them to concentrate on clear labelling and accuracy of content rather than attempting to be too sophisticated.

Children are adept at discovering the possibilities of IT software when left to their own devices. If they are new to the software, do not be too insistent on printed results, as several attempts may be necessary to begin with. In certain cases, children may use IT to produce only the words and turn to conventional means to produce the background and/or artwork. Inevitably, the IT task may take some time, but it may be a good idea to change over after 45 minutes.

If the children have access to a hand-held scanner, images from photographs can be inserted into their designs. Artwork can, of course, be produced within a graphics package, or the children may make use of available clip art to enhance their covers. Use their results to further discussion on style and presentation and to spur on the next pair of children using the computer.

### Suggestion(s) for extension
Some art packages offer sophisticated facilities for font and image manipulation and confident children can be given

further opportunity to explore these. They can extend their skills by designing covers for imaginary books, for example, 'Rocket Engine Manual', 'Time Machine Engine Diagnostic Booklet', 'Bungee Jumpers' Handbook' and so on.

### Suggestion(s) for support
Limit expectations with less confident children, perhaps to using IT for the production of text only. Pairing them with a more confident child may offer additional support.

### Assessment opportunities
This activity will enable you to assess children's ability at combining text and graphics. Look for their ability at finding the graphics images and inserting them into the appropriate place within their design. Are the text and images balanced, meaningful and correctly sized? There are also opportunities to make assessments in art as to how well the children select appropriate resources and experiment with the possibilities that these offer, and their selection of visual elements appropriate to the purpose.

### Display ideas
A collage consisting of a variety of the children's cover designs will be interesting and attractive. Enlarged examples imaginatively displayed will show off their efforts to good effect.

## FAMOUS PEOPLE

*To search a CD-ROM and select images and text for saving and downloading into word processing software.*

†† *Pairs.*

🕐 *30 minutes at the computer; 10 minutes demonstration.*

### Previous skills/knowledge needed
Children will need the ability to access information from CD-ROMs, and to insert saved text and graphics into a word processing or DTP application.

### Key background information
CD-ROMs are capable of storing enormous amounts of information and are a fast, cheap and efficient medium to use. Children need to develop the skill of accessing information from CD-ROMs, and this activity requires them to search for both text and graphical information, then to download and save it from the CD-ROM into a word processing or DTP application. It uses the context of famous people, offering excellent links to other curriculum subjects such as history or science. Once the children have obtained the appropriate information, the remainder of the activity centres on DTP formatting.

Children need to learn that different CD-ROMS have different ways of providing access to information. If it is an encyclopaedia type of CD-ROM then there will be a built-in routine to allow searches to be made. Other types of CD-ROM may be of the 'browse around' kind, where a search routine is not an integral part of the software. The routines for saving text and graphics will again depend on the type of CD-ROM used. Saving the material first, rather than dragging it straight into the word processing software, is good practice. Once the material has been collected, it could be transferred to a floppy disk for use on another machine.

### Vocabulary
CD-ROM, CD-ROM drive, access, image, text, search routine, download.

### Preparation
Collect a variety of CD-ROMs, including encyclopaedias such as *Encarta*, *Hutchinson's Encyclopaedia* and *Kingfisher Micropedia*, which include information about famous people, perhaps relating to the children's current work in other subjects. Make a copy of photocopiable page 131 for each child.

### Resources needed
A computer with a CD-ROM drive, a DTP or word processing application, a printer, paper, a collection of CD-ROMs containing information on famous people (see Preparation), photocopiable page 131.

INFORMATION TECHNOLOGY

## What to do

This task centres around the production of five (or less) short descriptions or 'portraits' of famous people. The children can each choose their famous people according to the particular curriculum context they are working within at the time. Start by telling them that they are going to do some research into these people using CD-ROMs as the source of information. Give each of them a copy of photocopiable page 131 to focus them on the basic facts they will need to gather about their famous people. This will help to keep their material relevant and interesting. Talk about any additional information that may be useful.

Now explain that you want the children to gather information from the collection of CD-ROMs you have provided, using the questions or headings on the photocopiable sheet to guide them. They must download the relevant text from the CD-ROM into a word processing application and re-work it to produce short passages of around 50–100 words for each of their famous people. They must also include a graphic downloaded from the CD-ROM as part of their page, preferably a picture of each character or something relevant to them. Emphasise that the text must be edited in some way and not merely left unchanged. If necessary, provide a demonstration showing the children how to access information from a CD-ROM and explaining the routines for downloading and saving text and graphics into a word processing or DTP file.

The children can present their finished portraits together as a series, perhaps in chronological order of birth or the date of the person's main achievement.

## Suggestion(s) for extension

The children could carry out a similar task choosing famous scientists, artists or musicians, famous places, animals, forms of transport and so on, depending on the current curriculum context. The emphasis should be on accuracy, brevity and quality of production. The skill to be developed is one of seeking out the important detail from the wealth of information available. The task may be further extended by the children concentrating on one famous person and finding additional material taken either from CD-ROMs or reference books. The idea is for them to build up a portfolio on their chosen character and produced using IT.

## Suggestion(s) for support

The task may be limited to focusing on one or two characters only and printing out immediately after downloading the text and graphics rather than editing onscreen. The children can then use a highlighter pen to mark the important information for later word processing. This allows them to make progress away from the computer. They can then return to working onscreen knowing what text to keep, amend or cut. Again, pairing with a more confident child can offer great advantages.

## Assessment opportunities

This activity will offer opportunities for assessment in IT capability in the combining of text and graphics and in redrafting and refining their work. Look to see how confidently your children are accessing the graphic images and how they are processing the textual information. Their formatting and layout should show evidence of organisation, especially the sizing of graphics and the balance of text and images. There are also opportunities to make assessments in writing, including their ability to edit the text, keeping it grammatically structured and clear, with acceptable punctuation and spelling.

**INFORMATION TECHNOLOGY**

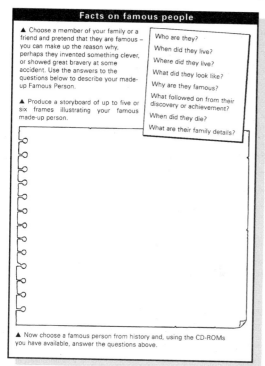

**Facts on famous people**

▲ Choose a member of your family or a friend and pretend that they are famous – you can make up the reason why, perhaps they invented something clever, or showed great bravery at some accident. Use the answers to the questions below to describe your made-up Famous Person.

▲ Produce a storyboard of up to five or six frames illustrating your famous made-up person.

Who are they?

When did they live?

Where did they live?

What did they look like?

Why are they famous?

What followed on from their discovery or achievement?

When did they die?

What are their family details?

▲ Now choose a famous person from history and, using the CD-ROMs you have available, answer the questions above.

### Display ideas

The children's work from this activity can enhance any project on people, places or things. By producing only brief descriptive text and including interesting graphics, displays will be visually appealing and accessible. The children's results could be collected and mounted into small books, for example 'Our Book of Famous Scientists'.

### Reference to photocopiable sheet

Photocopiable page 131 lists a variety of headings to help focus the children in the information collection exercise.

## THE CLASS NEWSPAPER

*To have the opportunity to select, write and illustrate within a specific context using IT. To provide the opportunity to edit, cut and paste and write in a variety of styles using IT.*

†† *Whole class working in pairs.*

🕐 *30 minute sessions at the computer; 20 minutes discussion.*

### Previous skills/knowledge needed

The children need to be confident in using word processing software and should be able to format text and images. They must have a knowledge of newspaper layouts and features such as headlines, subheadings and justified text.

### Key background information

The production of a class newspaper can be most rewarding. The idea is to involve the whole class in a team effort and, with older children, to have an editing team that

can delegate particular tasks. This acti[vity enables] children to write for a particular audienc[e and to] redraft text using a variety of IT skills. [...] within a historical context where the children [use] information to produce a newspaper relevant to a particular period. It could be presented as a 'real' daily paper with current local or world news. Alternatively, it could be a school newspaper reporting on internal events. The management and structure of the activity will be similar whatever the context. Use the exercise to awaken the children to real-life newspaper production and how IT dominates the process offering efficiency, speed and quality. A visit to your local newspaper office is an excellent start!

### Vocabulary

Copy (as in newspaper text), redraft, columns, justified text, centred text, headline, subheading, spacing, deadline.

### Preparation

If you plan to do this activity over several days you may need to borrow more computers. If possible, obtain some software which emulates news flashes coming down a telephone line, such as Extra. This software helps to

generate the situation within a newspaper office, where newsflashes occur regularly while the team is trying to meet its production deadline. If using this, you will need to load the various stories in a particular order and sprinkle them with irrelevant details beforehand. The addition of irrelevant material allows the children to prioritise and decide what makes a good story. Producing a newspaper for a real audience, such as for another class, will add greatly to the children's motivation.

Gather a good range of newspapers for the children to look at and use as a stimulus. If you choose a historical context for your newspaper, collect plenty of relevant reference material. For a newspaper relating to school events, you may need a longer period of time in which to gather suitable stories.

### Resources needed

A computer, or several if possible, to re-create a 'news room' atmosphere, word processing or DTP software, a printer, paper, editing room 'paraphernalia' (a scanner, tape recorders, notice boards, telephones and so on), software such as Extra which emulates newsflashes coming down a telephone line (optional), suitable reference material (for newspapers set in a historical context), a selection of different types of newspaper – weekly locals, daily nationals and so on.

### What to do

You can carry out this activity in several ways. It can be a full-time project for a couple of days, dedicating time to news gathering, editing and final production to meet a specific deadline (like the real thing). This may allow you to borrow extra computers or software to engage more children in the task at the same time. It also means that the inevitable disruption is short-lived! Alternatively, you can take a more measured approach, allowing more time to concentrate on the finished product.

Start by showing the whole class a selection of different newspapers. What different sections do newspapers include? What makes them different from each other? Look at the various features such as photographs, headings and subheadings and discuss the different layouts.

Now tell the children that they are going to work as part of a team to produce their own newspaper. Explain the newspaper's context – for example a newspaper set in a period long ago, a current 'local' newspaper or a school newspaper. Tell them who they are writing this for (children in another class, for example) to motivate them and to encourage them to think carefully about the audience. Provide suitable reference material for them to gather their stories from.

The 'team's' initial task is to produce the raw copy. Aim for a front page only, perhaps with a second page if there is sufficient material. Decide what news stories the children want to cover and let them think up some catchy headlines. If possible, have the 'journalists' writing copy at the keyboard. Other children could be working on scanned images, photograph insertion, advertisements, sections on sport, travel, leisure, a children's page or crossword and so on at the same time.

**INFORMATION TECHNOLOGY**

Depending on the children's capabilities, you can enter the copy immediately into a 'master' file where the final draft is gradually put together, or completed stories could be kept and shared out to produce a variety of editions. The organisation will depend greatly on the quantity of computers available and your chosen style of production. Whatever you choose, the children should be aiming for a high-quality final result.

### Suggestion(s) for extension
Confident children can be involved with the more demanding aspects of production, such as the manipulation of graphics or taking overall responsibility for a whole section.

### Suggestion(s) for support
Children who are less confident should be occupied with a clearly defined task. Examples could include producing a jokes or games section, or creating a 'wordsearch' puzzle on a particular theme.

### Assessment opportunities
You can assess how well the children use IT to convey ideas and information using text and graphics. Look out for their general confidence at the keyboard using the word processor facilities such as different fonts and layouts, and the inclusion of graphical material.

### Display ideas
The display of the finished newspaper(s) should generate much interest. Showing the stages that the children went through to achieve this result, perhaps with photographs, would add significance to the display. Placing first drafts or initial material alongside the completed newspaper would provide a comprehensive and stimulating insight into the making of a newspaper.

## FOUR-COLOUR EXERCISE

***To use flood fill techniques with accuracy.***

†† *Individuals or pairs.*

🕐 *30 minutes at the computer; 10 minutes demonstration.*

### Previous skills/knowledge needed
Little IT knowledge and few skills are necessary.

### Key background information
Graphics applications usually incorporate a 'flood fill' tool which fills a specified area with a selected colour. The icon on the button for this tool is often marked as a tilting can of paint with a stream of paint pouring out. It is a satisfying technique for children to use and is effective in filling both small and large areas with a variety of colours.

The idea in this activity is to use the flood fill tool to produce a variety of patterns according to certain rules which limit the number of colours that can be used. In this case, only four colours are allowed and the same colour should not touch both sides of any line or 'boundary'. This limitation is taken from what is known as the 'Map Colour Problem' – what is the least number of colours that can be use to colour a map without two different countries sharing the same colour across a boundary? The answer is four!

### Vocabulary
Flood fill, palette, selected colour, boundary.

### Preparation
Make one copy of photocopiable page 132 for each child.

### Resources needed
A computer, graphics software with flood fill tool, colour printer, paper, photocopiable page 132.

## What to do

Introduce photocopiable page 132 to a selected group of children who will later undertake a similar task on the computer, or use it as a whole class activity. Ask the children to colour the pattern on the sheet using as few colours as possible, making sure that no colour meets the same colour on either side of a line or boundary. Attempting this exercise on paper first will help the children to appreciate how much easier it is to do the same task on the computer using IT graphics tools.

Now show the children how to use the computer graphics program to 'take a pencil for a walk', filling the screen with a squiggly pattern containing many enclosed areas created with thin 'pencil' or 'brush' lines. Then demonstrate how to colour the pattern with the fill tool. Explain to the children that you want them to repeat this task on the computer, but emphasise that only four colours can be used and the same colour must not appear on both sides of any line or 'boundary'. If they find being limited to four colours too difficult, you may have to relent and allow them to use additional colours!

When all the spaces are filled in the children's patterns, including the background, let the children make colour printouts, perhaps using them to embellish a folder or an exercise book. Changing the colour selection on the same pattern looks effective when displayed beside the original, and the children could produce several versions using different colours.

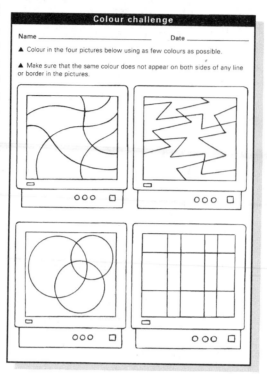

## Suggestion(s) for extension

More confident children could explore the use of the colour palette more fully. Using a range of different tones within a single colour can look very effective; but this will obviously depend on whether your software has this facility. If it does not, the children could try using different shades of grey or a variety of patterned fills.

## Suggestion(s) for support

Allow less confident children to use as many colours as they wish when filling in their pattern initially; then go on to limit their choice of colours as suggested in 'What to do'.

## Assessment opportunities

This activity will allow you to assess the children's ability to use IT equipment and graphics software while carrying out the above task. The links to the art curriculum can also be exploited for purposes of assessment.

## Display ideas

The children's patterns offer exciting opportunities for a display and, when imaginatively mounted, will enhance any area of the school. Ask the children to think up some unusual titles for their work.

## Reference to photocopiable sheet

Photocopiable page 132 contains a variety of simple patterns. The children must fill in the patterns using as few colours as possible, making sure that the same colour does not appear on both sides of any line or 'border'.

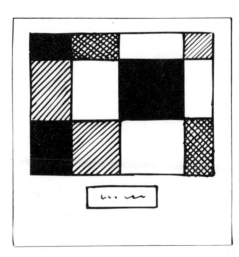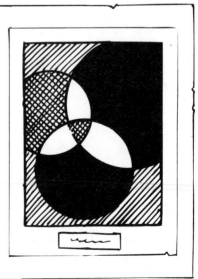

INFORMATION
TECHNOLOGY

# KANDINSKY PRINTS

*To become familiar with line, draw and flood fill facilities. To understand that using simple line and shape may produce simple results. To appreciate that background colours other than white can be used.*

†† *Individuals or pairs.*

⏰ *20 minutes at the computer; 10 minutes demonstration.*

## Previous skills/knowledge needed

The children need to be aware that the geometrical shape drawing tool in graphics programs produces a variety of shapes such as circles, squares and triangles.

## Key background information

IT graphics software offers an excellent opportunity to experiment with arranging colour, shape and form without the necessity of creating 'realistic' pictures. Such experiments can produce simple abstract drawings which look attractive and offer children instant success in that there is no right or wrong but simply an enjoyment of coloured shapes and forms. Historically, the Cubist Movement and the school of 'modern art' arose from this kind of artistic expression.

Children will need to see a variety of examples of modern art, such as pictures of works by Mondrian, Klee and Kandinsky, to appreciate the style and formulate their own ideas. Children are used to being given pieces of white paper on which to start their drawings but with IT they can start with a background or 'page' of any colour.

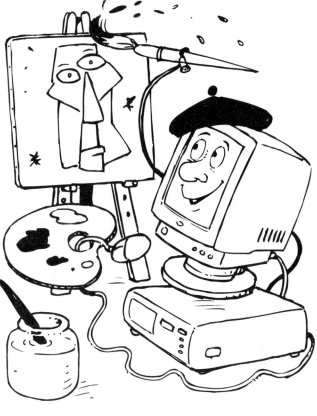

## Vocabulary

Drawing tool, flood fill, rubber banding, background, foreground, Cubism.

## Preparation

Make one copy of photocopiable page 133 for each child. Collect together some examples of modern art on posters or in books, particularly those by artists such as Kandinsky and Mondrian.

## Resources needed

A computer, graphics software with shape drawing tools to create squares, triangles and circles, a colour printer, paper (preferably special colour printer paper for brighter reproduction), some examples of Cubist art for discussion and stimulation, photocopiable page 133.

## What to do

Show the children the examples of modern art you have collected and point out the attributes which make it fit this category. Look at the shapes and colours that the artists used. Discuss how these pictures mostly concentrate on shape, form and colour and look at the balance between the areas of colour. Tell the children that you are going to paint your own piece of modern art using the computer. Starting with a blank screen, use the geometrical shape drawing tool to create a number of overlapping squares, circles and triangles. Show the children how, when using this tool, the first click of the mouse often fixes a corner of a shape or the centre of a circle. Moving the mouse outwards produces dotted lines showing what the shape would look like if you were to click the mouse for a second time. Explain that this is known as 'rubber banding', as the lines grow and shrink with each movement of the mouse. (The children will need to experiment later with different shapes and learn to relate the mouse movement with what is happening on the screen.) Leave plenty of empty areas within your shapes and use the colour fill tool to colour them. Don't forget to fill in all around to create a coloured background. If possible, try not to have the same colour on both sides of any border. The completed effect can look very appealing, rather like a stained glass window.

Having watched your demonstration, tell the children that they can now produce their own masterpieces. Before they start on the computer, however, give each child a copy of photocopiable page 133 to provide an opportunity to design their picture and experiment on paper first. (Make sure that they keep their drawings abstract rather than trying to create something realistic.) When they come to use IT, they should appreciate how much easier it is to make changes to their designs. Encourage them to start with a

INFORMATION TECHNOLOGY

coloured 'page' or background on the computer by flood filling the white screen.

This activity should not take too long – 15 minutes is plenty of time. The children may well have enough time to print out two or three examples of their individual designs, each filled with different colours.

### Suggestion(s) for extension

Invent rules for this activity such as using only three squares, three circles and three triangles in any one design, or eight rectangles only, according to the level of the children's ability. As in the previous task, 'Four-colour exercise' on page 37, you could also limit the number of colours used.

### Suggestion(s) for support

Suggesting that the children use only rectangles for their design will simplify the task. Once they have completed one design like this, they can then go on to try using different shapes.

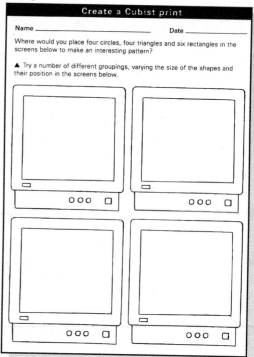

Create a Cubist print

Name _____ Date _____

Where would you place four circles, four triangles and six rectangles in the screens below to make an interesting pattern?

▲ Try a number of different groupings, varying the size of the shapes and their position in the screens below.

accept ordinary photocopying paper, superior colour reproduction can be achieved by using special colour printer paper. This paper does not absorb the ink but allows it to dry on the surface, resulting in much brighter colours. Including pictures of modern works of art by famous artists such as Kandinsky will add educational value to the display.

### Reference to photocopiable sheet

Photocopiable page 133 allows the children to produce some rough designs for their drawings before creating them using IT. This will help them to appreciate the greater flexibility that IT offers for such tasks over conventional art materials.

## MOOD PICTURES

*To experiment with a variety of graphic tools to achieve a specific outcome.*

†† *Individual or pairs.*

⏱ *20 minutes at the computer; 10 minutes discussion.*

### Previous skills/knowledge needed

A familiarity with the basic tools available within a graphics program (brush/pencil tool, line drawing tool, flood fill tool and so on) and the type of effects they achieve.

### Key background information

Colours have the power to affect our moods, although we may not always be aware of this. This activity allows the children to experiment with a variety of IT graphics tools to produce an abstract 'happy picture' without having to be

### Assessment opportunities

There are assessment opportunities during this activity to determine how well pupils use IT equipment and graphics software tools to produce pictures in a particular style. There are also opportunities to make assessments in art.

### Display ideas

The children's work from this activity can look most attractive when carefully mounted. Although most printers

particularly artistic. The children will soon discover that it is not only colours that generate a particular mood but also the type of patterns and shapes used.

This activity could accompany a conventional art lesson, offering a group of children an IT opportunity while the remainder use conventional media. Art produced by conventional means is difficult to change but IT offers much more flexibility for making alterations and correcting errors. The children should experience this 'fluidity' which is similar to that gained by using a word processor. In both types of software the children should learn to experiment, as nothing need be printed out until a satisfactory outcome has been achieved.

## Vocabulary
Brush tool, pencil tool, line drawing tool, flood fill, paint spray, colour palette.

## Preparation
Collect together a variety of abstract works of art which clearly convey different moods, such as Joan Miro's *Women and Bird in the Moonlight*, 1949 (silence and dreams), Picasso's *Three Musicians*, 1921 (sinister, solemn) and Paul Klee's *Park near Lucerne*, 1938 (display of experiences and sensations) to discuss with the children.

Before starting the activity, it is important to have talked about what makes the children happy or sad, and to have looked at a variety of abstract pictures, talking about how their mood is affected by these pictures.

## Resources needed
A computer, graphics software with a variety of drawing and colouring tools, a colour printer, paper, several examples of abstract art.

## What to do
Many pictures portray mood through their content but this activity concentrates on generating mood purely through colour and form. Show the children a variety of abstract pictures by well-known artists and discuss how each picture makes them feel. Try to identify what features create a particular mood, for example bright colours typically suggest light-heartedness, while dark or grey shades create more sombre atmospheres. How does pattern, shape or line define mood? (A good example is jagged lines which can be used to express anger.)

Now tell the children that they are going to produce their own 'happy picture' on the computer. Explain that rather than showing something 'real' the pictures must be abstract, focusing on line and colour. Let them work in pairs on the computer, producing their pictures together once they have agreed how the mood is going to be illustrated. They may be able to produce a picture each, depending on the time available, otherwise they should agree on content and technique and produce one picture between them. Encourage them to use a variety of graphics tools such as the brush/pencil tool, line drawing tool, flood fill tool and so on to produce their pictures.

Finally, ask the children to produce a short explanation on the word processor as to how their drawing suggests a particular mood.

## Suggestion(s) for extension
The children could extend their skills by portraying a sad or angry mood using graphics tools that they have not used in their previous picture.

**INFORMATION TECHNOLOGY**

### Suggestion(s) for support

Some children may not be familiar with the graphics tools. Ask a more confident child to demonstrate what effects these tools can produce but limit the number of tools used for less confident children.

### Assessment opportunities

You will be able to assess the children's ability to use IT to generate, amend, organise and present ideas in picture form using a variety of graphical tools. There are also opportunities to make assessments in art.

### Display ideas

The children's work could be used to create a comprehensive display, perhaps entitled 'Mood through pictures'. Placed alongside posters of abstract art, the children's work will look attractive and generate much interest. The addition of written explanations will create further discussion around your display.

## MONOCOLOUR PICTURES

*To become familiar with colour palette changes. To use a variety of tones of the same colour to produce a picture within a relevant context. To learn to use the subtleties of shade or tone within a single colour.*

†† *Individuals or pairs.*

🕐 *40 minutes at the computer; 10 minutes demonstration.*

### Previous skills/knowledge needed

A knowledge of how to use the basic tools available within a graphics program (brush/pencil tool, line drawing tool, flood fill tool and so on) and experience in colour mixing.

### Key background information

A common art activity is teaching children how to produce a range of shades of one colour by mixing paints. Graphics programs can offer children a similar opportunity to experiment with the colour palette – with the added advantage of no mess! This activity introduces children to colour mixing within a graphics program, encouraging them to think about the subtleties of colour and shading. The task involves painting a picture (within a relevant curriculum context) using a limited range of shades of one particular colour. The facility to produce a minimum of three shades of a particular colour within your graphics software is therefore essential.

Sophisticated graphics software may offer the facility to create thousands, even millions, of different shades of colours. It is important to remember that the colours will look different on screen from when they are printed out.

On screen the colour is transmitted and brighter, while on paper the colour is perceived through reflected light and therefore appears duller. Ultimately, the sensitivity of your colour printer will determine how many subtleties of tone are produced.

### Vocabulary

Palette, colour mix, shade/tone.

### Preparation

Find some examples of pictures which are dominated by one particular colour in several shades to use as a stimulus for the children's work. Some examples could include Braque's *Still Life with a Mandolin*, 1937 (mainly browns), Monet's *Rouen Cathedral*, 1895 (chiefly greys and light blue) and Picasso's *An Old Jew with a Boy*, 1903 (blue).

### Resources needed

A computer, graphics software which allows at least three different shades of a particular colour to be mixed, a colour printer, paper, examples of pictures that are dominated by a particular colour which appears in several shades.

### What to do

Show the children some pictures in which a single colour dominates, but appears in several different shades. Point out how, through using a range of shades of a single colour, shape and form are distinguishable in a picture. Explain that using this technique can produce attractive results.

Demonstrate to the class, or a large group, how to obtain various shades of one colour using the computer's colour mix facility. Tell them that you want them to produce their own pictures or patterns using shades of a single colour. They may like to use ideas from the previous activities, 'taking a pencil for a walk' (see page 38) or using the shape tool to produce areas to fill with colour (see page 39). Allow the children access to the computer in pairs, preferably with each pair choosing a different colour to use so that there is variety in the results. Once the children are happy with their results, they can make a colour printout.

## Suggestion(s) for extension

Challenge the children by changing the rules, for example by asking them to produce a pattern or picture using only two shades. They could create a new picture or work based on their original one, using fewer shades to provide an interesting comparison.

## Suggestion(s) for support

Ask less confident children to start by producing a pattern or picture with an unlimited palette. Having set out their design using the full range of colours, they then replace as many colours as they can with shades of their chosen colour, gradually reducing the number of shades used.

## Assessment opportunities

This activity will enable you to assess how well the children use the facilities available in graphics software to generate and communicate images. Focus particularly on their skill in using a variety of shades of one colour to produce their picture. There are also opportunities to make assessments in art.

## Display ideas

Carefully mount the children's pictures to create a bold, colourful display. Increase the impact of the pictures by clustering together those with similar colours. You could create a seasonal arrangement with browns for autumn, whites/greys or blues for winter, light green/pinks for spring and dark green/yellows for summer. Sunset shades could form another category.

# DESIGN A TAG

**To use the paint spray tool within a graphics program.**

†† *Individual or pairs.*

🕐 *20 minutes at the computer; 10 minutes discussion time.*

## Previous skills/knowledge needed

An understanding of how to access the paint spray tool within a graphics program and how to adjust the density of spray.

## Key background information

The urban subculture of 'tagging' – producing graffiti that forms the signature of the perpetrator – is generally considered highly undesirable. However, it has spawned an artistic style of its own that is unusual in its effects. The aim of this activity is for the children to use the paint spray tool to create their initials or name in this style, experimenting with control over the size and density of spray and colour change. An art lesson where your children are asked to design their own tag may appear questionable

initially, but it could be used positively to discuss the care of our environment and why we should treat property with respect.

Preferably, the children should see some examples of this art if they have not already done so. If you prefer, you can use examples of 'bubble' or hollow lettering. Photocopiable page 134 provides some examples of decorative letter styles that the children could use to write their names using the paint spray tool.

### Vocabulary
Paint spray tool, spray density, spray area.

### Preparation
Make a copy of photocopiable page 134 for each child.

### Resources needed
A computer, graphics software with a paint spray option and preferably the facility to change the density and size of spray, samples of 'tag' style lettering or bubble or hollow lettering – photocopiable page 134 provides some examples, a colour printer, paper.

### What to do
Start by showing the children the examples of 'tag' style lettering on photocopiable page 134 and any other examples you can find. Then demonstrate on the computer how to draw hollow letters using a single spray colour. Fill in the letters with a variety of spray colours, perhaps creating a 3D effect using shadowing if appropriate within the graphics package. A background such as a wall or door may be added later using other graphics facilities. Ensure that the children

keep to large lettering, this will offer them greater control over the process.

Now explain that the children will have the opportunity to write their initials on the computer using the paint spray tool. First, however, they need to practise their favourite type of lettering by drawing it on photocopiable page 134. Once they have completed some initial designs, let them work in pairs on the computer, using their hand-drawn designs to aid their onscreen work. As each pair finishes, post up their 'tags' for display to minimise repetition and help motivate the next IT users.

### Suggestion(s) for extension
More confident children could attempt to produce additional lettering, perhaps writing their full name or designing a title that is set within a coloured frame for a classroom display of the children's work from this activity. The process of using this technique for a particular purpose should extend their IT skills.

### Suggestion(s) for support
Children who are less confident may like to experiment freely with the paint spray tool for some time before attempting to paint their initials.

### Assessment opportunities
This activity will enable you to assess how well the children use IT to convey ideas through graphics, experimenting with a particular style of graphic art. Look to see with what degree of confidence the children choose and use the graphic tools. How do they handle errors? How much help do they need or are they happy to experiment and work

**Name tags**

Name _____ Date _____

Below are some examples of letters written in 'tag' and other decorative styles.
▲ Choose the style you would like to write your initials in and practise this in the space provided.

ABCDEFGHIJKLM
NOPQRSTUVWXYZ
Jack Gurinder Lucy
Gemma Peter Rajit

autonomously? Opportunities are also available to make assessments regarding art in their accuracy and attention to detail, and also in their identification of ways of improving their work.

### Display ideas
Create a street scene, painting brick walls and doors, as a backdrop against which to display the children's work.

### Reference to photocopiable sheet
Photocopiable page 134 provides some examples of 'tag' style and other decorative lettering for the children to base their designs on. The children choose their favourite style in which to practise drawing their initials.

---

## IMPRESSIONIST STYLE

*To provide further practise in using the paint spray tool to imitate a specific style of art.*

†† *Individual or pairs.*

🕐 *30 minutes at the computer; 10 minutes discussion.*

### Previous skills/knowledge needed
Some experience with the paint spray tool in graphics software (see 'Design a tag' activity on page 43). Some awareness of what Impressionist paintings look like.

### Key background information
The later French Impressionists (called Neo-Impressionists) succeeded in enhancing the realism in their paintings

through a technique called pointillism. This involved covering areas of their paintings with tiny dots or brushstrokes using a wide range of shades of a particular colour. This technique gives the colours a subtlety, creating an overall 'impression' of colour and supposedly a more vibrant effect, which broader brushstrokes lack.

The children can use IT graphics software to imitate this technique to a certain degree, producing areas of colour built up in this way, or even simple pictures. The paint spray tool will allow them to cover areas with small dots of colour and, if several layers are sprayed on top of each other, an Impressionist-style effect can be created. You can use this activity as part of a whole class exercise on Impressionist style, with the non IT users trying out genuine Impressionist techniques with paint and very small brushes.

### Vocabulary
Paint spray tool, dot density, shade, tone, overlay.

### Preparation
Make one copy of photocopiable page 135 for each child. Gather together some pictures or posters of works by Impressionist artists, such as Monet and Seurat, as a stimulus for the children's work. Collect several colour

photographs taken from newspapers which the children can look at with magnifying glasses to see how hundreds of tiny dots build up the overall image and colours.

### Resources needed
A computer, graphics software with a paint spray tool, a colour printer, paper, some pictures or posters of work by Impressionist artists, several magnifying glasses (optional), newspaper pictures (optional), crayons, felt-tipped pens, copies of photocopiable page 135.

**INFORMATION TECHNOLOGY**

## What to do

Show the children some pictures of works by Impressionist artists, pointing out how the artists built up images and colours by layering hundreds of tiny dots of paint on top of one another. If appropriate, introduce the name of this technique (pointillism). The children can use a magnifying glass to see the small dots of colour more clearly and look at how these combine to form a colour and/or image when viewed from a distance. Looking at newspaper pictures through the magnifying glass will reinforce this idea.

Next, give each child a copy of photocopiable page 135 which provides practice in producing a range of colours by applying small coloured dots or strokes of paint to gradually build up a chosen image. The children will find this difficult at first as they will be keen to colour large areas of paper with broad crayon or brush strokes.

When the children have mastered the technique, provide a whole class or large group demonstration on the computer. Show them how to use the paint spray tool to create Impressionist-style pictures, starting with a very simple scene of sky, land, trees and some water. Do not aim for detail. If you find that a particular colour or shade is wrong, you can easily correct it by adding another layer. Use a variety of colours and point out the overall effect the different colours have on the image.

Now tell the children that they will have the chance to try this technique for themselves on the computer by using the paint spray tool. Depending on their ability, the children can attempt simple paintings, perhaps centred around a particular Impressionist painting, or simply a particular range of colours, such as 'autumn colours'. You may wish to use any appropriate current curriculum themes for this activity or suggest themes such as 'Summer picnic', 'Firework

night', or 'Storm at sea'. Make sure that the children keep their pictures simple so that they are effective. When they are happy with their final pictures or colours, allow them to print these out.

## Suggestion(s) for extension

Children who are confident may like to try some more detailed painting. This could be done either by using a very small spray can tool setting or by using a small paintbrush and dotting the colour in the conventional style.

## Suggestion(s) for support

Less confident children may like to start by experimenting with a spray pattern of their own design. Once they feel more confident with the tool, they can go on to attempt 'painting' a scene.

## Assessment opportunities

This activity will enable you to assess the children's use of IT, especially their confidence in the use of graphics tools, to convey ideas in the form of colours and images. There are also opportunities to make assessments in art, both in their accuracy and attention to detail, and also in their identification of ways to improve their work.

## Display ideas

Mount copies of Impressionist paintings by well-known artists alongside the children's work.

## Reference to photocopiable sheet

Photocopiable page 135 gives the children practice in colour mixing and imitating the Impressionist technique of pointillism.

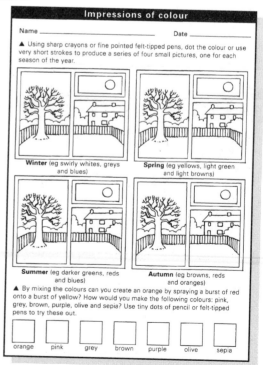

## PICTURE THE RULES

***To use a variety of IT tools for a purpose. To learn that bold, clear images communicate meaning more effectively.***

†† *Pairs.*

🕓 *30 minutes at the computer; 15 minutes discussion.*

### Previous skills/knowledge needed
The children should know either how to use graphics software tools to create simple images, or how to obtain appropriate images from clip art.

### Key background information
Symbols are an important way of communicating information. In a multicultural society where many languages are spoken, pictures are often more effective than words in conveying messages.

This activity encourages the children to devise their own symbols using IT. The aim is to illustrate a school rule, although they may think of other more general labels or notices that would be useful to display in the classroom. Using IT allows the children to experiment with a visual idea for their symbol on screen, resize the image easily, change its colour, invert it, rotate it and, if necessary, add text. The children should be able to use the IT tools to achieve a professional-looking result. You could use the activity as part of a topic on communications if appropriate.

### Vocabulary
Clip art, image, symbol, proportion, rotate, flip, resize.

### Preparation
Find (or draw) some examples of familiar signs or symbols which communicate meaning either in the street, in shops or at home. Make one copy of photocopiable page 136 for each pair of children.

### Resources needed
A computer, graphics software, desktop publishing software, a selection of clip art, a colour printer, paper, examples of familiar street/public place signs and symbols, photocopiable page 136.

### What to do
Show the children a collection of familiar signs and symbols such as washing labels, road signs, 'no litter' symbols and so on. Talk about why we use signs. Ask them to think of any other examples they have seen and to explain what these mean. Discuss what makes a good sign: are colours important? is the size of the symbol important? are words necessary and if so, what kind of words? Show the children an example which is particularly effective to emphasise the importance of clarity and unambiguity in the choice of a symbol.

Now tell the children that they are going to work in pairs to design their own symbols. Some will do this using IT and others will do the activity using conventional art materials to allow a comparison at the end of the activity. Give out copies of photocopiable page 136 – one each for children working conventionally, and one per pair for children using IT. The sheet provides a list of suggestions for school or classroom rules which the children can choose from to design and illustrate a matching symbol. Children working

Match the symbol to the rule

Never run with scissors

Don't chew gum in class

Never throw things indoors

Never give sweets to the hamster

Keep your desk tidy

on screen can use appropriate images from clip art (if you have access to a clip art library), or design their own using a graphics application. Words could be added via the graphics software, or designs could be saved and loaded into desktop publishing software to add in words at a later stage.

When the children have finished their signs, gather them together to judge the results, highlighting comparisons between those produced using IT and those drawn with conventional art materials. Discussdn the merits and drawbacks of each method. Use constructive criticism to discuss the attributes that make signs effective.

### Suggestion(s) for extension
More confident children could go on to use IT for producing a series of symbols to show safety in the kitchen, what not to throw in the dustbin (recycling symbols), symbols for a time machine's dashboard, symbols to look at while doing their homework (concentrate, turn the music down, no television, no sweets, no daydreaming, best handwriting only and so on).

### Suggestion(s) for support
Ensure that less confident children choose something straightforward and not too sophisticated, such as 'No running' or 'Paper towels go in the bin'. They could concentrate on the symbol only and try out various colours and sizes.

### Assessment opportunities
This activity will enable you to assess how well the children are using IT graphics tools to convey meaning using pictures appropriate to the context. There are also assessment possibilities in art.

### Display ideas
The children's work could be displayed in the appropriate place, according to the rule they have illustrated, so that it serves its original purpose. For work produced on the computer, use additional printouts to create a 'match the symbol to the rule' challenge by mixing together the pictures and the written rules.

### Reference to photocopiable sheet
Photocopiable page 136 contains a 'design a symbol' task. It provides a list of typical rules for the school or classroom which the children choose from to design and illustrate their own matching symbol.

**INFORMATION TECHNOLOGY**

# SWEET WRAPPERS

***To use the fine brush tool in a graphics program to produce detailed results.***

✝✝ *Pairs.*

🕐 *45 minutes at the computer; 10 minutes discussion/demonstration.*

## Previous skills/knowledge needed

Familiarity with art tools within graphics software including those for brush size, colour palette selection, colour fill, erasing and magnification.

## Key background information

A common art activity is to produce a detailed reproduction of an object, such as a sweet wrapper. Using IT to do a similar task is not so easy. The mouse becomes the paintbrush or drawing tool and children need time to develop skill in using it for detailed work. However, IT offers certain advantages in this kind of task. Mistakes can easily be rectified; detailed work is helped by a zoom or magnification facility which makes images appear larger on the screen. (Some software has several degrees of magnification available.) 'Global' changes can be made, such as changing all instances of one colour to a different one by a single click of the mouse.

## Vocabulary

Brush tool, drawing tool, magnification tool, zoom in, zoom out, pixel, colour fill.

## Preparation

Invite the children to bring in a variety of sweet wrappers. Make one copy of photocopiable page 137 for each child.

## Resources needed

A computer, graphics software including a paintbrush facility and preferably a magnification tool, a colour printer, a collection of sweet wrappers, art materials such as paint, brushes, coloured pencils and paper (optional), magnifying glasses, photocopiable page 137.

## What to do

Use photocopiable page 137 to introduce this activity. The sheet provides a picture of a key which the children must draw enlarged versions of, keeping as much detail as possible. They can choose their own scale, either reproducing the whole object, or better still, a small part of it. Using magnifying glasses will help them.

Once the children have completed this task, let them look at the collection of sweet wrappers. Again, provide magnifying glasses to enable the children to make a detailed observation. Then tell them that they are going to reproduce an enlarged detail from one of the sweet wrappers. To do this, they must concentrate on a small part of the design and choose an interesting area containing several colours or a particular pattern or logo, for example.

Show the children how to draw an outline of the wrapper on screen using simple crayon or brush tools, then use the

drawing or line tool to sketch roughly where the main features will be. The drawing need not be absolutely accurate, as adjustments can be made later when adding in the detail. Demonstrate how to use the magnification tool. Explain that choosing a narrow drawing tool or paintbrush while working under magnification, allows very detailed work to be done. Use fonts to reproduce any lettering and rotate them if possible to create a more realistic perspective.

Pairs of children can then work on the computer reproducing a single sweet wrapper, continuing to use a magnifying glass to see small detail clearly. Remember that precision is not the priority here. The children need the experience of using IT to perform detailed tasks so that they become familiar with the various tools and understand the opportunities and limitations of computer graphics software.

Resources and time will mean that some children will be using conventional art materials for this activity. This will provide an opportunity for the children to discuss the differences between using IT and 'standard' art tools. What are their preferences and what constraints did they encounter using these media?

INFORMATION
TECHNOLOGY

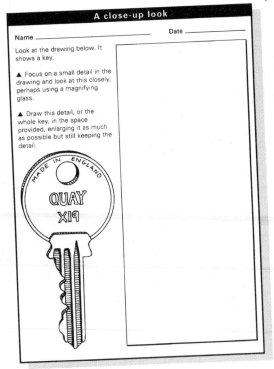

### A close-up look

Name _____                    Date _____

Look at the drawing below. It shows a key.

▲ Focus on a small detail in the drawing and look at this closely, perhaps using a magnifying glass.

▲ Draw this detail, or the whole key, in the space provided, enlarging it as much as possible but still keeping the detail.

## Assessment opportunities

This activity will enable you to make assessments in IT as to how well your children are using graphics software to reproduce a design in detail. There are also opportunities to make assessments in art.

## Display ideas

Placing the children's work alongside the original sweet wrappers will create an attractive display. It could be called something like 'Sweet wrappers – from small to large!'

## Reference to photocopiable sheet

Photocopiable page 137 provides a picture of a key which the children must draw enlarged versions of, keeping as much detail as possible. They can choose their own scale, either reproducing a small detail from the object or the entire picture.

## Suggestion(s) for extension

Confident children may like to use the graphics cutting tool to cut out their wrapper, shrink it and paste the reduced image in a tile formation.

## Suggestion(s) for support

Less confident children should choose a straightforward detail to copy from their sweet wrapper, with a minimum of lettering. Roughing out an approximate shape onto a piece of paper will help to guide their positioning of lines on the screen.

# FASHION SHOW

*To use the existing patterns available or to create patterns from the colour palette within a graphics program.*

†† *Pairs.*

⊕ *20 minutes at the computer; 15 minutes discussion/demonstration.*

## Previous skills/knowledge needed

Children should know how to access the existing range of patterned fills available from the colour palette and to be aware that new patterns can be made and stored.

## Key background information

IT is used widely in the design world when considering new ventures or products. The ability to model something on the computer screen before actually producing it allows changes to be made before finances are committed. In fabric design, computers allow different patterns and colour combinations to be tested out before production starts.

This activity allows the children to use IT to experiment with a variety of patterns and colours using fashion design as a context. It will help them to appreciate the importance of IT in the outside world and to appreciate that, though computers can generate any number of design possibilities, in real life perhaps only one of these may go forward for manufacturing.

## Vocabulary

Flood fill, pattern fill, model, colour combination.

## Preparation

Before this activity, you will need to use graphics software to produce a simple outline on screen of a boy and a girl wearing a jumper, shirt, shorts, trousers, skirt, socks and so on. Make sure that the clothes areas are bounded by unbroken lines, so that when the children use the flood fill tool to colour an area the colour does not leak out. Save the images for later retrieval by the children, keeping a copy of the file on a floppy disk in case it is accidentally deleted on the computer.

Collect pictures of patterned clothes from magazines and a selection of small fabric samples in different colours and patterns, including some that complement each other and some that clash when placed side by side. Make one copy of photocopiable page 138 for each child.

## Resources needed

A computer, graphics software with existing colour patterns available from the palette, a colour printer, paper, fashion magazine pictures, small samples of fabric in different colours, photocopiable page 138.

## What to do

Introduce the idea of colour matching to the children by looking at the fabric samples and some magazine pictures of clothes. Which colours or patterns do the children think go well together? Which ones clash? Which are their favourite colours and patterns? Explain that in the fashion world, computers are widely used to help with the design of patterns and shapes for clothes before they are manufactured.

Next, provide a demonstration for the whole class or a large group, showing how the computer can produce a wide variety of colours and patterns easily. Take an existing colour or pattern from the colour palette within your graphics program or mix your own, depending on the type of software you are using. Then use the flood fill tool to transfer the colour or pattern to the clothes on the boy/girl outlines you have already prepared.

Hand out copies of photocopiable page 138 to the children, asking them to complete the task as a preparation for their work at the computer. Using the photocopiable sheet will enable the children to appreciate the ease with which these functions can be completed using IT.

Working in pairs, let the children use the computer to fill in the outlines themselves, using either existing colours or patterns or ones that they have created. They may then like to print out a number of different colour/pattern combinations and use them for their project work.

**INFORMATION TECHNOLOGY**

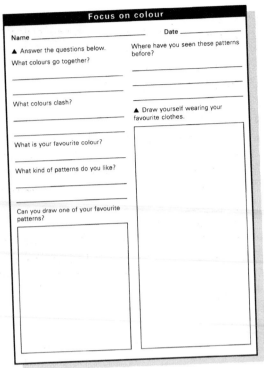

**Focus on colour**

Name _____    Date _____

▲ Answer the questions below.    Where have you seen these patterns before?

What colours go together?

What colours clash?

▲ Draw yourself wearing your favourite clothes.

What is your favourite colour?

What kind of patterns do you like?

Can you draw one of your favourite patterns?

## REPEAT PATTERNS

*To use the cut and paste facility to produce repeat patterns in graphics software.*

†† *Pairs.*

🕐 *30 minutes at the computer; 15 minutes discussion.*

### Previous skills/knowledge needed

The children should have used graphics software and be familiar with painting tools. They will need to have used cut and paste tools but not necessarily when producing patterns.

### Key background information

Many types of software offer a cut and paste facility where material on screen can be selected, then cut and moved or 'pasted' to another part of the document – the IT equivalent of using scissors and glue! This facility also allows an exact copy of any selected material (sometimes called a 'motif') to be repeated as many times as necessary. Used in a design context, this option can produce some attractive results.

In this activity, the children make use of the cut and paste facility in graphics software to produce a repeating pattern. When the children have mastered the technique, you could follow up the activity by asking them to produce a sheet of postage stamps, wallpaper, wrapping paper for a birthday present and so on. The children can initially work on a large scale to create their design, then reduce the scale before carrying out multiple pastes to produce their repeat pattern.

### Suggestion(s) for extension

Children could use the computer to create outlines for themselves of different items such as curtains/wallpaper, armchair/wallpaper and tie/shirt and so on and create pattern or colour matches for them.

### Suggestion(s) for support

Less confident children could carry out this activity using colours only to fill in the outlines on screen, since these are more obviously different than patterns.

### Assessment opportunities

This activity will enable you to assess how effectively the children can use appropriate graphics tools in IT to convey their ideas in the form of matching colours or patterns. Look to see with what degree of confidence the children choose or make up their own patterns and build up the completed images.

### Display ideas

The children's completed clothes' designs could be used alongside fashion photographs from magazines to create a display titled 'IT in the world of fashion design'. Make photocopied enlargements of the children's 'designs' to give the display greater impact. The display could be used as part of a project on clothing, colours or patterns if appropriate.

### Reference to photocopiable sheet

Photocopiable page 138 encourages the children to think about matching and combining colours and patterns effectively.

**INFORMATION TECHNOLOGY**

## Vocabulary

Cutting tool, paste tool, select area, resize, overlay (part of a pattern placed over another), motif, repeated paste, tile (a pattern placed next to another as in bathroom tiling).

## Preparation

Collect together some examples of repeat tiling patterns – these may be found in bathroom DIY brochures, reference books with sections on interior design or art books containing information on pottery and the production of tiles. Make one copy of photocopiable page 139 for each pair of children and sufficient card/paper tile templates to enable all pairs of children to participate in the activity.

## Resources needed

A computer, graphics software with a cut and paste facility, a colour printer, card or paper, examples of repeat patterns, tiling and so on; scissors, photocopiable page 139.

## What to do

The aim of this activity is for children to use IT to produce repeat patterns. Show them a collection of different tiling patterns and discuss how these are created. Start by using photocopiable page 139 to give them practice in manipulating a series of tiles in several ways. The idea is to use a single card/paper tile template to create several different layouts guided by the photocopiable sheet. This will give them experience of different tiling possibilities. Discuss what is meant by a drop pattern and let the children experiment with several kinds of this type of pattern, where each tile laid out is slightly lowered giving a staircase effect. Show how the degree of drop can be changed to produce a very different tiling effect.

Next, provide a whole class or large group demonstration of creating repeat patterns on the computer. Use the paintbrush to create a simple pattern in several different colours. Select a small part of the pattern to create a single 'tile' and show the children how this can be cut or copied and pasted somewhere else. If possible, show how to rotate the motif and reduce it in size before pasting. Then continue to paste the tile or motif to build up a repeating pattern. Show a variety of tiling possibilities, including straightforward side-by-side and drop pattern.

The children can now work in pairs to produce their own repeat tile pattern on the computer. They can use existing patterns from the colour palette or produce their own. They may like to construct a drop pattern where each pasted tile is lower than the preceding one. Or they could try re-creating a real tiling effect by placing the motifs side by side and leaving small gaps between them, which can be filled with coloured grouting using the flood fill tool. Some graphics software allows a motif to be used as a paintbrush; if you have this facility, let the children try painting rapidly across the screen to see what effects they can produce.

## Suggestion(s) for extension

Children may like to design a tile for a purpose such as to decorate a bathroom or kitchen. They could start by painting a number of small-scale patterns or scenes which, when tiled together, produce a larger scene.

## Suggestion(s) for support

For less confident children, ensure that their motif is larger. This means that they will create a pattern more quickly. Also, the larger the tiles, the less necessity for accurate placing on the screen.

## Assessment opportunities

This activity will enable you to assess how your children use the graphics software to produce different tiling patterns. There are also opportunities for making assessments in art.

## Display ideas

Repeat patterns can look most appealing when imaginatively displayed. Do not be tempted to crowd the children's work together; surrounding the patterns with plenty of space will increase their impact. You can enhance the tile patterns by adding one enlarged tile mounted beside the pattern. Mounting on complementary coloured paper will also further enhance the designs.

## Reference to photocopiable sheet

Photocopiable page 139 gives the children practice in manipulating tile patterns in order to produce different effects.

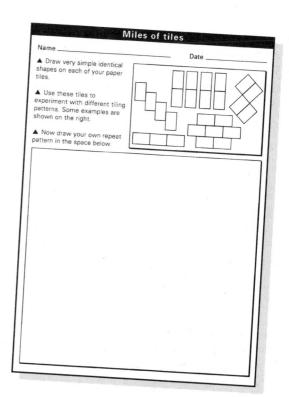

53

# SCAN A LEAF

**To use a hand-held scanner to produce an image.**

†† *Pairs.*

🕐 *30 minutes at the computer. 15 minutes discussion.*

## Previous skills/knowledge needed

Children need to understand that a scanner allows an image to be transferred into the computer software for saving and incorporating into other files or documents. They will also need the ability to use graphics software.

## Key background information

Scanners are becoming common additions to schools' IT resources. There are two main types; one is the-hand held variety which is drawn slowly across the image being scanned. These are quite cheap but tend to be only about 12cm wide and so the size of the image that can be scanned is fairly limited. The second type is known as the flatbed scanner. The image is placed under a lid (rather like a miniature photocopier) and is then scanned from within. Both black and white and colour scanners are available, although the latter are more expensive. The scanner is linked into your computer and accompanying software allows the scanned image to be processed and saved.

There are a number of settings that you can vary on your scanner and an important one is the scanning resolution. This is measured as the number of dots per inch (dpi). A resolution of 100 dpi will produce a rather coarse image, whereas 400 dpi will give a more detailed scan. For this particular activity the resolution (dpi) is not important.

The activity could be linked to part of a science project on plants or living things.

## Vocabulary

Scanned image, original image, resolution (dpi), scan rate, hand-held scanner, flatbed scanner.

## Preparation

If you are not familiar with using a hand-held scanner, it is important to practise before attempting to demonstrate scanning to the children. Scanning can often be a somewhat hit and miss process, so do not be put off by initial failure!

The choice of leaf for this activity is important. Choose examples with lots of detail such as a fern leaf or bracken leaf. A smooth-edged leaf will not give as good a result. Encourage the children to bring in their own leaves so that a good selection is available.

## Resources needed

A computer, a scanner (either a flatbed or a hand-held type), accompanying scanner software, graphics software, a printer, paper, a collection of leaves such as fern or bracken leaves (smooth edged leaves are not suitable), a sheet of acetate.

## What to do

The purpose is to use a scanner to produce an image – in this case a leaf – which can then be enhanced by colouring,

**INFORMATION TECHNOLOGY**

reducing, enlarging, tiling or manipulating within a graphics application.

Start by demonstrating to the children how to use the scanner. Hand-held scanners are more difficult to use as the movement necessary for scanning is provided by the person holding it. Some hand-held scanners will beep or flash if you move them too quickly. You will need to demonstrate the appropriate scanning speed several times.

Next, look through the collection of leaves with the children (see Preparation) and explain that you are going to scan in a leaf. Place the leaf under a piece of acetate to keep it flat so that the scanner travels smoothly across it. If you are using a black and white scanner, set it to scan in monochrome. This will give you a black and white image with no greys. Transfer the image to your graphics software. If you wish, use the colour fill tool to colour the leaf image and place it against a background in a different colour. Use the cutting tool to cut out, reduce and paste the leaf image to produce multiple tiled images. This is not the main aim of the activity but is useful to show the children what possibilities the scanning skill they are going to practise can lead to.

Now let the children work on the computer in pairs. Each child should scan in their chosen leaf and save the image on the hard disk or their own floppy disk. Although the leaf images could be used for a follow-up graphics activity, the main outcome is to ensure that each child achieves a successful scan rather than producing exciting artwork. Hand-held scanners will take a while to get used to and this activity will provide useful practice for the children.

## Suggestion(s) for extension

More able children can try scanning in several different objects to create a single motif for multiple pasting patterns. Scanners are more often used to process flat images, so the children could create their own images such as doodles, using a dark pencil or fine-tipped pen. They can scan these in for enlarging, colouring and manipulating in graphics software to produce some interesting effects.

They may also like to try scanning in flat objects such as doilies, stamps, pressed flowers and so on. Slightly three-dimensional objects can also be scanned provided they are held under acetate to ensure a smooth scanning movement. On a flatbed scanner, the thickness of the objects is not so important as the scanning takes place through a glass plate.

## Suggestion(s) for support

For less able children, keep the focus on the scanning process. Allow them plenty of time to achieve an acceptable scan. This can be printed out straight away without any graphics manipulation.

## Assessment opportunities

From this activity you will be able to make assessments as to how well the children are using IT to convey ideas through the use of their scanned images, and any later enhancement of these images. There may also be opportunities to make further assessments in art.

## Display ideas

The bold leaf images achieved by using monochrome scanning will make an attractive display if coloured or patterned using graphics software. Showing the original leaves alongside the scans will add further interest and help the children to appreciate the starting and finishing points.

## GROWING OLD GRACEFULLY

*To insert a scanned image into a graphics application for subsequent artistic manipulation.*
†† *Pairs.*
⏰ *40 minutes at the computer; 20 minutes discussion.*

## Previous skills/knowledge needed

Children need the ability to use a hand-held scanner and should be familiar with the functions of the different graphics tools available.

## Key background information

Video-fit images of missing persons or wanted criminals are commonly used in the media today. These realistic photographic images are nowadays generated by computer. Computerisation has vastly simplified the old process of gradually building up images of faces by matching together

each individual feature chosen from a library of thousands of separate pictures. Computers allow easy access to many millions of possible combinations through their ability to hold large amounts of information.

A recent IT development is the ability to reconstruct images, showing how children who have been missing for many years may look today. The original photographs are enhanced to give the impression of increased age, following recognised patterns of change that take place as human faces age.

This activity will provide children with a simple introduction to the power of IT to produce subtle changes in images. It would support any current work you may be doing on growth or perhaps a project on 'Ourselves'.

## Vocabulary
Original image, altered image, image enhancement.

## Preparation
This activity requires the children to be able to scan in pictures on the computer and so you may find it helpful to use the 'Scan a leaf' activity on page 54 to introduce them to the technique.

Before doing the activity, collect some photographs from magazines or catalogues showing a mix of older and younger generations so that the children can see how faces change with age. If possible, find a 'video-fit' picture from a newspaper. The children will also need to bring in photographs of themselves for scanning in. These photographs need to show their faces clearly on a reasonable scale, as small images will be too difficult to work with.

## Resources needed
A computer, a scanner, graphics software, a printer, paper, photographs of the children, photographs of faces of young children, teenagers, and young and old adults to show the ageing process.

## What to do
Look at the collection of photographs with the children and discuss the variety of changes that happen to faces as people grow older. Point out features such as receding hairlines, wrinkles, lines around the mouth and eyes, furrowed brows and thickening jowls. At this point, the children could try making some rough sketches on paper to show the differences between old and young faces.

If possible, show the children a 'video-fit' image of a face and explain how images like these are generated on computers. Tell them that IT can be used to make subtle changes to photographs that are scanned in, including photographs of faces. Then provide a whole class demonstration to imitate this process on your computer. First, scan in a child's face from a photograph and transfer the image into a graphics application. Then choose the narrow paint spray tool to make changes. (The paintbrush tool will be too harsh, especially if the scanned image is grainy.) Merely adding features such as glasses, different hair, cupid lips, a moustache or beard will show the children how easy it is to alter the original image and produce different 'disguises' for it.

Ageing the face is more difficult. Show them how to reproduce wrinkles by adding thin lines using the narrow brush tool. A receding hairline can be created by erasing hair fringes with the paint spray tool. Create lines around

the mouth and eyes using the narrow brush tool to complete the effect. (Adding glasses and changing hairstyles could also enhance the 'ageing' appearance.) Remind the children that using the undo button is available to erase any wrong moves made with the mouse.

Now let the children work in pairs on the computer each scanning in their own photograph and experimenting with altering the image. There is no clear completion point to this activity, but each child will probably need at least 20 minutes. The images can be saved and printed out if appropriate.

### Suggestion(s) for extension
Children could produce a dossier of themselves in various disguises by manipulating their photograph in different ways.

### Suggestion(s) for support
Less able children can concentrate on the facial disguises rather than the ageing process.

### Assessment opportunities
You will be able to assess how well the children use the scanner to produce their initial image and how they use IT to convey graphic ideas through the enhanced images they work on. Look out for how well they use the graphics tools to achieve the variety of features that indicate an ageing face. How well do they amend any mistakes – do they use the 'undo' tool?

### Display ideas
This activity can generate some intriguing artwork. Use it to make a 'Guess who?' game or a 'Rogues' gallery' display. Include the original photographs alongside the children's

manipulated images. You could also add in selections of photographs brought in by the children showing their grandparents or parents to illustrate the ageing process.

## MUSICAL ILLUSTRATION

***To provide an opportunity to use music composition software for a definite purpose.***
†† *Pairs or small groups.*
🕑 *40 minutes at the computer; 10 minutes demonstration.*

### Previous skills/knowledge needed
Children should have a basic appreciation of how musical compositions include a beginning, a middle and an end. Familiarity with compositional software would be helpful but is not essential.

### Key background information
Certain music software includes simple musical icons that allow children to make compositions without using standard notation. Every icon has a series of notes of varying lengths and pitch attached to it. Different icons are appropriate for the beginning, middle and end of tunes – usually, the children have to listen and choose the most suitable icon. Compositions are created by choosing a series of these icons. Usually, this type of software also has a tempo option providing easy control over the speed of compositions.

This activity involves using music software to demonstrate to the children the ease and flexibility that IT offers in creating compositions. The software allows easy editing of work through the immediate playback of chosen icons and the option to replace any icons in the sequence.

The children can therefore enjoy the process of composition without needing to know about musical notation. They can concentrate on the sounds and sequences to build up a particular tune. You may wish to centre the activity around creating a short appropriate piece of music for a poem or story, a work of art or perhaps a historical event.

## Vocabulary
Composition, sequence, edit, tempo, icon, melody.

## Preparation
It may be helpful to prepare a list of descriptive words relating to your chosen context for this activity. For example, words to accompany a historic battle scene could include: thundering (horses' hoofs), clashing (armour), swishing (arrows), loud, clamouring, calm (after the battle). Words to accompany Turner's painting of the *Fighting Téméraire* could include: light, mysterious, swirling, indistinct. Collect together any suitable visual material you wish to use as a stimulus.

Before doing the main activity, you will need to demonstrate to the children how certain musical phrases make good beginnings, some are appropriate for middle sections and others only suitable to end a composition. This is part of the wonder of music, how it creates tensions and then releases them. Play a particular phrase and ask them whether it would be suitable for a beginning. Give them a number of different phrases to provide practice in choosing appropriate positioning within a composition.

## Resources needed
A computer with in-built or external speakers, earphones may be used during their compositions to minimise classroom interruption, music software of the non-standard notation type such as *Compose* or *Compose World*, a colour printer (optional), appropriate stimulus material such as Georges Seurat's *La Grande Jatte* (1884), John Constable's *The Hay Wain* (1821) and Turner's *Hannibal Crossing the Alps* (1812).

## What to do
Explain to the children that they are going to use IT to compose some simple music to accompany a particular theme or event. Set the scene for them, such as 'a weary journey' or 'a sunny day', and show them a suitable picture as a stimulus. Display a list of appropriate descriptive words and encourage the children to suggest any others.

Provide a whole class demonstration of how to use the music software. Picking the icons and placing them in sequence is straightforward but emphasise that the children must pay attention to the sequence of the sets of notes. They may need prompting as to whether a particular sequence of notes is appropriate for a beginning, a middle or an end. Explain that you want them to use the sets of notes in their composition to evoke the chosen theme as effectively as possible. Help them to grasp the idea by demonstrating a variety of musical sequences and encouraging the children to comment on how appropriate these are to the theme. Can they give their reasons?

Tell the children that you would like them to compose their own pieces on the same theme, then let them work in pairs on the computer. Ask them to use your list of descriptive words as a prompt to help them choose sequences of notes and form some structure to their composition. (Provide a quiet area for them to work in or give them headphones to keep the noise level to a

minimum, allowing them to concentrate on their compositions.) If they are unable to finish their compositions within the time limit they can save them for future work.

Any completed pieces can be played back to the whole class to discuss which ones are the most appropriate and effective.

### Suggestion(s) for extension
Confident children may like to illustrate their musical composition visually using graphics software, or choose a more challenging picture or theme to extend their composition.

### Suggestion(s) for support
Ensure that less able children come to the computer with a list of words that are easily translatable into a musical sequence such as 'gradually going up', 'jumpy', 'regular beat', 'going down in stages'.

### Assessment opportunities
This activity allows you to assess the children's capability in using IT to create a musical composition that is appropriate to their chosen picture. There are also opportunities to make assessments in music in both performing and composing, and in listening and appraising.

### Display ideas
The children can perform their compositions to the rest of the class and, perhaps, to other classes in the school. Printing out the children's sequences of icons can provide a visual record of the music being played.

## LET'S DANCE!

*To use IT to compose a tune with an appropriate tempo and structure to accompany a short dance sequence.*

†† *Pairs or small groups.*

🕒 *30 minutes at the computer; 15 minutes discussion.*

### Previous skills/knowledge needed
The children will need a working knowledge of the type of music software that uses pictures (icons) to represent musical phrases (see the 'Musical illustration' activity on page 57).

### Key background information
Composing music is straightforward when using software that represents musical phrases in pictures. The children simply choose a particular sequence of icons to produce a composition. In this activity, they have the opportunity to concentrate on tempo and structure by composing music to accompany a short dance on a particular theme. They must link the structure and speed of their music to the chosen dance movements. They are encouraged to experiment with the software's tempo control to achieve a satisfactory speed and rhythm for their dance. It is important that the children know before they start what kind of movement structure they are setting the music to.

### Vocabulary
Tempo, phrase, pattern, repeat.

## Preparation

Tell the children that they are going to create a short dance for which they will later compose some accompanying music. Suggest some themes for their dances such as the discovery of Tutankhamen's tomb, the capture of Guy Fawkes in the cellars of the Houses of Parliament or the ascent of Everest – or let them think up their own ideas. Take plenty of time to discuss the kind of movement or pattern of steps they could use. Talk about the speed or 'tempo' of their dance – will it be fast, slow, or perhaps a mixture?

Now let the children work in pairs or small groups to create a dance lasting up to half a minute. Keeping their dances short will encourage them to be precise with their movements and more discerning when they come to choose the notes for their tune in the main activity below.

## Resources needed

A computer with in-built or external speakers, music software of non-standard notation type (such as *Compose* or *Compose World*), a colour printer (optional), an appropriate theme for a dance.

## What to do

Once the children have completed their movement sequences (see Preparation), they can go on to compose their tune using the computer. Emphasise that they must link the structure and tempo of their music as closely as possible to their dance movements. If necessary, remind them how to use the tempo control tool. They will need a quiet area around them during this activity, or a set of headphones to keep the noise level to a minimum and allow them to concentrate on their compositions.

When several dances and tunes have been completed, it may be possible to link several together to form a longer sequence. This would encourage the children to work co-operatively to prepare a performance for the rest of the class.

## Suggestion(s) for extension

The children can use the computer to type up some instructions for their dance, or use graphics software to provide simple illustrations of the dance movements.

## Suggestion(s) for support

You could assign the composition of one or two simple musical phrases to those children who are less confident. These phrases could act as an introduction to a dance. This will allow them to concentrate on the musical aspects, such as tempo and structure, without the necessity of linking their tune with specific movements.

## Assessment opportunities

This activity will enable you to assess how well the children use software to compose tunes that are suitable for movement or dance steps, paying particular attention to tempo and structure. There are also opportunities to make assessments in music in both performing and composing, and listening and appraising.

## Display ideas

The children's performance of their work can act as a display! It is important that they perform to an audience, whether to the rest of the class or perhaps in an assembly. You can also create a board display using the printouts of the tunes together with word processed descriptions of the dances and, perhaps, some simple graphics showing movements.

INFORMATION
TECHNOLOGY

## RECOGNISE THIS ONE?

*To use software using standard notation to compose.*

†† *Pairs.*

🕐 *40 minutes at the computer; 15 minutes demonstration/discussion.*

### Previous skills/knowledge needed

The children will find the activity easier if they have some previous knowledge of standard musical notation. Some experience of working on music software which uses standard notation would also be helpful.

### Key background information

Certain types of music software offer the facility to compose on screen using standard musical notation. This software offers a range of standard notes to work with and allows flexibility in inserting and deleting them. Some software also allows the entering of chords to accompany the notes. The addition of extra staves, the insertion of a percussion line and even the ability to transpose, are other features.

Initially, children will need plenty of experimentation in using such software but setting simple tasks will help them to gradually learn how to make use of the different

facilities available. If you have an electronic music keyboard, this software may allow output through the midi connection so that the music can be played using all the keyboard's features.

### Vocabulary

Note dragging, track, stave, bar, time signature, tempo.

### Resources needed

A computer with in-built or external speakers, standard music notation software, a printer (optional), headphones (if a quiet working space is not available), an electronic music or piano keyboard (not essential).

### What to do

The idea behind this activity is to encourage the children to use standard musical notation software. They will need a

quiet area around them, or the use of headphones to keep the noise level to a minimum, to allow them to concentrate on their compositions.

Explain to the children that they are going to re-create some short, recognisable tunes using IT. This could be an extract from something as simple as a well-known nursery rhyme or a Christmas carol. Ask the children to name or sing some popular tunes, then introduce them to the basics of the music software. Provide a whole class or group demonstration on the computer, show them how to insert notes by dragging them onto the staves and how notes are deleted.

Now ask the children to re-create their chosen tunes. Explain that they do not have to produce the complete tune, just a recognisable part of it. Asking them to limit the length of their compositions to ten seconds will reinforce this idea, providing motivation and speeding up computer access. When they have finished, the children should save their work so that a selection of tunes can be played later to the whole class or to a wider audience.

The outcomes of this activity will depend much on the children's musical ability and their understanding of standard musical notation. Reproducing a recognisable tune is a minimal expectation and the resulting tune may be very basic. Some children will need much support throughout the activity. By using IT to compose, such children may gain in confidence provided the initial expectations are realistic.

### Suggestion(s) for extension

Children who are more musically adept will enjoy exploring what other features the software has to offer. They could add chords or a percussion line to accompany their notes, or even a second track or stave to provide some harmony. If the software allows, words could be added to the music and the whole composition printed out.

### Suggestion(s) for support

With less confident children ask them to decide on a tune and then hum it to you before they begin on the computer. Suggest that they only compose the first few bars. Let them save their tune so that they can return to it for further work at another time.

Communicating information

## Assessment opportunities

This activity will enable you to make assessments of how well the children use IT to convey their ideas in sound, and how appropriate these are for a particular audience. Look out for how confidently the children use the software facilities to achieve their composition, especially deletion and insertion of notes, and repeated playback to test their results. There are also opportunities to make assessments in music, in both performing and composing, and in listening and appraising.

## Display ideas

The performance is the display element of this activity. Building up to a group performance will motivate the children, especially if it is for a wider audience. Printed-out music in standard notation is not particularly strong display material, but it may be enhanced with word-processed descriptions or pictures of how the children set about composing their tunes.

## MULTIMEDIA MUSIC

*To create a multimedia presentation and use standard notation software to compose some appropriate music.*

†† *Pairs.*

🕑 *45 minutes at the computer; 15 minutes demonstration.*

## Previous skills/knowledge needed

The children will need a working knowledge of how to use standard notation software. Activities such as 'Musical illustration' (see page 57) and 'Let's dance' (see page 59) will help to prepare them for the composition aspects of this activity.

## Key background information

There are multimedia packages which allow text, pictures and sound to be combined to produce a presentation. Information is accessed by clicking onscreen buttons and links can be made between relevant areas of information. Adding music files into the package (usually via music CDs) offers another layer of information which can be communicated through multimedia applications. If the children are putting together text and images from an event such as a school visit, a sports day or another major function, adding music into the IT package can enhance their presentation and help them to develop their IT capability.

## Vocabulary

Multimedia, presentation, sound file.

## Preparation

Explain to the children that they are going to use IT to produce a multimedia presentation which includes text, pictures and music. They will start by combining the text and pictures first. The music will be added in later. Let the children choose a theme for their presentation such as a class outing, a hobby, a holiday they enjoyed – or any other subject that inspires them! Then provide a whole class or group demonstration of the basic IT tools they will need to create their text and pictures in the multimedia package. Graphics files may come from a number of different sources, perhaps in the form of artwork done by the children in graphics software, scanned images of photographs they have taken or from commercially produced graphics files or clip art. The popular system of PhotoCD is a practical source of photographs, where film processing includes the copying of the images onto a CD which can be accessed by the computer. Most up-to-date multimedia computers have the facility to read these PhotoCDs.

## Resources needed

A computer with in-built or external speakers, standard musical notation software, PhotoCD software (optional), multimedia software, a scanner (optional), a printer (preferably colour), artwork and photographs for scanning.

## What to do

The children should have prepared the text and pictures in their multimedia presentations (see Preparation). Now ask them to identify parts of their presentation where short pieces of music would be appropriate. The children may think that, to produce a good multimedia presentation, all the music should be commercially produced. However, you want them to gain confidence in using standard musical

INFORMATION
TECHNOLOGY

notation software, so, instead of using audio CDs, encourage them to compose their own music. Emphasise that their compositions need to be suitable for the visual content and discuss the children's ideas for this.

Provide a whole class or group demonstration on the computer, reminding the children of the features in the musical notation software such as deleting and adding in notes, using the tempo control, adding chords and so on. Once the children have decided on the kind of composition required, they can go on to use the computer themselves. Encourage them to keep the pieces short so that the focus is sharper. The same piece could be used a number of times if necessary. Alternatively, the children could compose a number of pieces between them and try them all out while running their presentations, to see how well they match.

You can provide additional motivation by asking them to prepare their presentations for a real audience, perhaps for a parents' evening or an open day.

### Suggestion(s) for extension
Confident children will be able to exploit the facilities within the music software such as chords, additional tracks and percussion lines.

### Suggestion(s) for support
Ensure that less able children keep their pieces short. It is the appropriateness of the music to the multimedia context which is important.

### Assessment opportunities
This activity draws on many IT skills. Assess how well the children are using such skills to convey their ideas in text, graphics and sound in an appropriate way for a particular audience. Look at how confidently the children use the

software tools to achieve their composition, and how easily they make changes and rework their music to reach an acceptable outcome. There are also opportunities to assess the children within music, especially in the attainment targets of performing and composing, and listening and appraising.

### Display ideas
The multimedia presentation forms the display aspect of this activity. The children could choose the most visually appealing pages to print out from their presentations and these could form an attractive board display. The children could word process some descriptions of how they put their presentations together to add extra interest.

## WHEREVER I MAY ROAM

***To use the Roamer's music facilities to play tunes.***

†† *Pairs.*

🕐 *40 minutes at the computer; 20 minutes demonstration.*

### Previous skills/knowledge needed
The children should have some previous experience of using the Roamer's sound commands.

### Key background information
It may seem strange to think of using a programmable robot to create music, but the Roamer offers an excellent IT opportunity and demonstrates IT's wider use away from the computer. The activity involves the children entering long sequences of commands into the Roamer using the Roamer Logo language. The Logo language, including the

**INFORMATION TECHNOLOGY**

Roamer's version, allows us to interact with IT systems in a friendly manner. It consists of commands such as 'FORWARDS', 'BACKWARDS', 'TURN LEFT', 'WAIT', 'REPEAT' and many more. A command is usually followed by a number or value, for example 'FORWARDS 6'. (More activities involving the use of Logo feature throughout Chapter 3.)

This activity focuses on the Roamer's music facility by asking children to use it to re-create a well-known tune. To make the Roamer play a single note, the note key must be pressed followed by two numbers. The first is the duration of the note (numbers between 1 and 8), the second is the pitch (numbers between 1 and 13). A rest is obtained by entering the number 14 as the pitch value. The children will need to experiment with the notes before setting out to compose their tune.

### Vocabulary

Pitch, duration, rest, sharp, flat, repeat, clear entry.

### Resources needed

A Valiant Roamer (or several if possible), pens and paper or Roamer cards (these are available commercially).

### What to do

The aim of this activity is for the children to become familiar with some of the Roamer's commands through using them to re-create popular tunes. The quality of the children's tunes is less important here than the development of their IT skills. As music experimentation with the Roamer can be noisy, try to provide a space away from the rest of the class for those children using it.

Start by providing the children with a Roamer (or several if possible) and allowing them to experiment freely with the keys and their functions. After about ten minutes, explain that you would like them to use the Roamer to compose a short tune. Make sure that they choose a simple tune, such as a nursery rhyme or jingle. Hold a whole class or group demonstration showing them the basic commands that are necessary to create notes (see Key background information).

Point out that the Roamer has no record of which keys have been pressed; there is no screen or readout system

to tell the user what sequence has been entered. Also, once the Roamer is switched off, any tunes keyed in will be lost. For these reasons, it is essential that the children keep a record of the sequence entered. They can either write this down or use Roamer cards which contain all the Roamer keypad symbols. The children can lay these out to correspond with their chosen sequence. When the time comes to make corrections to their tune, these records will provide an essential reference point. Once the children have composed their tune, they will necessarily have to play it back immediately.

### Suggestion(s) for extension

More confident children may like to record the Roamer's music onto a tape recorder and then use other instruments – such as recorders – to accompany the playback. If there are any sequences of notes that are repeated in their tune, they may extend their IT skills through the use of the Roamer's repeat key. This facility could be used, for example, to play the repeat phrases in the tune of 'Three blind mice'.

### Suggestion(s) for support

Ensure that the less confident children choose a short piece. They could work in groups of four, with the first pair composing the initial part of a tune and the second pair continuing and completing it.

### Assessment opportunities

You will have the opportunity to assess how well the children are using IT to create sound for an audience. In particular, you can assess their ability to create, test, modify and store sequences of instructions through their use of the Roamer. There are also possibilities for making assessments in music.

### Display ideas

The display aspect is in the performance. If more than one Roamer has been used then a short performance may be possible. As it takes some time to enter a music sequence, do not have your performers entering their sequences while others are waiting!

# Handling information

As technology progresses and allows us to access ever-increasing amounts of information through media such as CD-ROMs and the Internet, it is imperative that the children develop skills to use their time effectively and focus on specifics when searching through large quantities of information. The activities in this section encourage them to use IT to help save, sort, display and search data held within various kinds of databases, and to increase their understanding and knowledge of IT storage and retrieval systems.

Teacher intervention is important in these activities. The children should be aware of the purpose in collecting the information and have some idea about what conclusions may be drawn from particular patterns in the data. The activities do not end with the graphical illustration but should continue with the interpretation of the patterns within the data.

Handling information is an aspect of IT which relies heavily on curriculum context for its success. To benefit from using IT in this way, the children should be involved with an information-rich subject area.

INFORMATION
TECHNOLOGY

## LOOKING AT US

*To collect accurate information and enter it into a computer database. To use the database to produce graphical illustrations.*

†† *Whole class and pairs.*

🕐 *Session 1: 45 minutes to collect data.*
*Session 2: 5 minutes per pair computer time; 15 minutes demonstration.*

### Previous skills/knowledge needed

The children will need to know how to measure their physical dimensions or attributes such as height, weight, foot length and so on.

### Key background information

Computers are highly efficient at processing large amounts of data and storing it in a small amount of space. Data is usually handled on computers using a database system that allows easy storage of information and access to it in an organised way. The data is usually stored under particular headings, for example in a database containing information about a class of children, these could include height, weight or hair colour. Headings are referred to as fields within the database. Many databases also offer facilities to illustrate the data, chiefly in graph form. Often there is a choice of the type of graph drawn such as pie chart, histogram or line graph. Certain graphs are more appropriate than others, depending on the type of data being displayed. A line graph is appropriate for displaying a variation over time (change in temperature, for example), a pie chart would be suitable to compare proportions such as the number of children with blue, brown or green eyes in your class.

A sophisticated database will offer search facilities which further simplify access to the required information. Searches may be carried out using either keywords or a logical search, depending on the sophistication of the database.

### Vocabulary

Data, information, database, field, interpretation, graphical illustration, data collection sheet, conclusion, cubit (forearm measurement), reach (fingertip to fingertip with outstretched arms), bicep, span.

### Preparation

Set up some facilities in the classroom for measuring physical attributes such as a vertical tape for height measurements, bathroom scales to measure weight, string and metre rules to measure reach, stride, head circumference and so on. You might also like to organise access to the hall so that the children can record timings of their pulse rates following exercise.

Photocopiable page 140 contains a data collection sheet which requires the children to collect measurements for a range of different physical attributes. Make one copy for each child, or use it as a basis for devising your own sheet. Once you and your class have decided what attributes will be measured, set up a suitable database for the children's findings so that they can type in their data. The way this is organised will depend on the database used. However, any field used must be either alphanumeric or numeric, meaning that the data entered is either in words or in numbers. When entering numerical data, ensure that only numbers are entered into the field – do not include the units. If a child is 123cm tall, then the number only must be entered. Prepare a list of short questions which will encourage the children

to use the database to draw some conclusions from their data. For example:

▲ Who are the four tallest children in our class?

▲ Who are the four shortest children in our class?

▲ By how much are the tallest group taller than the shortest group?

▲ Do the four in the tallest group have longer hand spans?

▲ Do children with big feet have longer index fingers?

▲ Is there any connection between height and reach?

## Resources needed

A computer, software in the form of a card-index type database which allows fields to be chosen and has options to display graphs, a printer (preferably colour), measuring equipment (bathroom scales, tape measures, a stop watch, metre rules and string), pens and paper, photocopiable page 140.

## What to do

In both sessions of this activity, the children are encouraged to compare a variety of measurements of physical attributes. There are opportunities to talk openly about similarities and differences and what makes each of us individual and unique.

### Session 1

In this activity the children collect data on a variety of measurements of their physical attributes and, in Session 2 enter the data into the computer and then examine it for any connections. For example, is there a connection between height and foot size, stride length, index finger length, reach or head circumference? Are tall children faster runners? The children should notice that there is a close connection between height and reach. Measuring

someone's reach provides a good estimate of their height. There are other connections between height and foot size, height and span, height and pace and height and cubit.

Before the children begin to collect data, raise their curiosity by asking them questions about their physical attributes, such as whether they think tall people have longer strides or whether big feet are found on tall people. Next, give each child a copy of photocopiable page 140 or your own data collection sheet and provide some measuring equipment (see Resources needed). Ask them to measure the items listed on the sheet and write these down.

Collecting data in this way will take time, especially if it involves time measurements during PE lessons. Ensure that the activity is carried out sensitively, as some children may be self-conscious about their weight or size. In these cases it may be wise to avoid such measurements.

### Session 2

Once the data has been collected the children need to enter it and then save it into the computer database. Provide a whole class or group demonstration of how to do this, then allow the children to work in pairs on the computer. The most important thing is that they learn the process of entering data. Once they are familiar with this, you may wish to ask an adult or older pupil to enter the remaining data to save time and to avoid the children losing interest.

When the data entry is complete, show the children how to use the database for information sorting and plotting graphs, so that they are able to access the database facilities themselves. The children will need to be able to access the graph plotting facilities and print out a variety of graphs from which to draw simple conclusions and comparisons. For example, by producing graphs of height and foot size, visual comparisons may be made which can be further

INFORMATION
TECHNOLOGY

## Suggestion(s) for support
Ensure that the less confident children have completed their data sheet (some measurements may not be accurate but this is not essential). They should be paired up with a more able child for the data input session.

## Assessment opportunities
This activity will enable you to assess how accurately the children classify and prepare information for IT processing. One would hope for accurate measurements here. However, any mistakes will be obvious from the graphs drawn and will add to the interpretational importance. You can also assess how well the children interpret and check the plausibility of information held in the database, especially from the graphical illustrations they use.

## Display ideas
Use the children's graphs and other printouts to create a display on the variety of physical attributes of your class, perhaps with some humorous illustrations. Brief conclusions drawn from the data can be enlarged and printed as headings for the display. If the database allows the combined totalling of the children's height, you can repeat the measurements at a later date to see how much the whole class has grown.

## Reference to photocopiable sheet
Photocopiable page 140 is a data collection sheet which requires the children to take measurements of different physical attributes such as height, weight and so on. They fill this in and enter the data into the computer.

substantiated by adding up the totals of the children concerned. You may also use a particular graph, say the length of pupils' cubits, and ask the children to think up three or four facts obtained from the graph. These may include 'Most of the class have cubits between 25 and 35 centimetres', 'Only three children have cubits above 37 centimetres'. This gives them opportunities for interpreting the graphs in a more open-ended fashion. Provide a short questionnaire requiring them to use the database to draw these types of conclusions (see Preparation). Asking them to plot different graphs in response to your questions will help the children to understand how the database can help with these inquiries.

## Suggestion(s) for extension
More able children could collect additional data such as their heartbeat measured before exercise and after a 50 metre sprint. They could extend their IT skills by setting up their own database to contain these additional findings. They could measure the 'index of Elegance' (length of arm plus extended hand divided by the length of the middle finger); the 'index of Strength' (circumference of biceps divided into the chest circumference) or the 'index of Power' (distance jumped from a standstill divided by circumference around calf). Looking at these aspects gives the children the opportunity to compare and discuss their physical attributes.

# WATCHING IT GROW

**To enter data into a database and interpret graphical information.**

†† *Pairs and small groups.*

🕐 *15 minutes at the computer; data collection over a period.*

## Previous skills/knowledge needed
An ability to measure attributes, such as the weight of an animal and the height of a plant, is needed for this activity.

## Key background information
This activity involves a science investigation, looking at growth. Usually, the growth of living organisms is a slow process and can only be measured over a period of time. The activity will show the children how IT can be used to illustrate the growth process clearly. They will see how data can be collected gradually and entered into a database to produce graphs illustrating the rate of growth. In a sophisticated database, the drawing of several graphs for immediate comparison may be possible. The activity will reinforce the idea that using IT allows data to be easily stored and accessed, and enables information to be presented clearly in the form of graphs.

## Vocabulary
Data, database, storing, illustrating, rate of growth, line graph, bar chart, data collection sheet, conclusion.

## Preparation
You will need to prepare a suitable database on screen for the children to input their data. A simple frequency type database would be sufficient to log the heights/weights on a regular basis. In the case of a pet, weekly weighings should bring in adequate data to measure any increase in growth. However, with plants you may wish to introduce some strong influencing factors such as the amount of light provided, the type of soil used and the frequency of watering. If so, you will need to decide on these aspects of the investigation in advance and make suitable preparations. Separate databases will have to be used where different conditions prevail. If appropriate, prepare a data collection sheet for the children to record their measurements on. Make one copy of photocopiable page 141 per child.

## Resources needed
A computer, database software with the facility to plot graphs, a printer (preferably colour), paper, measuring equipment (including rulers or tape measures and kitchen scales – digital scales are best), a classroom pet such as a hamster to be weighed or plant to be measured over time, a jam jar (for weighing small pets), pens and paper, photocopiable page 141.

## What to do
Introduce the activity by giving the children copies of photocopiable page 141 which illustrates the growth patterns of a hamster using a line graph. The variations seen in the graph may be interpreted in different ways. Discuss this with the children and encourage them to offer some explanations as to why the graph is that shape. This will focus them onto the interpretation of graphs. The bump on the graph may have been a result of more feeding (the mother feeling more maternal, or a member of the litter dying so there is more milk all round) and decline in weight gain between weeks five and six could have been due to an illness of the hamster or its mother, or perhaps the hamster spent more time moving around rather than feeding!

Next, introduce the investigation by discussing with the children what changes take place when living things grow. Does growth happen slowly or quickly? If slowly, how might it be recorded? Explain that they are going to measure the growth of a plant and/or animal over the next few weeks, and then enter the data into the computer to produce some graphs.

Ask the children to start taking measurements and recording them initially on paper. These measurements will need to be made at regular intervals over a chosen period of time. Organise a rota so that pairs of your children do the measuring. Have the class watch to ensure a similar routine is followed. If you decide to measure the growth of a class pet such as a gerbil or hamster, it is best to use digital kitchen scales that can be set to zero. Place an empty jar on the scales and set to zero, then place the pet in the jar and re-weigh to give the animal's weight. If looking at the growth of a plant such as a bean or sunflower, discuss with the children some of the influencing factors such as amount of light, type of soil and frequency of watering.

INFORMATION TECHNOLOGY

Once all the measurements have been made, let the children work in pairs to enter their data. If necessary, provide a whole-class or group demonstration of how to input the data and save it. Once the children are familiar with the entry and saving process, you may prefer to save time by asking an adult or older child to enter the remaining data. When this is complete, demonstrate the graph plotting facilities available on the database. The children will see how IT can help them to produce different types of graphs. Encourage them to discuss which type is the most appropriate for their needs in this situation; then allow them access to the computer in pairs to produce their own graphs.

You may wish to devise a questionnaire which asks the children to interpret their graphs and investigate particular aspects of the growth patterns, especially if growing conditions have varied. If two plants have been grown close to each other, but with varying watering conditions, the accompanying graphs will look different. You may have asked the children how they might expect the graphs to look if one plant was going to struggle while the other was given full care. Rate of growth is rarely linear: there are accelerations and decelerations. As the organism becomes established, growth increases. As the organism reaches its growth limits, then the rate of growth will diminish. All these points are pertinent and should be apparent from the graphs. The children may not reach these conclusions by themselves, and so you will need to explain them at the appropriate time. Some software allows different graphs to be plotted at the same time for comparison, and this can provide an interesting exercise.

Finish by helping the children to draw some conclusions from their graphs. In the case of the plant investigation, these could relate to the conditions that affect plant growth.

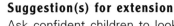

For the animal investigation, these could relate to comfort and well-being, an established feeding routine and general living conditions.

### Suggestion(s) for extension

Ask confident children to look at their graphs and work out how tall their plants could be if they had continued to grow at their fastest pace. Or, in the case of the gerbil or hamster, how heavy it could be if the maximum increase in weight was sustained over a period of time.

### Suggestion(s) for support

Check the measurements made by less confident children and allow them to enter their data alongside a more confident child.

### Assessment opportunities

This activity will allow you to make assessments of how well the children use IT to organise and analyse graphical information, and to interpret the plausibility of the information. You will also be able to assess how accurately they enter their growth data.

### Display ideas

Place the children's computer graphs alongside the original data, together with some written explanations of how the investigation was carried out. The use of a colour photocopier to enlarge the graphs will enhance the display. Photographs of the children carrying out the investigation can be used to add further interest.

### Reference to photocopiable sheet

Photocopiable page 141 provides a graph showing the weight measurements of a hamster taken over a ten-week period. It can be used to help the children focus on interpreting graphs.

INFORMATION
TECHNOLOGY

# TRAFFIC PATTERNS

*To gather data using data collection sheets. To enter this into a database and then plot graphs to draw conclusions.*

†† *Pairs.*

🕐 *20 minutes at the computer; Data collection over a week.*

## Previous skills/knowledge needed

The children should know how to complete a tally chart and how to enter information into a simple database.

## Key background information

Using IT to handle data collected from a simple traffic survey may seem unnecessary in the classroom. However, such an activity provides a scaled down version of what happens in the real world, where IT is often essential to handle millions of items of information in large scale research. Only through using computers can any patterns in the data be identified and illustrated. The children will obviously collect a much smaller amount of data but hopefully it will be sufficient to enable them to identify some trends in the traffic flow near to your school. For example, it may be that there is a daily difference in the frequency and types of traffic that go past the school, caused by factors such as market day, weekend travel on Mondays and Fridays, early closing mid-week or other local influences. The activity will allow the children to practise their IT information handling skills, enabling them to plot graphs and draw some conclusions from these. It could form part of a geography study or project on traffic or the environment.

## Vocabulary

Tally, frequency, field, database, trend, histogram (frequency block graph).

## Preparation

You will need to organise a suitable rota and arrange adult supervision for when the children go out to collect the traffic data. Working in pairs rather than small groups will help the children to stay more focused on the task. You may wish to create some simple data collection sheets for the traffic survey, or ask the children to design their own.

The software required for this activity is a straightforward frequency chart type with graph drawing options. Examples could include Data Plot (Archimedes) or Counter for Windows (PC). Before the children carry out the traffic survey, set up a simple tally database on the computer, adding in the survey times and the types of vehicle to be logged. Possible vehicle categories could include bicycle, motorbike or scooter, car, van, lorry, bus and other (mobile crane, JCB, dumper truck, tractor and so on).

## Resources needed

A computer, a printer (preferably colour), frequency chart database software with graph drawing options (see Preparation), spreadsheet software (optional), a data collection sheet (prepared by the teacher or children), pens, a stopwatch.

## What to do

Tell the children that they are going to carry out a traffic survey over a period of one week. Start by discussing the local traffic flow and what influences it. Encourage the children to make some predictions as to how traffic may be affected by factors such as people going to work, market day, early closing and so on. What would be a good time to log the traffic flow? How long should each survey session last? Would there be an advantage in logging more than once each day? Whatever their final decisions, the children will need to log the traffic for the same amount of time and at the same time of day throughout the week to make it a fair test. Help the children to decide on the types of vehicles to be logged, and reach a consensus on when a van becomes a lorry! Make sure they are clear about how to keep a tally of the traffic and that they know their position on the rota. Allow each pair to carry out the survey, using the data collection sheets to gather the information (see Preparation). Each day, the children can feed the data into the computer database ready to print out histograms of the traffic frequencies. If several logs are made each day do not add them together on the database as it is important to compare the traffic at the same (separate) times each day. Ask the children to plot graphs so that the traffic totals are clearly illustrated on a daily basis. Patterns should emerge as the week

71

progresses. For example, the volume of traffic may lessen on early closing days but increase on market days. By the end of the week the children should have produced a minimum of five graphs for comparison. Produce a short questionnaire to make them examine their graphs and draw some conclusions. For example, on which days are there more bicycles? What is the trend in numbers of lorries during the week? Which vehicle is the most commonly/ least commonly used?

### Suggestion(s) for extension
More able children could enter their findings into a spreadsheet. Graphs of the totals of particular vehicle types could then be plotted to see how these vary across a week.

### Suggestion(s) for support
Ensure that less confident children are paired with a more confident friend. Depending on the volume of traffic, ask each child to tally one type of vehicle.

### Assessment opportunities
This activity will enable you to assess how well the children use IT to organise and analyse the information from their traffic survey. Look for how confident they are in entering the data, plotting the graphs and using the graphs to make conclusions.

### Display ideas
Print out the children's graphs in colour and place these alongside their findings to create a colourful display. If possible, add some photographs of the children logging the traffic and print out some extracts from their conclusions printed using large, bold text.

## WHAT'S ON THE MENU?

*To devise a questionnaire using appropriate software. To reach conclusions by analysing the results.*

†† *Whole class and pairs.*

🕒 *30 minutes at the computer.*

### Previous skills/knowledge needed
The ability to use word processing software to devise a questionnaire would be an advantage although it is not essential.

### Key background information
This activity models the larger poll investigations carried out amongst the public. Public opinion polls are useful not only as a mechanism for gauging opinions and attitudes, but also as a marketing tool for companies researching new products and so on. Using IT helps to streamline the process, allowing large amounts of information to be stored and trends to be illustrated. Usually, the questionnaire is presented in a 'yes or no' answer format for ease of data collection. The skill is in ensuring that the right kinds of questions are asked.

In this particular case, the children are investigating the food preferences (likes and dislikes) among the class. However, they could choose any other area of likes and dislikes to investigate, such as books, TV programmes, football teams, films, TV personalities, famous people (present or past) or music. The children have the opportunity to devise a poll questionnaire and set it up on the computer, thinking of sensible and effective questions which will help them to reach interesting conclusions. They can then use the appropriate software to present or illustrate the results in a meaningful way.

### Vocabulary
Questionnaire, response, database, multiple choice, open ended, sample, trend.

### Preparation
You will need to set up a suitable database in which the children can enter the answers from their questionnaires. The software Junior Pinpoint (Archimedes/PC) or Survey (PC) allows the design of the questionnaire to be carried out. This can then be printed out and each child asked to collect and enter the relevant data onto the paper questionnaire. This data can later be fed back into the computer for analysis using Junior Pinpoint and, where necessary, for producing graphs. However, the children may like to devise a questionnaire using word processing, collect their data and then feed their findings back into a different kind of database such as Junior Database (Archimedes) or Information Workshop (PC).

**INFORMATION TECHNOLOGY**

## Resources needed

A computer, software such as *Junior Pinpoint* (Archimedes/ PC, Longman Logotron) or *Survey* (PC, SPA) for designing the questionnaires, entering the data and producing graphs, or word processing/DTP and database software.

## What to do

Talk to the children about opinion polls. Do they know what opinion polls are? Can they think of any examples of when these are used, such as at election time, in market research and so on? Now tell the children that they are going to carry out a class poll on food. Ask them to work in groups of four or five to produce separate questionnaires, each tackling a different aspect of food. Examples could include fruit, cakes, cereals, biscuits, breakfasts, lunches, suppers, Sunday lunches, picnics, Christmas dinner and birthday parties. Rather than a simple like/dislike investigation the children could also look at reasons for the given responses, such as the taste and consistency of food.

Software such as Junior Pinpoint allows the children to design the questionnaire on screen, then enter the collected data into the software which will in turn count up the input responses and produce graphs to illustrate the findings. If such software is not available, the children can design their questionnaire using a word processing or DTP package and enter the answers into the database software.

Once the groups of children have entered the data from their questionnaires, they can produce graphs to help them reach some conclusions. These will be fairly simple, such as, 'more children prefer toast than cereal' and 'two out of three boys prefer a banana to an apple', but the overall process will show the children how opinions can be gathered and illustrated, and the significance of the results can be interpreted, using IT.

## Suggestion(s) for extension

More able children may like to design additional questionnaires on connected topics such as sweets or ice-creams or perhaps produce a resumé of the results for a class poster or flyer.

## Suggestion(s) for support

Ensure that the less confident children work with others who can support them in their group.

## Assessment opportunities

This activity will enable you to assess how well the children use IT to organise and analyse the information collected from their questionnaires. Note how they devise their questions and set them out within the software. Having collected the data, with what degree of confidence do they interpret their findings? Do they use graphs to help draw conclusions? Can they spot inaccurate data?

## Display ideas

The results from this investigation will make an interesting display when enhanced by the children's art work depicting favourite foods. You could add large headlines to the display stating some of the class 'poll' findings and perhaps produce a flyer giving a resumé of all the results.

**INFORMATION TECHNOLOGY**

# BOOK REVIEWS

**To use a database that has a keyword facility. To become familiar with the keyword option.**

†† *Individuals and pairs.*

🕐 *15 minutes at the computer; 15 minutes discussion.*

### Previous skills/knowledge needed
The children will need to know how to enter information into database software.

### Key background information
Some databases have a keyword facility. This feature plays an important part in the categorising and retrieval of information in the outside world, particularly when large amounts of data need to be sorted. The process of using keywords is simple. For example, if you wished to sort the children in your class according to particular characteristics or 'categories', such as blue-eyed, left-handed, dark-haired, and so on, you would enter all their names into the database, together with the appropriate characteristics which act as keywords. You could then use these keywords to search the database for the names of those children who are blue-eyed, left-handed and so on. (However, the number of keywords used should not be too large otherwise it defeats the purpose.)

This activity is necessarily a small-scale project but it will show the children how keywords can help to sort database information according to various categories.

### Vocabulary
Keyword, category, attribute.

### Preparation
You should explain that this activity involves the children in setting up a database of class library books to help them choose their books in the future. If you wish, you can share the database among children from several classes, perhaps including the intended age range of the readers as an additional keyword.

Book Title: *Asterix the Gaul*

Author(s):

Comments:
• John Dee

  *I specially liked the funny bits*
• Mary Jones

  *I really like the pictures most*

Keywords:
fiction, illustrated, humorous, cartoon, history

To enable children to collect data you will need to produce a comment sheet for each book in the class library which the children must fill in when they finish reading a book. A possible format is suggested below which also lists the keywords appropriate for the particular book.

INFORMATION TECHNOLOGY

You will also need to set up a suitable database in which the children can enter the various book details and keywords. This database can follow the same structure as the comment sheet.

### Resources needed

Database software with keyword facility, *Data Card* from Datasweet 3 (Archimedes and PC).

### What to do

You should discuss with your children what attributes are going to be useful and which will act as fields and keywords. Hold up examples of a range of books and decide on some basic categories (keywords), such as fiction, non-fiction, humorous, illustrated, adventure, crime, travel and historical. Show them the comment sheets (see Preparation) and ask them to fill in the appropriate one with a short 'review' whenever they finish a book. Once there are a sufficient number of comments for each book, ask the children to work in pairs to enter the details in the library database. Each database entry will contain the agreed keywords in the form of basic categories such as fiction, history and so on, and brief comments or 'reviews' to guide the children in choosing a suitable book. When this is complete, demonstrate how to use the keyword facility to search for the type of books that the children are interested in. The children can then use the keywords to search for information on the type of books in which they are interested. Repeated searches each time the children wish to find out about a new book will help to reinforce the idea of using keywords.

As the children will need to read the books before writing their reviews, building up the database will be an ongoing activity. However, it is the process rather than the finished product which is important.

### Suggestion(s) for extension

More able children may like to extend their IT skills by seeking out keywords for different collections of objects and setting up an additional database.

### Suggestion(s) for support

Make sure that less confident children are given adult support in writing the correct information on the comment sheet, and are supervised when entering the data into the computer.

### Assessment opportunities

This activity will enable you to assess how well the children use IT to prepare, classify and organise information on their reading books for carrying out database searches using keywords. Look to see how well they can access information from the completed database by using the keyword search facility within the software.

### Display ideas

Use enlarged database printouts to create a display close to your class library or in the school library. Such display material will help the children to learn about the processes involved in handling information and how routines, such as the use of keywords, allow us to access particular information.

INFORMATION
TECHNOLOGY

# WHATEVER THE WEATHER

*To use an appropriate database within which data may be stored for comparison.*

✝✝ *Pairs (collecting data) and small groups (analysing results).*

🕐 *5 minutes data entry into the computer per day; 15 minutes for daily data collection over about two months.*

## Previous skills/knowledge needed

The children will need a basic familiarity with databases. They will also find it helpful to have some experience of taking weather measurements.

## Key background information

Serious weather forecasting relies on the accurate collection of data on which to base predictions. The activity below involves the children in collecting weather data on a daily basis. To gather a meaningful amount of data they should be collecting observations over at least two months. The activity will illustrate the importance of making accurate measurements and show the children how IT can be used to identify patterns within the data collected.

As the weather data is collected, the children can eventually compare one month with another and investigate the trends. Totals and averages across months may be compared by using the graph plotting facilities within the database software. If you are using a spreadsheet database, the children will find it easier to read the weather data and to make comparisons of data from month to month or week to week as much of the data can be seen on the screen at one time.

## Preparation

A simple card index type of database will suffice for this activity. Set this up with one card per day containing fields for the weather data to be recorded. Typically, these may include maximum/minimum temperatures, temperature at a fixed time each day (such as noon), wind speed and direction, cloud cover, visibility and, possibly, humidity and air pressure. (If possible, discuss different fields/headings with the children to decide on the most suitable ones.) Make one copy of photocopiable page 142 for each child.

## Resources needed

A computer, database software such as a card index type database (examples include *Junior Database* (Archimedes) and *Information Workshop* (PC), or spreadsheet software such as *Sheetwise* (Archimedes and PC), a printer (preferably colour), equipment to collect weather data, photocopiable page 142.

## What to do

Give each child a copy of photocopiable page 142. Ask them to look carefully at the data to explain what the weather is doing on each particular day. Use the photocopiable sheet to help familiarise the children with the different weather variables such as rain, temperature, cloud cover and so on. Can they find links between any of the variables on the photocopiable page? For example, does it mean rain is more likely if the wind is in a particular direction? Or what is the connection between cloud cover and rainfall?

Explain to the children that they are going to gather their own weather data over the next two months or so. Provide a whole class introduction to the organisation for this, discussing what is to be collected, at what time of day and

who is to carry it out. Make the weather data collectors responsible for entering their readings into the database. Once the children start collecting the data, it can be difficult to sustain their interest over such a long period. You can keep their motivation up by discussing the findings in a superficial way as time goes on. For example, perhaps there is a trend in the daily noon temperature as winter approaches, or the pattern of clear night skies leading to cold and frosty nights.

Once all the data is collected and fed into the computer, the children can begin their analysis in earnest. Guide them through this process or allow them to investigate the results themselves, depending on their age and ability. Ask them to seek out the possible patterns in temperature and cloud cover, air pressure and cloud cover, a trend in the maximum temperature (depending on the time of year), rainfall and wind direction, rainfall and air pressure, cloud and rainfall, wind direction and maximum temperature and so on. Can they discover any other connections or trends? As far as possible, they should produce graphs to illustrate their findings.

### Suggestion(s) for extension

Confident children may like to include some more unusual recordings such as the temperature 10cm below the ground surface (using a half-buried thermometer or digital thermometer probe) or pond water temperature. They could use their database to find out how such additional data relates to other more conventional weather readings.

### Suggestion(s) for support

For less confident children provide some initial help with their measuring and recording. Pair them up with a more able child and check their results for accuracy (although

mistakes can lead to some important discussions, bringing children's attention to the fact that computers are still more limited in many ways than the human mind and will not warn you of careless mistakes!).

### Assessment opportunities

This activity will enable you to assess how well the children use IT to analyse information, check its accuracy and interpret it, choosing elements required for specific purposes such as finding connections and relationships within the data and considering the consequences of mistakes caused by entering erroneous data. Look to see how confidently the children enter the data and begin to make comparisons of the various findings. Real connections between weather data cannot be made until they have collected information over at least two months; it should then allow them to draw conclusions from their graphs – how accurate are they in their graphical interpretations?

### Display ideas

Display the children's results in graph form together with some colourful artwork and word processed descriptions of various weather types. You can also add in some photographs or posters of different weather conditions.

### Reference to photocopiable sheet

Photocopiable page 142 provides six different sets of weather data measured at different times of the year. The children are asked to look at each set of data and describe what the weather conditions are like. They can then try to spot any patterns in the different weather variables.

---

**What kind of weather?**

Name _____  Date _____

▲ Describe what the weather is doing from these weather readings. Cloud cover is measured in octas (eighths of sky covered).

| October 23rd | |
|---|---|
| Wind speed on Beaufort scale | 5 |
| Wind direction | SW |
| Cloud cover | 7/8 |
| Minimum temp | 4°C |
| Maximum temp | 10°C |
| Noon temp | 8°C |
| Rainfall | 1mm |

| July 3rd | |
|---|---|
| Wind speed on Beaufort scale | 1 |
| Wind direction | S |
| Cloud cover | 0/8 |
| Minimum temp | 12°C |
| Maximum temp | 25°C |
| Noon temp | 23°C |
| Rainfall | 0mm |

| June 4th | |
|---|---|
| Wind speed on Beaufort scale | 6 |
| Wind direction | W |
| Cloud cover | 8/8 |
| Minimum temp | 10°C |
| Maximum temp | 14°C |
| Noon temp | 12°C |
| Rainfall | 12mm |

| January 3rd | |
|---|---|
| Wind speed on Beaufort scale | 0 |
| Wind direction | |
| Cloud cover | 0/8 |
| Minimum temp | −5°C |
| Maximum temp | 0°C |
| Noon temp | 0°C |
| Rainfall | 0mm |

| April 15th | |
|---|---|
| Wind speed on Beaufort scale | 3 |
| Wind direction | W |
| Cloud cover | 4/8 |
| Minimum temp | 7°C |
| Maximum temp | 10°C |
| Noon temp | 8°C |
| Rainfall | 14mm |

| March 24th | |
|---|---|
| Wind speed on Beaufort scale | 6 |
| Wind direction | SE |
| Cloud cover | 6/8 |
| Minimum temp | 7°C |
| Maximum temp | 13°C |
| Noon temp | 12°C |
| Rainfall | 0mm |

---

INFORMATION TECHNOLOGY

# FINDING THE FACTS

***To search a database to find out facts which allow conclusions to be drawn. To become familiar with search routines.***

†† *Pairs.*

🕐 *40 minutes at the computer; 15 minutes discussion/demonstration.*

## Previous skills/knowledge needed

The children should be familiar with using databases and understand the possibilities of investigating the facts that these contain.

## Key background information

There is a wide range of computer databases available that offer different options for the handling of information stored within them. The simplest type works on the card index principle – a computerised version of the pupil card index system found in many school offices, or the patients' card index used in doctors' surgeries, for example. Each card contains an identical set of headings or fields which may contain words or numbers. A set of such cards can be sorted on any field; an alphabetical sort if the field contains words, or a numerical sort if the field is numeric. Certain card index databases will offer a search facility on any field. The user enters a search word (or search number) and the result is that all cards containing the searched word or value will come up to the top of the collection, or may even form a separate set of cards.

More advanced databases have a search facility known as a logical search. This allows you to search for several words at one time. Once you state the words you wish to search for, and which headings or fields they fall within (such as name, address, and so on), the software will pull out all the entries that contain these search words. This kind of search uses AND and OR. For example, if you wished to search for all cases of boys AND Year 4, this will produce all cases of boys who are in Year 4. If you search for boys OR Year 4, the result will be a larger group consisting of all boys and all Year 4 pupils. The logical search is a powerful tool and will need careful explanation to enable the children to grasp the concept. The database that you provide for this activity should allow them to use this facility. As more and more information becomes available on IT systems such as CD-ROM and the Internet, the development of IT searching skills is important.

## Vocabulary

Sort, search, narrowed down search, search word, logical search, AND, OR.

## Preparation

You will need to prepare at least two databases in advance for this activity. The first is based on photocopiable page 143 which provides a simple 'spreadsheet' style list of a group of children with a variety of different attributes. The children are asked to carry out a logical search to answer the list of questions on the photocopiable sheet, so you will need to prepare a database which contains the same details as the sheet. Make one copy of the photocopiable sheet for each child.

The second database can contain information on any subject, perhaps linked to your current topic. This will enable the children to practise logical searches once they have grasped the technique. There are many prepared databases

available commercially dealing with topics such as monarchs, British birds, volcanoes of the world, counties and so on and these can save you a lot of preparation time.

It will also be necessary to prepare some question sheets relating to the database to encourage the children to interact with it and use the search options. Choose the searches carefully to suit the children's abilities.

## Resources needed

A computer, two pre-prepared databases, one with appropriate question sheets (see Preparation), a printer, paper, a small manual card index system (perhaps from the school office), photocopiable page 143.

## What to do

Explain to the children that a computer database can be used to sort through large amounts of information. To help them understand how a simple database works and the processes it goes through when searching, show them a manual card index system – your school office may have one and this would provide an excellent example. Using the card index, demonstrate the information retrieval process by pulling out all the cards that contain a particular word and placing them at the front of the pile. Explain that this selection of cards is the result of a particular search. You may go further and narrow down the search by picking out cards from the result of your first search which contain a second search word. For example, the result of your first search could be 'all boys'. The second search could be 'Year 4', so the result would be 'all Year 4 boys'. Make sure the

children understand the term 'narrowed down search'.

Now use photocopiable page 143 to introduce the children to the idea of logical searches done on computer databases. Give each child a copy of the sheet and provide a whole class demonstration of how to use the AND/OR search routine on the computer (see Key background information) to answer the questions on the sheet. Question 1 is an introductory question to get them used to the searching process. The search is a simple one not requiring the use of AND or OR. In question 2, the search is for blue AND cat, so the children must look for all cases of children with blue eyes and ensure that these children also have a cat. The logical operator OR means there are alternatives. In question 4, the search is for all those children who either have brown eyes or have a cat (this must include even the blue-eyed cat owners!). It may take some time for the children to understand logical searches so they will probably need plenty of support in answering the questions on the photocopiable sheet when they come to work at the computer.

Once the children are sufficiently familiar with using logical searches, they can go on to use the other database that you have prepared for them. Your question sheets (see Preparation) should encourage them to use search routines for interrogation purposes and to draw some conclusions.

## Suggestion(s) for extension

As this exercise is largely steered by you through the work sheet activities, you have control over the complexity of the children's IT tasks. The more confident children may

be able to find answers to such questions as 'Is there any connection between average length of a bird and the number of eggs it lays?' 'Is there a connection between the density of population of a county and the type of local industry found there?'

### Suggestion(s) for support

Again, you can offer the less confident children appropriate tasks by tailoring your question sheet to suit their ability. It may not be appropriate for them to carry out logical searches but they could establish facts by using simple searches based on keywords rather than the 'AND/OR' routine.

### Assessment opportunities

You will be able to assess how well the children use IT to analyse information held in a database and to interpret the plausibility of information in order to draw conclusions. Look to see how effectively they analyse the data through the use of search routines – are they skilled in the use of search tools? do they produce accurate results?

### Display ideas

Printouts from databases usually require supplementing with colourful illustrations to ensure an attractive display. Much will depend on the context and substance of the database. Banner headlines such as 'Did you know that ...?' and 'Smaller birds lay more eggs – can you think why?' will help to make the display eye-catching.

### Reference to photocopiable sheet

Photocopiable page 143 introduces the children to a logical research routine using AND/OR.

**Spreadsheet challenge**

Name _____
Date _____

Can you sort out your ANDs from your ORs?

| | A | B | C | D | E |
|---|---|---|---|---|---|
| 1 | Name | Eyes | Hair | Pets | Boy/girl |
| 2 | Tom | Blue | Brown | Cat | Boy |
| 3 | Ann | Brown | Brown | Dog | Girl |
| 4 | Susan | Brown | Black | Dog | Girl |
| 5 | Jo | Brown | Black | Fish | Boy |
| 6 | Peter | Blue | Black | Canary | Boy |

▲ Using the data in the spreadsheet, answer the following questions:

1 Who has blue eyes? _____
2 Who has blue eyes and a cat? _____
3 Who has brown eyes? _____
4 Who has brown eyes or a cat? _____
5 Who has brown hair or a canary? _____
6 Is there a girl who has a dog and blue eyes? _____
7 Is there a boy who has a fish and blue eyes? _____
8 Who has brown eyes or brown hair? _____
9 Who has brown eyes and brown hair? _____
10 Which boys have black hair or blue eyes? _____

## CD-ROM SEARCH

***To search the information held on a CD-ROM encyclopaedia for specific facts from which to draw conclusions.***

†† *Pairs.*

🕐 *45 minutes at the computer; 15 minutes discussion/demonstration.*

### Previous skills/knowledge needed

The children will find it helpful to have worked with a variety of search routines in databases, including a logical search. Doing the CD-ROM activity 'Famous people' on page 33 first would be an advantage.

### Key background information

The CD-ROM has almost become a standard classroom resource. There is an ever increasing variety to choose from, including interactive and encyclopaedia-type CD-ROMs. The encyclopaedia type are an excellent classroom resource for reference work and there are CD-ROMs to cover most areas of the curriculum. The ability to access a wide variety of information in textual, picture, sound or video format makes reference and research activities using CD-ROMs enjoyable and rewarding. Usually, the text and images can be selected and placed into word processing or DTP software.

Different CD-ROMs have different ways of allowing you to access the information. The encyclopaedia type usually

has an efficient search routine and, sometimes, a logical search facility. Other types may be of the browse around kind where a search routine is not an integral part. With the enormous amount of information available, the children need to develop skills that allow them to search such IT systems efficiently. It is all too easy to browse around irrelevant areas of information within CD-ROMs, jumping from link to link. Clear tasks set by you, perhaps even timed activities, will limit the temptation to wander off course! For this activity, the children work to a set time limit and have clear instructions about what to find out from the CD-ROMs in the form of a question sheet.

## Vocabulary
Search routine, AND, OR, limited search, link, section, back track.

## Preparation
As with any useful classroom resource, it is essential to have a good knowledge of the contents of the CD-ROM that you plan to use with the children. Search it to identify the type of information that you would like the children to find out about. Prepare a number of question sheets which will help the children to target specific areas of information and to reach suitable conclusions from this, depending on their ability. A typical context may be finding out about nocturnal animals. Your questions could ask the children for information on habitat, food, types of movement, hibernation and so on. The second part of the sheet could direct them towards drawing some suitable conclusions,

such as 'Do most nocturnal animals inhabit woodland?' or 'Are there any special features that nocturnal creatures need to have?' The questions should direct them to use the search routines and links available and to save a variety of images and text for importing into word-processing applications.

A strategy for focusing the children's searches is to limit the number of links used on each page to just two, perhaps. This would mean that from a page on owls, for example, the children must use only two of the links available to access further information on the CD-ROM. This restricts the amount of information they have to deal with, but, most importantly, it forces them to choose carefully the most useful links. You can frame your questions to guide the children into taking particular link routes. It is difficult to be familiar with all the contents of a CD-ROM, but the better your knowledge, the more accurately you will be able to pitch the questions for the children.

## Resources needed
A computer with a CD-ROM drive, an encyclopaedia-type CD-ROM, preferably with a search facility, copies of question sheets to focus the children's searches, a printer (preferably colour).

## What to do
CD-ROMs present information in an attractive, varied way and can tempt children to start browsing indiscriminately rather than focusing on the task in hand. The object of this activity is to ensure that they use their time efficiently and

INFORMATION
TECHNOLOGY

search for information in a more discerning way to reach some suitable conclusions. The setting of a time limit for the task is recommended.

Start with a whole class or large group demonstration of how to search your chosen CD-ROM for information. Show the children the search routine(s) available and remind them of how to use the different links and download text or images into other software if necessary. Give each of

them a copy of the appropriate question sheet you have prepared (see Preparation) and allow them access to the computer in pairs to complete these. Set a time limit of around 45 minutes for them to complete the activity. If you have framed your questions to limit the amount of links that the children can use, draw their attention to this. When they have completed the questions on their sheets, check that they have accessed the appropriate information before they move on to the next part, where they are required to draw suitable conclusions.

## Suggestion(s) for extension
The question sheets should be tailored to the children's specific abilities. This means that you can give the confident children more challenging tasks to carry out, perhaps in the form of a logical search if possible, and the saving of text or pictures to complete their questions sheet.

## Suggestion(s) for support
Similarly, the task for less confident children could be simplified by limiting them to simple searches in response to more basic questions such as 'How many nocturnal creatures can you find on the CD-ROM?' or 'Choose two nocturnal creatures, what do they eat? '

## Assessment opportunities
This activity will allow you to assess how well the children use IT software to analyse information on the CD-ROM and how well they search and choose elements required to complete a question sheet.

## Display ideas
Graphics obtained from a CD-ROM can enhance any display. What your children display as a result of this activity obviously depends on the tasks you set them. It would be helpful if the activity supports an ongoing topic so that the information from the CD-ROM can be used to enhance other work produced by the children.

## LOOKING AT SPREADSHEETS

*To use a spreadsheet to store information. To use spreadsheet facilities such as total, average, sort and graph to illustrate their findings.*

†† *Whole class (data collection) and pairs (at the computer).*

🕐 *20 minutes at the computer; 15 minutes demonstration.*

## Previous skills/knowledge needed
The children should be able to make measurements of their own dimensions. It would be helpful to have already covered the activity 'Looking at us' on page 66.

## Key background information
Computer spreadsheets are powerful IT tools which present information in a clear, easily accessible format. All spreadsheets consist of numbered boxes or cells within which data in the form of words or numbers is placed. A single spreadsheet may contain hundreds of cells which means that the whole sheet may be too large to see all at once. However, the cells can be moved around, with the computer screen acting rather like a small window through which we look at one part of the sheet at any one time. Usually, around the top and left-hand sides there are labels which define what each column or row contains.

Spreadsheets have various functions which can process the data held within them. For example, the totalling or averaging of a column is easily carried out. Graphs of the column contents can also be produced to illustrate patterns within the data and enable conclusions to be drawn.

Searches, and narrowed down searches, can be carried out within rows to identify particular cases which fall between certain ranges. Some spreadsheets offer the facility to identify the maximum or minimum within a column.

The activity below introduces the children to using spreadsheets. They are asked to collect measurements of their own physical dimensions and to input this data into the spreadsheet. They are then encouraged to use the total/average and graph facilities.

### Vocabulary
Spreadsheet, cell, narrowed down search, cell address (the co-ordinates of each cell, usually in the form of A1, B16, G7 and so on), maximum, minimum, range, column, row, sum.

### Preparation
Set up a computer spreadsheet with one row for each child in the class and approximately six columns, each one headed as follows: Name, Height (cm), Weight (kg), Foot (cm), Reach (cm) and Cubit (forearm measurement) (cm) – or any other attributes that you wish the children to measure. If you have already done the activity 'Looking at us' on page 66, then you can re-use the data obtained.

If you have not yet carried out the above activity, refer to Session 1 of the 'What to do' section on page 67 to collect the data in preparation for the main activity below. You may also wish to make copies of photocopiable page 140 to help the children gather their data. Alternatively, you can make copies of photocopiable page 144 and use this data to complete the activity.

### Resources needed
A computer, spreadsheet software, preferably with a column totalling and averaging facility, a printer (preferably colour), paper, pens, measuring equipment such as tape measures and bathroom scales, photocopiable page 144 (if you have not already done the 'Looking at us' activity on page 66.

### What to do
In this activity the children use a simple spreadsheet to store data about themselves and then use some of the functions available to illustrate and interpret the data. The children will need to have collected various measurements of their physical dimensions first (see Preparation).

Start with a whole class demonstration showing the children a printout of the spreadsheet structure you have set up on the computer (see Preparation). Point out the cell structure, and the way that the columns and rows are arranged. Explain that only a small part of a spreadsheet can be seen on the screen at any one time. Show them how data is typed into the cells and how to move around between the different cells by clicking on a particular cell using the mouse pointer. Demonstrate how to save the information. Now tell the children that they are going to use a spreadsheet format to enter the measurements of their physical dimensions/attributes. Explain that they will also use some spreadsheet facilities to interpret and

OUR CLASS WEIGHS AS MUCH AS **1000** BAGS OF SUGAR

illustrate the data. Next, allow the children access to the computer in pairs to type in the measurement data collected. If the children have not had the opportunity to collect their own measurement data, perhaps due to time constraints, they can key in the data from photocopiable page 144 to enable them to participate in this activity.

Make a printout of the spreadsheet once all the data is entered. Talk about the sum/total and average of a column if your spreadsheet has these facilities. Finding the total height or weight of the class can be an amusing concept! The children should graph the data, to illustrate class heights or cubits, for example. If the spreadsheet has a scattergram facility (a graph that displays the connection between two variables – height and foot size, say), then some interesting comparisons may be made. Ask the children to plot reach against height; there should be a close connection between the two shown by a narrow spread of dots. Compare the average height of boys and girls.

## Suggestion(s) for extension

To extend the confident children, encourage them to make greater use of the scattergram feature. What other attributes that relate to each other can they find? They could enter into their spreadsheet the additional attributes mentioned in 'Looking at us', such as the index of Elegance, and look for connections – for example, are all elegant children tall?

## Suggestion(s) for support

The less confident children may need you to work alongside them for a short while to ensure that they enter their data correctly into the spreadsheet, or have a more confident

friend work with them to ensure the process is understood. They will be involved in straightforward analysis of the data in the spreadsheet such as printing out graphs of class attributes and totalling columns.

## Assessment opportunities

This activity can allow you to assess how well the children prepare information for IT processing, checking for accuracy as the data is entered. (Establishing a routine such as saying 'All children in this class are between the heights of x and y' may help with this).

You can also assess how well they interpret information, and how well they use and understand functions such as the total and average values of a column of data. Look at how confidently the children interpret the data in graphical form, and how realistic their conclusions are.

## Display ideas

The children will enjoy building up a display about themselves. The central focus could be the spreadsheet itself, enlarged. Use coloured cotton to link parts of the spreadsheet to illustrations or word processed explanations. Ideas for illustrations could include the total height of the class ('Our class is as long as six double-decker buses'), the total weight of the class ('Our class weighs the same as 1200 bags of sugar') and so on. Such comparisons will enable the children to improve their estimation skills in an enjoyable way.

## Reference to photocopiable sheet

Photocopiable page 144 can be used to help the children to experience the simple spreadsheet processes.

---

### Spreadsheet challenge

Name _____ Date _____

▲ Look at this spreadsheet example and answer the questions below.

|   | A | B | C | D |
|---|---|---|---|---|
| 1 | pupil | height (cm) | weight (kg) | reach (cm) |
| 2 | Tom | 123 | 34 | 120 |
| 3 | Helen | 137 | 39 | 139 |
| 4 | Sarah | 134 | 32 | 132 |
| 5 | Thomas | 136 | 38 | 135 |
| 6 | Lizzie | 122 | 28 | 122 |
| 7 | Jo | 124 | 29 | 120 |
| 8 | Eleanor | 130 | 35 | 132 |

1 Can you find the total of the height column – what is the sum of the height column? _____

2 What is the average height of the children? _____

3 How much taller are Helen and Sarah together compared with Tom and Lizzie together? _____

4 What is the average reach of the children? Is this similar to their average height? _____

5 What is the total weight of the children? _____

6 What is the average weight of the children? _____

7 Who is less than the average weight? _____

8 Who is above the average weight? _____

9 Who is above the average height? _____

10 Who is below the average height? _____

# WHAT ARE WE EATING?

*To collect and practise inputting data into a spreadsheet. To use the sort facility to draw conclusions.*

†† *Individuals (to collect data) and pairs (at the computer).*

🕐 *40 minutes at the computer; 15 minutes demonstration.*

## Previous skills/knowledge needed
The children should be able to enter information into a spreadsheet and save it. Doing the previous activity 'Looking at spreadsheets' (on page 82) will help to prepare the children.

## Key background information
Information held within a spreadsheet column may be sorted in alphabetical or numerical order. For example, data listing the children's heights (from the previous activity) could be sorted so that the name of the tallest child rises to the top of the column and the shortest goes to the bottom. All the data connected to every pupil across the spreadsheet follows the sort sequence.

Most spreadsheets also contain a facility for finding the maximum and minimum values within a column. This is easy to use and provides a useful feature for helping the children draw conclusions from their data. This activity will be most appropriate for work on nutrition, growth or farming.

## Preparation
Ask the children to bring in nutritional information from the backs of cereal packets. Ensure that a good range of cereals is covered; try to obtain details from at least a dozen different ones. Set up a spreadsheet with the appropriate headings for nutritional values including protein, carbohydrate, fat, fibre, iron, calories, vitamins, and so on. Make one copy for each child of the cereal questionnaire on photocopiable page 145, or devise your own if a more differentiated approach is required. These questionnaires should encourage the children to draw graphs and sort the data to form conclusions.

## Vocabulary
Maximum, minimum, cell, entry, value, numerical sort, alphabetical sort.

## Resources needed
A computer, spreadsheet software including sort, graph and minimum/maximum value facilities, a printer (preferably colour), paper, pens, data collected from cereal packets (see Preparation), photocopiable page 145 or your own cereal questionnaire for the children to use.

## What to do
The aim of this task is to provide the children with further practice in entering data into a spreadsheet and then to sort the data to make comparisons and draw conclusions from any patterns identified. The children should bring in the nutritional details printed on the packets of cereals (see

Preparation). These details all follow a similar pattern, but care needs to be taken over whether the values given are per 100g or some other weight. Keeping to nutritional values based on 100g will make comparing the data much more straightforward. Allow the children to work on their own or in pairs to enter into the spreadsheet the nutritional values they have collected. Alternatively, you could use the data from the spreadsheet on photocopiable page 145 to speed up the data collection process.

Once all the data has been keyed into the spreadsheet, give each of the children a copy of photocopiable page 145 or your own cereal questionnaire. Then provide a whole class or large group demonstration of how to answer such questions by sorting within the appropriate column. For example, finding out which cereal gives us the most energy, which cereal provides us with the most fibre and so on, can all be solved by sorting within the relevant column. To carry out a sort on a particular column, usually the column is first highlighted and then the sort option clicked with the mouse pointer. Some spreadsheets offer alphabetical sorts either from A to Z or in reverse order Z to A. The routine is similar with a numerical sort and again, the option of a reverse numerical sort is offered so the column can be in ascending (largest at the top) or descending order (smallest at the top). Next, show the children how to produce graphs to illustrate the total values within a particular column. Sorting a column will bring the biggest value to the top and the smallest value to the bottom of the column, so immediately the children can see these values within a column. This process will enable them to draw conclusions quickly. For example, in the photocopiable data, the cereal containing the most fibre can be identified easily by sorting on the fibre column with values in ascending order and, in this case, finding that Brantime contains the most fibre and Sugared Rice the least.

## Suggestion(s) for extension

Devise a questionnaire to offer more able children an appropriately challenging range of questions. They could be asked to work out the costs of each cereal per 100g, for example, or perhaps compare the nutritional value of cereals with other foods such as biscuits.

## Suggestion(s) for support

You may have to help less confident children to enter their data or pair them up with a more able child. Devising appropriate questions to match their ability closely will help to ensure that they experience success with the activity.

## Assessment opportunities

This activity will enable you to assess how well the children use IT to organise and analyse information. Look to see with what level of confidence the children use the spreadsheet tools, such as the sorting facility, to make decisions and draw conclusions. Also, how well they prepare information for IT processing and whether they check for accuracy; are they aware that the computer will not check for any mistakes?

## Display ideas

The children could use their findings from the questionnaires to create banner headlines for displaying alongside other work they have completed on food or nutrition. Using an enlarged printout of the cereal spreadsheet, along with coloured cottons linked to captions, will add to the instructional aspect. Add questions printed in large type, such as 'Can you find ...?', 'In which column is the ...?', to make the display more interactive.

## Reference to photocopiable sheet

Photocopiable page 145 provides a spreadsheet layout of the nutritional values of a range of imaginary breakfast cereals The children can key in this data to find the answers to the questions, or they can try it as a pen and paper exercise first to appreciate how much easier it is to do the same task on screen. The questions can also be used to analyse data keyed in from the nutritional panels of a number of real breakfast cereals or other foods.

### Eating our breakfast

Name _____ Date _____

▲ Look at the spreadsheet below. It shows the nutritional values of a range of different breakfast cereals.

| | A | B | C | D | E | F | G | H |
|---|---|---|---|---|---|---|---|---|
| 1 | Cereal | Energy (kJ) | Protein (g) | Carbohydrate (g) | Fat (g) | Sodium (g) | Fibre (g) | Cost per 100g (p) |
| 2 | Brantime | 1150 | 15.0 | 45.0 | 3.0 | 1.00 | 24.0 | 16 |
| 3 | Teamsters | 1300 | 9.2 | 65.5 | 2.6 | 0.60 | 17.5 | 20 |
| 4 | Oaties | 1460 | 12.0 | 60.0 | 8.0 | | 14.0 | 8 |
| 5 | Freddies | 1410 | 9.8 | 72.8 | 2.1 | | 10.5 | 17 |
| 6 | Vitalise | 1456 | 9.2 | 72.3 | 2.4 | | 10.5 | 25 |
| 7 | Wheaties | 1510 | 10.5 | 69.8 | 2.7 | 0.30 | 9.4 | 21 |
| 8 | Raisin Bix | 1450 | 9.0 | 71.0 | 2.0 | 0.01 | 9.0 | 28 |
| 9 | Muesli | 1537 | 12.0 | 65.6 | 5.0 | | 8.4 | 18 |
| 10 | Toppers | 1506 | 9.0 | 74.0 | 2.0 | 0.01 | 8.0 | 26 |
| 11 | Sugared Clouds | 1554 | 6.0 | 88.0 | | 9.00 | 7.0 | 26 |
| 12 | Starter | 1550 | 8.0 | 77.0 | 1.2 | | | |
| 13 | Wheeties | 1615 | 6.1 | 78.4 | 2.0 | 0.50 | 6.0 | 29 |
| 14 | Porridge | 1014 | 8.2 | 43.6 | 4.0 | 0.30 | 6.0 | 23 |
| 15 | Frosted Flakes | 1650 | 5.0 | 89.0 | 5.4 | | 3.8 | 7 |
| 16 | Corn Twists | 1600 | 6.4 | 82.2 | 0.4 | 0.80 | 2.2 | 23 |
| 17 | Malted Slims | 1600 | 15.0 | 76.0 | 1.4 | 0.80 | | 17 |
| 18 | Cocoa Chips | 1600 | 5.0 | 87.0 | 1.0 | 1.00 | 2.0 | 29 |
| 19 | Sugary Rice | 1650 | 4.0 | 90.0 | 1.0 | 0.80 | 1.0 | 31 |
| | | | | | 0.5 | 0.80 | 0.4 | 31 |

▲ Now answer these questions on the back of this sheet:

1 Which cereal contains the most fibre? How much fibre per 100g?
2 Which cereal contains the least fibre and how much is it per 100g?
3 Which is the most expensive cereal?
4 Which is the cheapest cereal?
5 Which cereal give you the most energy? How much energy is that?
6 Which cereal gives you the least energy?
7 Which is the fattiest cereal?
8 Can you spot any connection between energy and carbohydrate?

**INFORMATION TECHNOLOGY**

CHRIS CHROME'S
# CAR WASH

## BUSINESS PLANS

*To use a spreadsheet to model the running of a small business. To be able to ask 'What if..?' and make decisions from conclusions drawn.*

†† *Pairs or small groups.*

🕐 *45 minutes at the computer; 20 minutes demonstration.*

## Previous skills/knowledge needed

The children should have used a simple spreadsheet before and will need to be at Level 4 or above in Maths.

## Key background information

Spreadsheets are a useful tool to monitor how a business is functioning. By entering all the income and expenditure, spreadsheets allow us to keep careful track of the flow of cash. Most importantly, spreadsheets enable us to model the consequences of any changes – by making a single change in one entry, all the values that depend on that entry are updated across the spreadsheet. Additional calculations can be made on the data through the use of various functions, such as 'sum' and 'average'. The only function required for this activity is the sum function. (The 'Party time' activity on page 92 explores this modelling aspect of spreadsheets in more detail.)

This activity is based on a spreadsheet for an imaginary car wash business, for which the children have to consider expenditure and income to work out the profits, and model what would happen if certain changes took place to affect the cashflow. The children have the opportunity to use some of the formula options within the spreadsheet to help them with their calculations. Although the activity is based around the business figures provided on photocopiable page 146, the children could set up their own imaginary car wash business and produce appropriate figures for this to use in the activity.

## Preparation

Photocopiable page 146 provides some sample figures for the first month of a car wash business, together with some questions which will encourage the children to make use of the spreadsheet facilities. Make one copy of the photocopiable sheet for each child. Prepare a spreadsheet based on this, perhaps asking the children to input the data as part of the main activity – a good test of their accuracy skills! If you wish, adapt the sheet or produce several of your own to suit the children's abilities. Alternatively, a more able group of children could sort out their own spreadsheet labels and enter some realistic data based on their perceptions of the possible business cashflow. In this case, you will need to produce your own question sheet to direct the activity.

A visit to the school office to see a real spreadsheet modelling the school's cashflow is a good way to prepare for this activity, if possible. A local business or shop may be willing to demonstrate how a spreadsheet is used in the running of their business.

## Vocabulary

Cell, formula, calculation, cashflow, model, expenditure/outgoings, income, profit.

## Resources needed

A computer, spreadsheet software, a printer, paper, photocopiable page 146 or your own data/question sheets.

## What to do

Provide each child with a copy of photocopiable page 146. Explain that this shows the income and expenditure for a car wash business and includes some questions which you would like them to answer. Tell them that these questions relate to various changes in the business, and they are going to use a computer spreadsheet to find out what would happen as a result of these changes.

Start by providing a small group demonstration to remind the children how the spreadsheet software operates and how data is entered and saved. Now show them how to enter a formula into the spreadsheet; for example, to find out the total amount of money made per day or week is 'cost per wash x number of cars'. In this function, the product of the two cells will be calculated and placed in a

**INFORMATION TECHNOLOGY**

# Handling information

cell. The children will also need to know about the sum function. Show them how this adds up any number of values held within a column or part of a column and how the total can be placed into a cell. Next, point out how easily changes in circumstances can be modelled – for example, if the business costs were to rise or fall, the spreadsheet can show exactly how this would affect the profits once you have entered the relevant figures. Show them a few examples so that the children can see how the software updates the relevant values automatically. Then allow them access to the computer in pairs or small groups to complete the photocopiable sheet, inputting the data as part of the activity if you have not already done this for them. Most children are likely to need support in using the spreadsheet functions to answer the questions.

The children should enjoy using the different spreadsheet formulas to answer the 'What if ...?' type questions on the photocopiable sheet, and will start to appreciate the ease with which changes can be modelled.

## Suggestion(s) for extension

Children who are confident with the spreadsheet's facilities could model more complex situations such as: 'The boss decides to give himself a 50% wage increase. How does this affect the weekly profit?', or 'The landlord decides to charge the car wash company one-fifth of its takings as rent. How many more cars must be washed to keep the profits level?'

## Suggestion(s) for support

Less confident children will need much adult support during this activity, and it may not be appropriate for them to use a function. They could be asked, for example, to note down how well the business is doing from looking at the weekly profits. They could also be asked to alter the amount spent on advertising and see how that affects the weekly profits.

## Assessment opportunities

This activity will enable you to make assessments as to how well the children interpret, analyse and check the plausibility of information held on the IT system, and in choosing elements required for specific purposes. Look to see how confidently the children use the spreadsheet facilities to model the cashflow. Do they fully understand how making a change in one cell of the spreadsheet will affect any total that relies on that cell?

## Display ideas

Use an enlarged copy of the car wash spreadsheet as the central focus of your display, and ask the children to add explanations as to what the contents of specific cells mean and how the flow of cash is modelled. Word processed and graphic work could enhance the display.

## Reference to photocopiable sheet

Photocopiable page 146 shows the income and expenditure for a small car wash business. It contains questions relating to various changes in the business, encouraging the children to use formulas in a computer spreadsheet to find out the consequences of these changes. As only the sum and product functions are used, the task is straightforward.

### Chris Chrome's Car Wash

Name _____  Date _____

This spreadsheet shows a month's business figures for a small company.

▲ Enter the data into a computer spreadsheet. Your teacher can help you with this.

| | A | B | C | D | E |
|---|---|---|---|---|---|
| 1 | Chris Chrome's Car Wash | | | | |
| 2 | | Week 1 | Week 2 | Week 3 | Week 4 |
| 3 | Cost per wash (£) | 5 | 5 | 10 | 10 |
| 4 | No. of cars | 12 | 24 | 34 | 27 |
| 5 | Total income (£) | 60 | 120 | 340 | 270 |
| 6 | Equipment (£) | 5 | 10 | 20 | 5 |
| 7 | Advertising (£) | 10 | 5 | 10 | 5 |
| 8 | Rent (£) | 10 | 10 | 10 | 10 |
| 9 | Wages (£) | 0 | 0 | 50 | 50 |
| 10 | Total outgoings (£) | 25 | 25 | 90 | 70 |
| 11 | Profit/week (£) | 35 | 95 | 250 | 200 |
| 12 | Profit carried fd. (£) | 35 | 130 | 380 | 580 |

▲ Now answer the questions by using the appropriate formulas in the computer spreadsheet. Use the back of this sheet for your answers.

1 What is the profit after the first week?
2 Why hasn't Chris Chrome paid himself for the first two weeks?
3 How much in wages could Chris have paid himself for the last two weeks?
4 Why has expenditure on equipment gone from £20 to £5 from week 3 to week 4?
5 How might Chris get more cars through his car wash?
6 Is Chris's business succeeding?
7 What is the increase in profit if you double the charge per car?
8 If you can only clean 20 cars per day how can you maximise your profits?
9 If it rains for a whole week and your takings are zero, how does this affect the profits at the end of the month?
10 The rent doubles after two weeks, how does this affect your profit?

INFORMATION TECHNOLOGY

# Controlling, monitoring & modelling

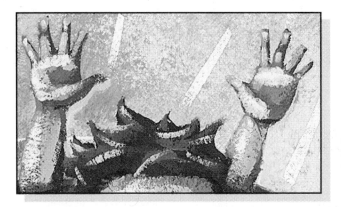

The second strand of the Programme of Study for IT at Key Stage 2 is in three parts. The first part involves modelling activities. Modelling software can have a profound impact on the curriculum; it can motivate, colour, enrich and stimulate children's work. Modelling software, adventure games and simulations are usually not open to teacher interpretation. They come with a clearly defined purpose, and offer the children opportunities to make choices and solve problems. The modelling aspect in the two activities provides an opportunity for children to make changes to a situation. By carefully adjusting values within the model, they can fulfil a desired outcome.

Control activities encourage children to develop sequencing skills through the use of a control language (Logo). These activities offer progression towards their understanding of the use of sensors and a control box. They will learn to appreciate the importance of accuracy in entering sequences of commands. Their understanding of the Logo control language will allow them to use a control box and to experiment with sensors (inputs) and outputs such as lights, motors and buzzers.

Monitoring activities encourage children to explore how IT can be used to collect data over a period of time. This data can be displayed by the computer and the patterns then interpreted. The children will question, observe, predict, measure and reach conclusions through such activities, giving them an insight into how IT is being used increasingly in the outside world to control and monitor our environment.

INFORMATION
TECHNOLOGY

software allow the children to experiment with lists of instructions. Rather than just entering a series of commands to draw a particular shape, instructions can be packaged into what is known as a procedure. A procedure is usually given a name, for example 'SQUARE' or 'PATTERN'. Rather than rewriting a whole set of instructions each time, the user simply enters the name of the procedure. If the instructions within the procedure are incorrect, changes can be made and tested out. The software is designed to encourage trial and error until a suitable end result is obtained. This is a useful characteristic of IT which is not limited to Logo software alone. Such software is known as modelling software – trying out a variety of inputs and seeing what happens.

In this activity, the children use Logo software to build a procedure (a series of instructions) that will make the computer draw a square. If their procedure is inaccurate, it is very straightforward to make adjustments and re-test until a satisfactory output is obtained.

### Preparation
Make a copy of photocopiable page 147 for each child. Before teaching the activity below, make sure that you are familiar with the Logo commands and the process of building a procedure.

### Vocabulary
Procedure, Logo software, Logo language, REPEAT.

### Resources needed
A computer, Logo software, a printer (preferably colour), photocopiable page 147.

### What to do
Use the photocopiable sheet as a way of introducing the idea of a procedure. Ask the children to look at the first example on the sheet which deals with making tea. Discuss how to do this, encouraging the children to break the process down into the separate stages, then let them write out the appropriate instructions on the sheet. Discuss some other everyday activities which could be written in a procedural form – for example, brushing our teeth, feeding the cat or programming a video machine to record a favourite TV programme. Ask the children to complete the other examples on the photocopiable sheet.

Next, tell the children that you would like them to build an IT procedure to draw a square on the computer. Provide a whole class or large group introduction to the various commands within the Logo software that they will need to use: FORWARD, RIGHT, LEFT, REPEAT. They should understand that to draw a square, the same commands are repeated four times and the Logo software uses a 'REPEAT' command to handle this. Explain that a set of commands – such as those for drawing a square on screen

## SQUARES ALL OVER

***To use a Logo program to build a procedure using the 'REPEAT' facility.***

†† *Pairs.*

🕑 *30 minutes at the computer; 15 minutes discussion/demonstration.*

### Previous skills/knowledge needed
The children should have some knowledge of sequencing commands, either from playing robot games and inventing their own commands or from using an IT robot.

### Key background information
The software known as Logo, of which there are many versions, allows children to draw on the computer screen. Instructions are entered via the keyboard using the Logo language. The pointer on the screen moves and draws in accordance with the commands entered. The joy of using the Logo language is that the commands are very straightforward, for example: 'FORWARDS', 'BACKWARDS', 'RIGHT', 'COLOUR', 'REPEAT', and so on. A command is usually followed by a value, for example 'FORWARD 40', 'RIGHT 90'. Turns are usually measured in degrees, but distances can be in arbitrary units, for example in mm or screen pixels. Most versions of Logo

INFORMATION TECHNOLOGY

– can be packaged into what is known as a procedure. This saves having to repeat all the commands individually each time. Demonstrate the PROCEDURE building routine to draw a square; the procedure may typically look like this:

```
TO SQUARE
REPEAT 4
FORWARD 50
RIGHT 90
END
```

Finish by showing the children how to name and edit the procedure.

Allow each pair of children about 30 minutes or so at the computer to carry out the activity. Throughout this, it is important to emphasise the modelling aspect of the software – that is, the opportunity to make changes to a series of commands, to test out the result and repeat this until the outcome is acceptable. Using a procedure is a very neat way of doing this.

Once they have mastered drawing a square, suggest that the children try drawing squares in different colours and sizes. Give them time to experiment, drawing attention to any interesting work so that others can learn from this. Through experimentation, the children will learn to appreciate the power of Logo, and see how commands entered can have surprising results! As far as possible, the children should record their procedures on paper as they progress. However, not all Logo programs have a straightforward printing routine.

### Suggestion(s) for extension

The more able children could try a more demanding task; for example, drawing squares within squares, using the 'REPEAT' command within a procedure to draw hexagons and so on.

### Suggestion(s) for support

It is important that the less able children understand the process of the 'REPEAT' command. Going over this with

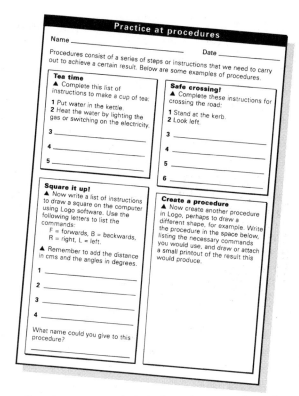

pencil and paper may help before they use the software. You could also ask them to pace out on the floor the route that would make a square while saying aloud: 'Repeat 4 times, forward two steps, right 90 degrees...' Comparing a procedure to a re-usable shopping list may help – we write it once but can use it again and again and it has the name 'shopping list'.

### Assessment opportunities

This activity will enable you to assess how well the children recognise patterns and relationships from the results obtained from the software, and how well they predict outcomes of various decisions when they adjust their procedures. Look out for their ability to make changes to their procedures, and for their understanding that such changes can be made repeatedly until the desired outcome is achieved.

### Display ideas

Logo patterns can look most attractive when carefully mounted for display. It would be interesting to have a series of printouts of the children's procedures for producing the squares, showing the various changes they went through and accompanied by the relevant list of commands. This would enable the children to link the commands with the outcome.

### Reference to photocopiable sheet

Photocopiable page 147 can be used to introduce the children to procedures in control technology. They are asked to write clear instructions, in the form of words or symbols, in order to achieve a specific result.

**INFORMATION TECHNOLOGY**

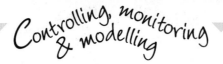

# PARTY TIME

*To use simple formulas to enter information into a spreadsheet. To see the immediate result of any changes to the information.*

†† *Pairs.*

🕐 *30 minutes at the computer; 20 minutes discussion/demonstration.*

## Previous skills/knowledge needed
The children should have had experience in using a simple spreadsheet and be capable of finding the totals or averages of columns of data. They should know that a spreadsheet allows them to store information.

## Key background information
The use of spreadsheets is included on page 82 of the chapter on Handling Information in this book. Their use is also included in this modelling software chapter because they enable real situations to be modelled. The joy of such software is that by making a single change in one entry, all the values that depend on that entry are automatically updated across the spreadsheet. This makes spreadsheets very powerful tools in considering 'What would happen if ...?'.

This activity models some basic costings of a class party. The children are encouraged to make changes within the spreadsheet, such as the number of items ordered or price alterations, to see how this affects the total cost.

## Preparation
The activities 'Looking at spreadsheets' on page 82 and 'Business plans' on page 87 should be carried out before asking the children to do the activity below. Set up a 'class party' computer spreadsheet in advance, as illustrated in the 'What to do' section, but do not include subtotals at this stage. (The idea is to use this for a whole class or large group demonstration on how to use formulas to calculate subtotals.) Depending on the children's ability and experience, you may also need to set up the same spreadsheet without numbers for the children to type in their own figures from photocopiable page 148. Make one copy of this sheet for each child. You should also prepare a sheet of questions (or several to provide differentiation) to encourage the children to use the modelling opportunities offered by spreadsheets. As all the children's items will be different, you should refer to these by their number in column A. Include questions such as: 'By how much would the grand total increase if you bought five more of item 1?', 'What is the difference between the total costs of item 2 and item 3?' and so on. Alternatively, you can ask all of the children to work on the spreadsheet example below and focus your question sheets around this.

## Vocabulary
Cell, cashflow, formula, total.

## Resources needed
A computer, spreadsheet software, a printer, a copy of your question sheet for each child, items of food for a class party, pens or pencils, photocopiable page 148.

## What to do
It would be best to set this activity within the context of planning for a real class party. Give each child a copy of photocopiable page 148 and explain that you want them to write down five things they would like to eat at the class party. Ask them to fill in an estimate of the cost and quantity for each item. Some likely responses are already indicated in the spreadsheet on the photocopiable sheet.

Next, explain that the children are going to enter their figures into a computer spreadsheet to find out the total cost of their chosen food items and to see what would happen if any of the prices or quantities were to change.

**INFORMATION TECHNOLOGY**

Open up your computer version of the spreadsheet below (see Preparation) and provide a whole class or large group demonstration of the formula facility to explain how to subtotal the food costs. The chart below shows the correct formula:

|  | A food | B cost per Unit | C No. required | D Subtotal |
|---|---|---|---|---|
| 1 | crisps | 35 | 20 | B1xC1 |
| 2 | peanuts | 40 | 5 | B2xC2 |
| 3 | biscuits | 85 | 4 | B3xC3 |
| 4 | oranges | 15 | 30 | B4xC4 |
| 5 | fizzy drink | 45 | 30 | B5xC5 |
| 6 |  |  |  |  |
| 7 |  |  |  |  |
| 8 |  |  |  |  |
| 9 |  |  |  |  |
| 10 |  |  |  |  |
| 11 |  |  |  |  |
| 12 |  |  |  |  |
| 13 | grand total |  |  | SUM [D1:D5] |
| 14 |  |  |  |  |

The formula is used to calculate the subtotals in column D. This formula need only be entered once, as the spreadsheet can then be asked to replicate it in each cell of column D. In this case, the general formula is B1 X C1, which is then replicated as B2 X C2 in the next row down and so on. Finish by showing the children how to calculate the grand total. This will be a 'sum' function which adds up all the subtotals, as shown in the chart above. The grand total may be placed in cell D6 and the function to calculate it will be 'SUM (D1:D5)' placed into the cell D6.

Now let the children work in pairs to enter their own figures from their photocopiable sheets into the computer. They can either use the spreadsheet structure you have prepared or set up this up for themselves (they will need plenty of support with this). They can then answer the questions on the photocopiable sheet and go on to play the modelling game, prompted by your question sheet. What if the cost of item 1 went up by 5p, for example? They will see that if they change the entry in cell B1, then every cell containing a value which is dependent on B1 will be updated right through to the grand total. A list of these types of questions, depending on the children's abilities, should provide plenty of opportunities to model the results of such changes.

## Suggestion(s) for extension

The more able children could include in their spreadsheet an additional cell relating to the number of children attending the party. The value within this cell could be used to calculate the values in column C. Can they plot a graph illustrating the connection between the number of children at the party and the total cost? They may also like to add further items of food to create a larger spreadsheet. Finally, they could produce a before and after-party spreadsheet, with the after-party sheet detailing what food was left and how much could be paid back if the goods were returned!

## Suggestion(s) for support

The less confident children will require a greater degree of support during the setting up of the spreadsheet. Their series of questions should reflect their ability concentrating on the given spreadsheet rather than enlarging it.

## Assessment opportunities

This activity will allow you to make assessments as to how well the children use IT software to organise, analyse and interpret information held on the spreadsheet. Are the children able to use the spreadsheet facilities to model the party cashflow with understanding? Do they appreciate that by making a single change of value in one cell all other cells that depend on its value will also be changed? Can

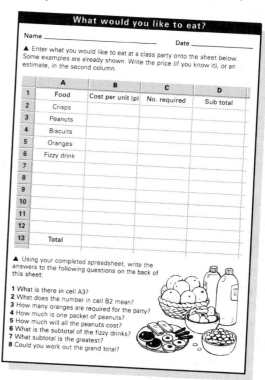

they work out 'What if we made a change here ... how would that affect something here?'

## Display ideas

Use an enlarged printout of the spreadsheet as a focus of your display, with coloured threads leading out to word processed captions explaining how the values within the sheet are reached. Pictures of various party food items produced on graphics software would brighten the display and add further interest.

## Reference to photocopiable sheet

Photocopiable page 148 provides a spreadsheet for the children to fill in the prices and quantities of food items that they would like to include in the party. They then enter these figures into a computer spreadsheet as part of the activity above. Some simple questions relating to the spreadsheet are included.

INFORMATION TECHNOLOGY

they can be switched on and off via the control software running on your computer. Typically, the outputs are numbered on a control box: 1, 2, 3 and so on. A large control box may have the capacity to deal with eight outputs, allowing up to eight devices to be connected at one time.

You will need to check the exact command that will switch an output on or off. Typically, it will be something like 'OUTPUT1 ON'. This command would only switch on the output numbered 1 for a fraction of a second. If you wish it to remain on, say for up to 3 seconds, then another command would have to be entered such as 'WAIT 30', where the computer counts time in tenths of a second (as is often the case).

### Preparation

Make one copy of photocopiable page 149 for each child. You may also wish to prepare some prompt cards with command and sequence suggestions for the less confident children. Make sure that the control box is connected to the computer, the appropriate software is loaded, and a variety of output devices, such as bulbs and buzzers, are available.

### Vocabulary

Logo, control box, control software, output, device, switch, sequence.

### Resources needed

A computer, control software, a control box that is compatible with your computer, a printer, paper, bulbs (6 volt torch bulbs will usually suffice), a 6 volt electric motor and/or a 6 volt buzzer, prompt cards (see Preparation), photocopiable page 149.

### What to do

When you have set up the computer and control box, start the activity with a large group or whole class demonstration

## ON/OFF – CONTROLLING OUTPUTS

***To become familiar with the control box. To switch outputs on and off in a pre-determined way.***

†† *Small groups of 3 or 4 children.*

🕐 *45 minutes at the computer; 20 minutes discussion/demonstration.*

### Previous skills/knowledge needed

The children should have had some experience of Logo, either through the use of a floor robot or screen turtle graphics software.

### Key background information

The logical progression from using a robot or screen turtle is to learn to use a control box attached to a computer, or a control box attached to a floor robot such as a Roamer. The control box can be controlled through the computer or robot keys by using the appropriate Logo type software that accompanies it. This particular activity concentrates on the control box attached to a computer.

Control boxes have connections for inputs and outputs. In this activity, we are only concerned with outputs. An output is an electrical device that can be switched on or off. Examples of outputs are lights (torch bulbs), motors or buzzers. These devices are readily available at low cost. When they are connected to an output on a control box

**INFORMATION TECHNOLOGY**

of how to use the control box. (see Key background information). Show the children how to attach a device to an output on the control box, and then enter the commands that will switch the output on and off. Keep this very simple at first, concentrating on how to control a single output. Demonstrate some of the more straightforward tasks on photocopiable page [149] such as entering:

```
SWITCHON 1
WAIT 30
SWITCHOFF 1
```

This should switch a light on that is connected to output 1 for three seconds. Or, in order to flash a light attached to output 1, try the following:

```
REPEAT 30
SWITCHON 1
SWITCHOFF 1
END
```

This should switch the light on and off rapidly. You may control the rate of flashing by inserting a 'WAIT 5' command between the 'SWITCHON 1' and 'SWITCHOFF 1'.

Give each of the children a copy of photocopiable page 149. Allow them to work in small groups to try out some of the simpler activities, using the control box with a single output. Once they have had some time to grasp the basics (usually over several sessions), you can provide more devices for them to connect to the control box, increasing the variety of possibilities available. They will enjoy activities such as connecting several bulbs and programming them to light up one by one in sequence; this is known as a 'running light', and can be obtained with a sequence of instructions such as:

```
SWITCHON 1
WAIT 5
SWITCHON 2
WAIT 5
SWITCHON 3 ...
... Up to SWITCHON 8
WAIT 5
SWITCHOFF 1
WAIT 5
SWITCHOFF 2 ...
... Up to SWITCHOFF 8
```

Part of the fun of this kind of Logo control activity is trying to predict what will happen. We know what we want to achieve, but it does not always work out as we would like! This activity allows your children to try out, observe and then make adjustments accordingly until the desired outcome is reached.

Alternatively, they could program the lights to turn on and off in sequence:

```
SWITCHON 1
WAIT 5
SWITCHOFF 1
WAIT 5
SWITCHON 2
WAIT 5
SWITCHOFF 2 ...
... Up to SWITCHOFF 8
(if there are eight
outputs on your control
box).
```

Adding more lights to the outputs of the control box will make the sequence longer but not necessarily more complicated.

Within a design and technology context, all eight outputs could be connected, for example to create lights for rooms in a house, a buzzer for a front door and a motor to work a

ceiling fan. The organisation of these activities will have to be carefully considered. If the children have produced several different models with output devices in place, then they will need to connect up the control box when it is their turn and then disconnect it ready for the next group to use. This will take time and such activities are likely to run into several weeks. Ensure that the children record their control sequences or keep a printout to use for display purposes.

**Suggestion(s) for extension**
This activity presents a good opportunity to offer the confident children more complex tasks. They could make use of the 'REPEAT' command, and possibly use the

95

INFORMATION TECHNOLOGY

procedure-building facility (see 'Squares all over' activity on page 90.

## Suggestion(s) for support

For the less confident children, you will need to offer a more straightforward task to match their ability. It is best to limit them to using one output until they gain more confidence. Providing them with simple prompt cards showing command and sequence suggestions will help to support them during this activity.

## Assessment opportunities

You will have the opportunity to assess how well the children create, test and modify their sequences designed to switch the outputs on and off. Look to see how confidently the children enter the commands and how well they can predict what the outcome might be.

## Display ideas

The main display is watching the process working and then swapping ideas and discussing possibilities. Photographs of their design and technology models connected to a control box would enhance a board display, although the opportunities are limited. However, adding some printouts of the children's control sequences would add to the educational content of the board display.

## Reference to photocopiable sheet

Photocopiable page 149 contains a range of activities to introduce the children to using outputs and devices on a control box. Progress to more difficult tasks is possible by using more than one output.

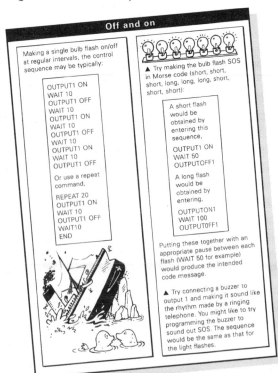

# TRAFFIC LIGHTS

***To emulate a traffic light sequence using a control box. To write a 'LIGHTS' procedure.***

**†** *Pairs or groups of three.*

🕐 *40 minutes at the computer; 20 minutes discussion/demonstration.*

## Previous skills/knowledge needed

The children should be familiar with Logo commands and need to have carried out the activity 'ON/OFF – controlling outputs' on page 94 so that they are familiar with building procedures.

## Key background information

Using a control box gives the children the opportunity to try out their knowledge of the Logo language. Different control boxes make use of slightly different Logo commands, but they all adhere to the general Logo syntax. The children should have no difficulty in making the small adjustments required for your particular control box. For this activity, the commands required are 'SWITCHON', 'SWITCHOFF', 'WAIT' and the procedure-building command 'TO LIGHTS', where 'LIGHTS' is the chosen name for this particular traffic lights sequence.

Building a procedure allows your children to model their sequence. If the sequence is not satisfactory for some reason, they can 'EDIT LIGHTS' and then re-test until the desired outcome is achieved. Without using a procedure, they would have to rewrite the whole sequence each time. Writing sequences in the form of procedures is an effective way of handling long series of commands, especially when

INFORMATION TECHNOLOGY

it comes to making changes. You will need to organise it so that pairs or groups of three children take it in turn to enter their commands. Either allow them to start from the beginning by setting up the equipment themselves, or set it up in advance yourself, depending on the children's confidence and experience.

## Preparation

To give a taste of realism, the three output lights could be painted red, amber and green. Alternatively, use coloured Cellophane around each bulb. As a design and technology exercise, the children could make a miniature set of traffic lights – black plastic 35mm film containers make excellent bulb holders and look very realistic. For demonstration purposes in the main activity, set up the traffic lights, connecting each bulb to an output and testing to make sure that all is working. Make a copy of photocopiable page 150 for each child.

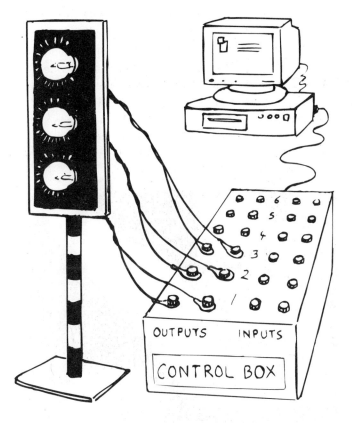

## Vocabulary

Sequence, procedure, outputs.

## Resources needed

A computer, control software, a control box, a printer, torch bulbs (6 volt), coloured Cellophane (see Preparation), photocopiable page 150.

## What to do

Start by discussing traffic lights with the children. Do they know what the sequence of the light changes is? Explain

that you are going to recreate this traffic light sequence using IT. Show the children the 'traffic lights' attached to the control box (see Preparation) and provide a large group or whole class demonstration of how to control these lights. Start by demonstrating how to switch the lights on and off, then show them the whole sequence working up in stages. To guide you with the necessary programming, a typical sequence may look something like this:

```
TO LIGHTS
SWITCHON 1 (red)
WAIT 50 (wait 5 seconds)
SWITCHON 2 (amber)
WAIT 10
SWITCHOFF 1
SWITCHOFF 2
SWITCHON 3 (green)
WAIT 50
SWITCHOFF 3
SWITCHON 2
WAIT 10
SWITCHOFF 2
LIGHTS (calls the procedure again)
```

This sequence would run until interrupted. If we miss off the last line, the procedure could be repeated a number of times as shown below:

```
REPEAT 4
LIGHTS
END
```

This would run the sequence four times.

Make sure that those children who are going to do this activity know how the Logo commands work and are familiar with the process of building a procedure. You may need to demonstrate how to write a procedure in your version of Logo. (The activity 'ON/OFF – controlling outputs' on page 94 introduces the idea of building procedures as an alternative to giving single instructions.)

Now provide the children with photocopiable page 150. Ask them to use this to list their commands for the traffic light sequence. It does not matter at this stage whether their sequence of commands is correct, as they can edit the procedure later.

Next, allow pairs or groups of three children at a time to enter their commands for the sequence and then demonstrate it. This will show them that their efforts are valued and allow you to raise any general points. Ask them to print out a copy of their sequences and procedure so that they can review this and edit it accordingly. It is more important that the children construct and use a procedure successfully than produce an absolutely correct traffic light sequence.

INFORMATION
TECHNOLOGY

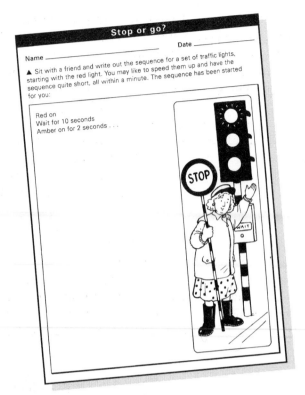

## Suggestion(s) for extension

To extend the confident children you may ask them to include a flashing amber pedestrian light. This could be done using a second procedure.

## Suggestion(s) for support

Ensure that the less confident children have successfully completed the photocopiable sheet and that they are working with a supportive friend.

## Assessment opportunities

This activity will allow you to assess how well the children create, test and modify commands to simulate a traffic light sequence. Look to see how well the children understand the various commands within the control language and why we use a procedure. Do they understand that a procedure need only be written once and then called up at any time?

## Display ideas

The display potential is mostly in the demonstration of the children's results. It may be possible to set up a display for a parent's evening and have the lights working for a long period of time or to demonstrate them during an assembly. The children could write up their activity and make illustrations to go with their printed out sequences as part of a wall display.

## Reference to photocopiable sheet

Photocopiable page 150 asks the children to write out the sequence for traffic lights in their own words, and if possible in the Logo language. They should estimate their times in seconds and minutes.

# PRESS ME AND WATCH!

*To use one input, such as a switch, and a variety of outputs. To control several outputs by activating one input.*

**†† ** *Pairs or groups of three.*

**🕐** *45 minutes at the computer; 20 minutes discussion/demonstration.*

## Previous skills/knowledge needed

The children need to have used Logo before and should feel comfortable with programming a robot and using Logo with turtle graphics. They need to be familiar with building procedures (see the 'Squares all over' activity on page 90).

## Key background information

A control box can have inputs (sensors) connected to it as well as outputs. This activity introduces the children to the use of inputs. An input is a device which can tell the control box that it has been switched on or off. For example, if we connected an ordinary switch, such as a small light switch, to an input terminal on the control box, then using the control software we could ask the computer to detect whether the switch had been turned on or off.

A typical command in Logo would be: 'IF INPUTON 1'. This asks the computer if the switch connected to input number 1 is on or off. The next part of the sequence in Logo would contain the command THEN, for example: IF

**INFORMATION TECHNOLOGY**

INPUTON 1 THEN SWITCHON 3. This finds out firstly if the switch at input 1 is turned on and, if this is the case, it then turns on the number 3 output. If a bulb had been attached to output 3 then it would light up.

However, there is one other control command that we would have to set up first. In order to make sure the computer has enough time to do the search as to whether the input is on or off, it must be placed within a repeat loop to give it time to detect the state of the input. This is easily done by asking it to repeat a number of times:

```
REPEAT 50
IF INPUTON 1 THEN SWITCHON 3
END
```

Depending on the timing units of your control software, REPEAT 500 may give it about 5 seconds worth of search time.

Once the children are confident with how the input commands work, they can begin to use the function of the control box in an exploratory way.

## Preparation
Have a collection of different outputs available and a variety of switches, both for demonstration and for the children to use, such as slide switches, push switches or home-made paper-clip/drawing pin switches. Make one copy of photocopiable page 151 for each pair or group of three children.

## Vocabulary
Output, input, switch, control language.

## Resources needed
A computer, control software, a control box, input switches and output devices such as lights, buzzers and motors, photocopiable page 151.

## What to do
Start by reminding the children what an output on a control box is, if necessary demonstrating how it can be turned on and off through the control box and the computer control software. Tell them that they are going to experiment with using inputs on a control box, and explain how inputs work (see Key background information). The children may wonder what advantage using switches through a control box has over ordinary switches. The answer is that using a control box allows greater flexibility and opens up more possibilities – for example, we can delay the turning on of a device, keep it on for a specified length of time (as in the 'Traffic Lights' activity on page 96 and use a number of outputs at the same time.

Now demonstrate the input control command and how the control box needs to search during a REPEAT loop to

check whether an input has been turned on. Show how by switching one input on, a number of outputs may be turned on at the same time or even after a chosen delay. The control box is put into a repeat loop with the commands:

```
REPEAT 5000 ....................END.
```

As it goes round and round within this loop, the command 'IF INPUT1 ON ...' ensures that the control box constantly checks whether the input number 1 has been turned on. The remainder of the control sequence tells the control box what to do when this happens:

```
........THEN OUTPUT1 ON
```

This will turn on the light or whatever output is connected to output 1. If there were output devices connected to outputs 2–8, they could all be turned on at the same time. Another important demonstration is to turn a light off that

was already on by turning an input on! It appears illogical but is all part of the wealth of possibilities using the control software.

Remind the children of how to build a procedure, then hand them copies of photocopiable page 151. This sheet contains a long sequence of commands which the children have to build into a running lights procedure using six lights ('RUNNING'). The children need only write this once and can then save it, illustrating the usefulness of procedures.

INFORMATION
TECHNOLOGY

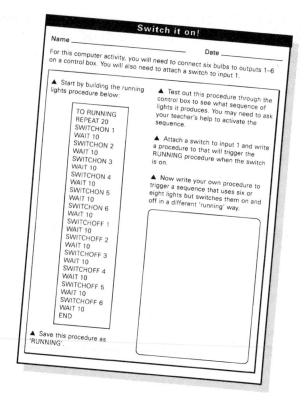

Allow them to work in twos or threes to write the RUNNING procedure and, once complete, to trigger it by switching on an input. The commands would look something like this, depending on your version of the control software:

```
REPEAT 500
IF INPUT1 ON THEN RUNNING
END
```

The REPEAT loop is to ensure that the control box checks for an 'on input' over a period of time; if the switch at input 1 is turned on, then the RUNNING procedure will start.

Once the children have mastered this procedure and worked out what light sequence it produces, they can design a different sequence (as part of the photocopiable activity), for example stepping through the six or eight outputs in turn lighting only one bulb at any one time. When they feel secure with the operation of inputs controlling outputs they may like to experiment with a variety of different set-ups. For example, they could try using two inputs, each triggering a different procedure.

## Suggestion(s) for extension

The more able children will enjoy trying out a variety of combinations of inputs and outputs, perhaps having several inputs each triggering off a different procedure, as mentioned above. Different inputs could be used to produce different flashing light sequences in Morse code, for example.

## Suggestion(s) for support

For less confident children, you can produce lists of sequences for them to enter. It may not be appropriate to involve them with the writing of procedures.

## Assessment opportunities

This activity will allow you to assess how well the children create, test and modify sequences of instructions, linking inputs with outputs, and in their use of the control software. Make a judgement as to how fully your children understand the linking between input and controlled output: do they appreciate that the control box actually controls the output?

## Display ideas

The display opportunities are provided mostly by watching the children's results. You need to allow others to see how their use of the control activity has produced a particular outcome. In a general display of control work, including robot and screen turtle pictures, word processed accounts of how the children have used inputs and outputs would illustrate the progression of activities within this area of IT.

## Reference to photocopiable sheet

Photocopiable page 151 contains a long sequence of commands which the children have to build into a running lights procedure using six lights. They then have to devise their own sequence by building a suitable procedure for this.

# JEWEL SECURITY

**To use the control box as a security alarm.**

†† *Pairs or groups of three.*

🕐 *45 minutes at the computer; 15 minutes discussion/demonstration.*

## Previous skills/knowledge needed

The children should have had experience with the use of inputs and outputs on a control box and be familiar with the relevant control software. They also need to know how to write procedures in the control software.

## Key background information

Control activities are much more meaningful and enjoyable when they happen within a design and technology context. In this activity, the children make a security system using sensors and an alarm. Different types of sensors are available and the type used will depend on the context. There are sound and light sensors that will turn on or off at a particular volume of sound or brightness of light; some of these allow the triggering level to be adjusted. Other

sensors include ordinary switches, pressure pad switches, magnetic switches, vibration detectors or tilt switches; all of these are either on or off and have no level of input determining their switching point.

Commercial switches are reasonably priced and available from local computer or radio repair shops. Alternatively, the children may like to make their own simple switches, such as a drawing pin and paper-clip type of contact switch. They can also make simple pressure switches by using tinfoil, thin layers of sponge and card.

## Preparation

You will need to ensure that the sensors and outputs are appropriate to the context. If you have purchased a more unusual sensor, test it first to confirm that it behaves in the way you would expect. Make one copy of photocopiable page 152 for each child.

To provide a context for the burglar alarm activity below, encourage the children to make a model of a building, perhaps as part of a design and technology task.

## Vocabulary

Security, sensor, detector, alarm.

## Resources needed

A computer, a control box, an appropriate variety of sensors and outputs, some wire, a model or artefact within which an alarm system is to be installed (see Preparation), photocopiable page 152.

## What to do

Use photocopiable page 152 to introduce the activity to the children. This should help them to appreciate the process of using electronic devices to make an area secure. Talk about security systems and burglar alarms in general. Perhaps there is one installed in your school. Tell the children that the detector most commonly used within a home or school system is placed up high in a corner of the room and flashes a light whenever it detects movement. This device detects the heat from our bodies; and whenever it senses a change in the heat pattern, as produced by any movement, it switches and sends a signal to the central alarm control box. These devices are easy to fit into buildings and have replaced the magnetic switches which used to be installed into window frames and door jambs. Mention that these types of sensor are also used in backyard security lights.

Now ask the children to design their own burglar alarm for their model building (see Preparation) using the computer control box and sensors. They will have to install the sensors into their models and run sufficient wire so that connections can be made to the control box on a temporary basis. Ask them to discuss what kind of alarm would be suitable: will it will be a flashing warning light or a noisy buzzer?

The children can then work in twos or threes to write the alarm sequence for the control box. The sequence for detecting an input being turned on could be fairly straightforward, for example:

```
REPEAT 500
IF INPUTON 1
THEN SWITCHON 1
END
```

**INFORMATION TECHNOLOGY**

Depending on the time REPEAT 500 takes to complete, this allows a limited amount of time for the alarm to be active; however, this duration is easily changed. The children could devise a method of switching off the alarm by installing a second input which, when turned on, switches off output 1. Some groups may like to write a procedure for the alarm to go off:

```
TO ALARM
REPEAT 30
SWITCHON 1
WAIT 20
SWITCHOFF 1
WAIT 10
END
```

This will turn on a buzzer for three seconds then off for two seconds and so on for a total of thirty times.

### Suggestion(s) for extension
The more confident children will enjoy devising different sensors for switching on different alarms. Could they also write a procedure for the sensor sequence?

### Suggestion(s) for support
Less confident children will enjoy using a straightforward sequence for their alarms, as suggested in 'What to do' above.

### Assessment opportunities
This activity will enable you to assess how well the children create, test and modify sequences of control commands in the devising of their security alarms. Make a judgement as to how confidently the children understand the use of a procedure. Are they able to use the Logo commands to

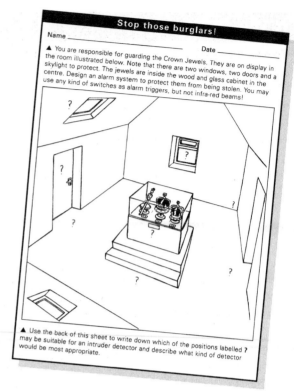

Stop those burglars!

Name _____ Date _____

▲ You are responsible for guarding the Crown Jewels. They are on display in the room illustrated below. Note that there are two windows, two doors and a skylight to protect. The jewels are inside the wood and glass cabinet in the centre. Design an alarm system to protect them from being stolen. You may use any kind of switches as alarm triggers, but not infra-red beams!

▲ Use the back of this sheet to write down which of the positions labelled ? may be suitable for an intruder detector and describe what kind of detector would be most appropriate.

achieve the intended outcome and can they predict what will happen through the use of particular commands? There may be opportunities for design and make assessments within Design and Technology depending on the context of this activity.

### Display ideas
The children's finished models will be a rich source of interest. The children will be able to demonstrate their alarms and have opportunities to test them out to see which is the most reliable.

### Reference to photocopiable sheet
Photocopiable page 152 challenges the children to design a burglar alarm to protect the Crown Jewels. You can use it to introduce the main activity.

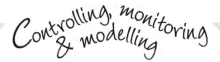

# HOT SPOTS

***To become familiar with using a temperature probe.***

**††** *Pairs or groups of three.*

🕑 *30 minutes at the computer; 15 minutes discussion/demonstration.*

## Previous skills/knowledge needed

It will be helpful if the children have previous experience of setting up the monitoring equipment although this is not essential.

## Key background information

Monitoring or data logging equipment is robust and easy to use, making it ideal for science investigational work. Typically, it consists of a data logging box that connects to the computer. This box has three or more sockets into which various sensors can be plugged. The sensors are usually temperature, light and sound. Other sensors may detect twist (amount of turn), pH (alkalinity/acidity of liquid) and movement.

The equipment can be used to log data over short or long periods of time depending on the context of the investigation. The data logging software displays the data in different graph forms. The key element is the interpretation of the resulting graphs, and the children's ability to link what these show to the actual physical changes that take place during the data logging process. Initially, the children should predict what the graph may look like and hypothesise, then collect the data and see whether their hypotheses were correct.

This activity comprises three simple investigations based around heat/temperature. In the first one, the children should find that the hot water in the polystyrene cup is kept warmer longer. Polystyrene is an excellent thermal insulator as it has microscopic bubbles of trapped air inside it. This substance is used throughout the building industry to insulate houses. In the second investigation, the children should find that a large object keeps warmer longer. Heat can only be lost from the surface of an object. Small objects have a large surface area compared with their volume. Large objects have a comparatively small surface to volume ratio so they lose heat less quickly. The third investigation

demonstrates why, in hot countries, houses are painted white and the inhabitants wear light-coloured clothes in order to keep cool. Dark fabric absorbs infrared light and warms up as a result, while light-coloured fabrics reflect infrared and remain cooler.

## Vocabulary

Data logging, temperature monitoring, rate of loss of heat, thermal insulation, graphic display, probe, sensor, input.

## Preparation

Make one copy of photocopiable page 153 for each child or pair of children. Introduce a small group of children to the data logging equipment before doing the investigations below. Explain what the sensors measure, the importance of where they are placed, how you can ask the software to collect over a variety of times and how the data collected is displayed in graph form.

## Resources needed

A computer, a data logging box, a printer, data logging software, two temperature probes, several very similar polystyrene and plastic cups, two balloons, a large tray (in case the balloons burst!), two small pieces of fabric (white and black) to wrap over the ends of the two temperature probes, photocopiable page 153.

## What to do

This activity involves the children in some simple temperature investigational work, looking at:

▲ Why some materials are better heat insulators than others.

▲ How large objects keep their heat longer than smaller objects.

▲ Why dark materials absorb heat while light materials reflect it.

The children should work in pairs or threes to set up the investigation and then use IT to log their readings. You will probably only have one group of children working with IT at a time, so this activity will only be carried out by a few of your class.

### Activity 1

This activity could support curriculum science work on fabrics, clothing, heat or insulation. Begin with a general discussion centred around photocopiable page 153 which introduces them to a variety of temperatures. Talk about

**INFORMATION TECHNOLOGY**

the different ways that we keep ourselves warm and what types of materials make good thermal insulators. Discuss some ways that could be used to test for good insulators. Now let the children use the data logging equipment to carry out a fair test. They should put the same quantity of hot water in both a plastic cup and a polystyrene cup, insert a temperature probe in each cup, and take readings over a similar period of time to compare how the temperature varies. Using IT will make it easy to produce graphs of the findings, and, with two temperature probes in use, both sets of readings can be displayed at the same time using the monitoring software.

### Activity 2

In this activity, the children can find the connection between heat loss and surface area, and how this is a factor in the survival of some animals over winter. Small creatures need extra insulation to survive and often they group together to share their warmth, creating a larger surface area from which less heat is lost. The children can test out this idea using balloons. Fill the balloons with different amounts of warm water, so that there is considerably less water in one balloon. The water should be of the same temperature in both balloons. Tie them so that the water does not escape and place them on a tray with a deep lip in case either one bursts. Ask the children to predict what they think will happen, then ask them to place the temperature probes underneath each balloon and take temperature readings every five minutes or so. As time progresses and both graphs are plotted, it will be found that the larger mass of water cools less quickly. Encourage the children to interpret the graphs and draw their conclusions.

### Activity 3

Start by asking what the children notice about clothing and house styles in hot countries. Are light or dark colours most often used? Explain that light objects are brighter because they reflect more light, whereas dark objects absorb light. If there is also heat in the light, in the infrared spectrum, then the heat is either reflected or absorbed as well. So, if the same amount of light was shone onto both temperature sensors, one with a light piece of fabric wrapped around it and the other with a dark piece, could the children predict what might happen over a period of time? Provided a good heat source is used, either sunlight through a window or a strong reflector type bulb, then the results should be conclusive.

A whole class discussion after the results have been obtained will enlighten the remainder of the children who have not participated in the IT activity. You could provide the whole class with the series of readings and graph from the activity and devise a questionnaire to encourage them to interrogate and interpret the findings.

### Suggestion(s) for extension

The more able children may extend the first activity to investigate the thermal properties of other materials. The third activity could be extended to investigate differences between the same coloured fabric but with differing textures.

### Suggestion(s) for support

Ensure that the less confident children are grouped appropriately. Check that the data collection is working properly and offer them less sophisticated questions requiring the interpretation of the graphs.

### Assessment opportunities

This activity will allow you to assess how well the children use IT to monitor external events in the form of temperature

measurements in the various activities. An important feature here is how well they interpret the graphs and draw conclusions from these findings.

## Display ideas
The graphs produced by the monitoring software will make an interesting focal point for a display and you could include the children's word processed explanations of their data logging activities.

## Reference to photocopiable sheet
Photocopiable page 153 gives the children practice in finding out the temperatures of a variety of items and places, in either degrees Celsius or degrees Fahreheit.

# 24 HOURS IN CLASS

*To monitor environmental conditions over a 24-hour period using data logging equipment.*

†† *Whole class and pairs or small groups.*

⏱ *30 minutes computer set-up time; 30 minutes discussion/demonstration.*

## Previous skills/knowledge needed
The children will find it helpful to have used a sensor before and should be familiar with the monitoring software. The 'Hot spots' activity on page 103 would help to prepare the children for the task below.

## Key background information
The automatic monitoring of environmental conditions through using IT is becoming commonplace. Computer control of air conditioning, temperature, humidity and light in our working or leisure environments helps to ensure that safety and comfort are maintained. In aircraft flight, for example, monitoring the weather conditions from the flight deck is an essential part of the safety of all involved. All this is achieved by positioning sensors in strategic places.

This activity will make the children more aware of the daily changes that take place around them in the classroom. Through initial discussion and the possible use of the photocopiable sheet, they are encouraged to predict and then monitor, through IT, what changes may take place during a 24-hour period, concentrating on sound, light and temperature levels, especially during their absence. The interpretation of the graphical findings is important and you wish to make these findings the focus of a questionnaire.

## Preparation
Check that the software will operate over a 24-hour period; the commonly used primary monitoring software such as *Junior Insight* will do so. Choose the group or groups of children who are to be active in this task and make a copy of photocopiable page 154 for each child.

## Vocabulary
Sensor, temperature probe, environment, conditions, monitor, data logging, graphical display.

## Resources needed
A computer, monitoring software such as *Junior Insight*, data logging equipment, a printer, light, sound and temperature probes, photocopiable page 154.

## What to do
Distribute one copy of the photocopiable sheet to each child. Explain that the three different graphs reflect the changes in conditions in a classroom over a 24-hour period and then discuss together some possible interpretations of these graphs. What changes do the children think may occur in their own classroom and what could cause these changes? For example, how do they think the light levels would vary during the day or during the night, and how may the noise levels change during the day?

Now tell the children that they are going to monitor the temperature, light and sound in their own classroom over 24 hours using data logging equipment. If they have used the data logging equipment before, ask them how they could monitor such changes and where the sensors could be placed. Those children who have not been involved in this kind of investigation before will learn from the demonstration and feedback process if this is introduced as a general whole class discussion.

Although only a small group of children will be actively involved in the IT part of the activity, you will need to share all aspects of it with the whole class after the data has

INFORMATION
TECHNOLOGY

been collected. Try to involve the children in the setting-up of the equipment, especially if you are to run the activity again for different groups. The experience gained by the first groups of children will allow them to guide and help later groups. Ensure that they are familiar with the fair test rule and if comparisons are to be made over more than one day, then the sensors must be in the same place each time.

Run the monitoring over the 24-hour period or periods chosen. The data collected in the form of values or graphs will be useful as a focus for questions set by you. These questions should enable the children to use their interpreting skills. You will have discussed the graphs on the photocopiable sheet at the start of the activity and this experience should help them with their interpretations of the real data collected.

## Suggestion(s) for extension

Involve confident children in a daily comparison of data and ask them to investigate reasons for any variations – is the class out of use for any significant time, for example in games/swimming lessons? Could changes in weather patterns affect temperature and light levels? A day where there is much class movement (reading groups in and out) could also affect conditions. Increase the challenge by offering them more difficult questions and asking them to make more complex predictions.

## Suggestion(s) for support

Less confident children should be grouped with friends who can support them in this activity. When you devise questionnaires based on the gathered data, ensure that the questions for these children are of a more straightforward nature.

## Assessment opportunities

This activity will allow you to assess how well the children use IT to monitor environmental conditions in the classroom and their ability to interpret the results obtained from the monitoring activity. Make judgements as to how well your children interpret the graphs and make conclusions from these findings.

## Display ideas

You could choose a title such as '24-hour class timeline' and display enlarged graphs of how the various classroom conditions change. Ask the children to produce word-processed explanations as to why conditions change and to link their writing with coloured thread to the appropriate position on the graph.

## Reference to photocopiable sheet

Photocopiable sheet 154 presents a 24-hour timeline for temperature, sound and light conditions in a classroom. The children can be asked to tackle just one of these aspects and plot approximate values throughout the day. They may be comparatively accurate in plotting temperature expected as there is a proper scale in degrees for temperature, but for light and sound only the variation can be expected – light and sound data is usually expressed as a percentage.

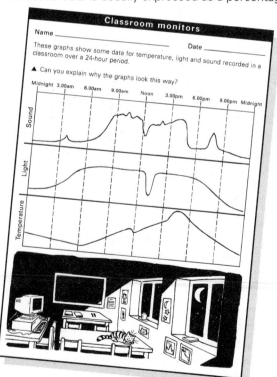

# HAMSTER WATCH

***To link a variety of sensors together to gather information.***

🕐 *Whole class and pairs or small groups.*

✝✝ *20 minutes computer set up time; 15 minutes discussion.*

## Previous skills/knowledge needed
The children should be familiar with using data logging equipment and would find it useful to have experience in interpreting graphs produced by data logging software.

## Key background information
In this activity, a vibration detector and sound sensor are connected to a data logging box to monitor the nocturnal activity of your class hamster (or similar!). The graphs produced through the monitoring software will provide opportunities for the children to practise their interpretational skills. The children may be able to suggest other methods of monitoring the class hamster; for example, if there is a treadmill wheel inside the cage, is there any way the number of revolutions can be counted? Some monitoring software includes the facility to count the number of times a switch has been opened/ closed. The addition of a magnetic switch connected to the treadmill could serve as another interesting monitoring opportunity.

The whole class can be involved with this activity, although it is best if only a few children at a time are put in charge of installing the sensors and setting up the data logging box. Different groups can be involved on a day-to-day or night-to-night basis. The collection of data over several nights will provide opportunities for making comparisons. The activity could form part of your science work on Life and Living Processes.

## Preparation
You will need to ensure that the detectors are effective by plugging them in and running the software. Make one copy of photocopiable page 155 for each child.

## Vocabulary
Monitoring, detector, sensor, vibration, data gathering, graphical interpretation.

## Resources needed
A computer, data logging equipment and software, a printer, a hamster (or similar nocturnal caged creature), photocopiable page 155.

## What to do
Start by discussing with the children the use of monitoring in the outside world. They will be familiar with the use of closed-circuit television (CCTV) and video monitoring in shops, for example. Ask them what other conditions can be monitored, for example the respiration and heartbeat of patients in hospital. Talk about other uses, such as the monitoring of global weather conditions for the forecasting of weather, traffic flow monitoring where the operation of traffic lights is 'controlled' by the number of vehicles, and smoke alarms where the purity of the air is constantly monitored for minute particles caused by combustion.

Next, give the children copies of photocopiable page 155. This shows a hamster's cage, and will help them to focus on what sensors would be appropriate for logging a particular activity and where they should be placed. For example, a sound sensor will monitor general noise level. A light sensor could be used to monitor where the creature is. The sensor would need a small torch bulb focused on it so when the creature passes between the light and the light sensor, the beam is broken and the resulting dip in light level is monitored by the equipment. If you decide to do this, put the torch bulb inside an open ended cardboard tube. This would shield any extraneous light and be less disturbing for the creature. A temperature probe could be placed close to the creature's sleeping quarters to monitor when it is asleep.

Once the children have completed the photocopiable activity, they can set up the real monitoring activity. Ask a small group to set up the sensors in the chosen places on or near the cage. Ensure that any probes placed within the

INFORMATION TECHNOLOGY

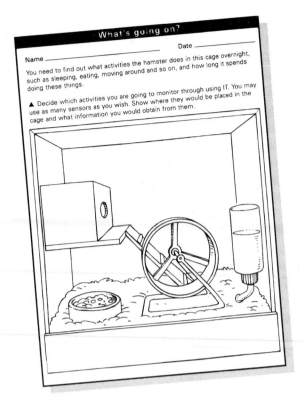

**What's going on?**

Name _____ Date _____

You need to find out what activities the hamster does in this cage overnight, such as sleeping, eating, moving around and so on, and how long it spends doing these things.

▲ Decide which activities you are going to monitor through using IT. You may use as many sensors as you wish. Show where they would be placed in the cage and what information you would obtain from them.

## Assessment opportunities

This activity will enable you to assess how well the children use IT to monitor external events, especially in the use of sensors and the interpretation of the resulting data. Look out for their degree of confidence in the placing of sensors to log particular activity and how well they interpret the graphical results.

## Display ideas

This activity could offer rich opportunities for creating and displaying the children's written and graphical work, as part a 'Life and Living Processes' topic. Their designs for cage monitoring on the photocopiable sheet could form interesting additional material.

## Reference to photocopiable sheet

Photocopiable page 155 shows a hamster's cage and requires the children to think about which sensors to use and where to place them. It can be used to prepare them for the main IT activity.

cage are not endangering the creature. The children should then choose the frequency of sampling data, so that meaningful results are obtained; this may prove to be a process of trial and error. If the results are disappointing, use these apparently negative findings as motivation to proceed further, having adjusted or changed the set-up. The children will need to decide whether the sampling will be at frequent intervals throughout the night or for a set period such as 1.00am to 3.00am, for example.

Hopefully, the children should obtain some results which will be useful for interpretation. Whole class discussion on these should follow, with general writing-up and illustrated explanations as to what the creature spends its night doing. If the treadmill count works, there is a good opportunity for some interesting mathematics: how far or fast does the hamster travel?

## Suggestion(s) for extension

The confident children may suggest further ideas for monitoring. Even if these are far-fetched or unlikely to work, let them try these out nonetheless. A lack of satisfactory results will generate discussion and motivate the children towards further investigation.

## Suggestion(s) for support

The less confident children do not need to be involved with the more critical interpretation of the findings. For example, they might comment on the data obtained from one sensor only, or comment on the creature's general activities without working out the timings or durations of these activities.

# TWIST AND TURN

*To enter a sequence of commands that guides a floor robot.*

†† *Pairs or groups of three.*

🕐 *30 minutes at the computer; 15 minutes discussion/demonstration.*

## Previous skills/knowledge needed

The children need to know the basic commands to control the robot. These are: FORWARDS, BACKWARDS, RIGHT, LEFT, CLEAR, ENTRY.

## Key background information

Often, we interact with technology through key pressing. From mobile telephones to sophisticated camcorders, we press a variety of buttons to transmit our instructions. Practice at entering sequences of commands is important for children and has good educational value. A Logo type of language (see 'Squares all over' activity on page 90) is often used in the programming of classroom floor robots. This activity offers the children opportunities to build on experience gained in Key Stage 1 in the programming of robots. The calculation of sequences of commands helps the children to develop particular mathematical skills and so using a robot provides many opportunities to develop estimation skills in distance, rate of turn, time and clarity in direction of turning.

## Preparation

Set up the IT equipment and ensure that a smooth clear floor area is available for the robot activity.

**INFORMATION TECHNOLOGY**

## Vocabulary
Input, direction, heading, angle, turn, command, route, sequence.

## Resources needed
A computer, Logo software, a floor robot, a printer, several paper cups, a clear smooth floor area.

## What to do
Provide a whole class demonstration to introduce the activity to the children. Place the robot between two paper cups and tell them that the cups mark out a 'garage'. Set up another paper cup nearby. Initially, the task is to programme the robot to leave the garage and then to go around the nearby paper cup before returning to the garage. The route can be made as complicated as you wish, for example by adding a second cup the route becomes a figure of eight around and between the two cups before going back to the garage. You could also label a number of paper cups 1, 2, 3, and so on, and set a slalom task to be done in numerical or, perhaps, reverse order. There is no limit to the degree of challenge and intrigue in the route that you could set up for the children.

Now allow the children access to the robot to try out the different route challenges for themselves. To enable all of them to participate will take time. It is important that they experiment and although 30 minutes is recommended it could take some of the children longer. It is essential that they record their sequences and include plans of the route taken by the robot. These plans will help them to think through the sequence, choose appropriate distance values and sort out left from right turns (easy to confuse!).

The robot has no screen to remind the children which keys have been pressed, so it is easy to lose track of where they are in the sequence. Emphasise to them the importance of recording their commands. Arrange it so that one child enters the key presses, one writes down the sequence and a third paces out the route bit by bit. The child pacing out should ensure that the right and lefts are sorted out.

## Suggestion(s) for extension
By introducing further challenge into the route the confident children should be stretched appropriately.

## Suggestion(s) for support
Keep the activities straightforward for the less confident children by requiring the robot to make short journeys.

## Assessment opportunities
This activity will allow you to assess how well the children create, test and modify sequences of instructions to control the robot. Look for clear thinking with their sequencing and an understanding of the various Logo commands.

## Display ideas
Enlarge the children's plans of the robot routes and display them alongside the corresponding sequence of commands.

INFORMATION
TECHNOLOGY

# ROBOT RUMBA

***To enter a longer sequence of commands. To write sequences for making two robots 'interact' with each other.***

†† *Groups of three or six.*

🕐 *30 minutes at the computer; 15 minutes demonstration/discussion.*

## Previous skills/knowledge needed

The children should be confident in programming a robot.

## Key background information

This activity will enable the children to work together and plan longer sequences of commands so that two robots can be made to interact in a dance-like routine. This offers opportunity for careful group planning, the estimation of distances and turns and using the children's knowledge of the robot's capabilities to choreograph the dance. This activity will help to consolidate their robot programming skills. It is an open task, allowing the children to be creative and inventive.

## Preparation

It would be beneficial to discuss and demonstrate with the children some simple dance movements such as approach, back, approach, turn round each other.

## Vocabulary

Routine, movements, sequence, pattern.

## Resources needed

Two robots (although a limited amount could be done with just one).

## What to do

Tell the children that they are going to create a sequence to make two robots 'dance' together. Discuss with them how the two robots may perform a dance routine, suggesting particular moves, but emphasising that they must keep their sequences short. The idea is not to let the robots actually touch, but to make their moves as intricate

as possible. If there is only one robot available, it would be better to have a static object for the robot to dance around. The object will also act as a marker around which the sequences can focus.

Allow three children at a time to work with each robot and to devise their sequences together:

▲ one child entering the commands;

▲ a second child writing down the sequences;

▲ the third physically pacing out the routes.

Set a time limit of about 20 minutes for this, and then draw the other children around to judge the final dance sequence. Before they make the judgement, discuss with them the criteria for judging. These could include how well the pair of robots move together, or how complicated the sequence is.

If you are fortunate to have access to more than two robots, then an even more complex dance routine can be programmed, carried out and evaluated.

## Suggestion(s) for extension

The more confident children may like to consider writing sequences for 'synchronised' robot dance routines and placing some sequences into procedures.

## Suggestion(s) for support

Make sure the less confident children are grouped with a helpful friend. Encourage them to start with relatively simple sequences.

## Assessment opportunities

This activity will enable you to assess how well the children create, test and modify their sequences in order to produce successful robot dance routines. Look out for a clear understanding of the robot commands, and an ability to predict what the robot should do once a particular sequence has been entered.

## Display ideas

The display of this activity is in the watching. You could have a robot dance show where groups enter their recorded sequences for display in turn. Judges could assign scores to the performances.

# ROBOT SHEEP DOG

**To command the robot by using a variety of longer sequences.**

†† *Groups of three.*

🕐 *30 minutes at the computer; 15 minutes demonstration/discussion.*

## Previous skills/knowledge needed

The children should have had experience of programming the robot and be familiar with degrees of turn.

## Key background information

This activity offers opportunities for an open-ended activity, with plenty of practice in estimation and collaborative working. The context is a rural one of rounding up sheep, in the guise of inverted paper cups, which have to be manipulated back into an enclosure. Paper cups make excellent objects for the robot to push along, provided that the floor surface is smooth. A small additional 'sheep catcher' made from card needs to be attached to the front of the robot, allowing it to scoop the 'sheep' and keep it trapped, even when the robot is turning round.

The object of the activity is for the children to involve themselves in entering longer sequences of commands with a challenging but amusing end goal. Again, it is important that they draw plans of their routes and record their sequences. As in the previous activities, tasks should be divided between a group of three, with one child entering the commands, the second writing the sequence and the third pacing out the intended route.

## Preparation

Bend a length of stiff card into the shape shown below and tape it to the robot. The bent ends are crucial to keep the cup in place as the robot turns. Ensure that the card is stiff enough not to bend during use and that it is well taped to the robot. Lay out the paper cups as shown below.

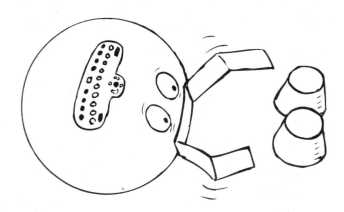

## Vocabulary

Sequence, direction, turn, route.

## Resources needed

A computer, Logo software, a robot, paper cups, a piece of card attached to the robot with sticky tape to act as a 'sheep catcher' (see Preparation).

## What to do

Introduce the children to the idea of rounding up sheep by discussing the work of sheepdogs on farms. Explain that the children are going to programme a robot to round up

'sheep' in the form of paper cups (laid out as shown in the Preparation section). Demonstrate how the 'sheep catcher' on the robot works by showing how it can be used to scoop up the paper cup 'sheep'.

Following the demonstration, allow small groups of children to place the robot within the 'field' and devise a sequence to make it go through the gate (two inverted cups), out into another field to round up a sheep which it then returns to the first field. The basic situation can have many variations and the children may wish to invent their own. If you have two robots, then it is possible to swap over 'sheep' by making the first robot back off and leave a sheep while the second robot approaches and scoops it up.

### Suggestion(s) for extension
Once again, the complexity of the task needs to reflect the capability of the group. More confident children will be able to construct a complex scenario, perhaps gathering several 'sheep' within a set time whilst a marauding robot, disguised as a fox, runs across the path and randomly snatches a sheep!

### Suggestion(s) for support
The less confident children should be given tasks appropriate to their abilities such as working with a single 'sheep'.

### Assessment opportunities
This activity will allow you to assess how well the children create, test and modify more complex sequences of robot commands. Look out for clear thinking with respect to their

various sequences, can they predict what should happen on entering a sequence of commands?

### Display ideas
Create a display called 'Lost sheep', with diagrams of the 'before' and 'after' situations that the shepherd and his robot sheepdog had to cope with. Further material in the form of the children's word-processed explanations and lists of sequences, plus graphical illustrations, will all help to enhance the display.

## PATTERN REPEATED

*To create a procedure that will draw a specified design.*

♦♦ *Groups of three.*

🕐 *30 minutes at the computer; 15 minutes discussion/demonstration time.*

### Previous skills/knowledge needed
The children should be familiar with programming a robot. It would also be helpful if they had experience in the use of procedures (see 'Squares all over' activity on page 90). In this activity, it is presumed that the children have access to a Roamer.

### Key background information
The 'Squares all over' activity incorporated the use of a procedure. A procedure is a list of commands which is given a name. This list can be saved and then retrieved at any time merely by entering its name. This is an effective use of programming power as the list need only be written once but can be used as many times as necessary. A procedure may contain a short or long sequence of commands. The Roamer robot has a useful facility for procedure building. The procedures are given names: P1, P2, P3, up to P99, which is the Roamer robot's maximum limit.

Some exciting patterns or designs can be drawn by entering these procedures into the Roamer, with relatively few commands needed. Such designs may appear complicated, yet they are produced through the repetition of a simple pattern. As in different versions of Logo, the entering and naming of a procedure into the Roamer has its own routine, and this is outlined below.

### Preparation
Make sure that the children have a smooth, clear space in which to lay out the card or paper for the robot pattern drawing activity.

### Vocabulary
REPEAT, procedure, repetition, rate of turn, degree, repeat pattern.

## Resources needed

Roamer robot, large pieces of card (for robot pattern drawing), Roamer drawing pack, Roamer Cards.

## What to do

Tell the children that they are going to use the Roamer robot to draw a repeated pattern. Demonstrate how to enter a procedure into the Roamer. The children need to know the function of the REPEAT key and the necessary commands to make the Roamer draw a square:

REPEAT 4 [ F1 R90 ].

Where 'F' is the forward arrow, 'R' is the right arrow and '[' or ']' is the square bracket key. This whole sequence can be entered as a procedure. To do this, first enter P1 (procedure number 1), then the square bracket key followed by the sequence outlined above:

P1 [ REPEAT 4 [ F1 R90 ] ].

Both the contents of a procedure and a repeat are placed within square brackets. The Roamer will remember all procedures, even when its 'CM' (clear memory) key is pressed. Having entered the above procedure for making a square, the Roamer can be made to carry it out by entering P1 GO.

The next stage is to demonstrate how to make the Roamer create a pattern with the squares, commanding it to draw a square, then move round a small angle, then draw the square again and so on. This will go to form the multiple square repeats and so build up a pattern. This sequence of events can be carried out by the children using

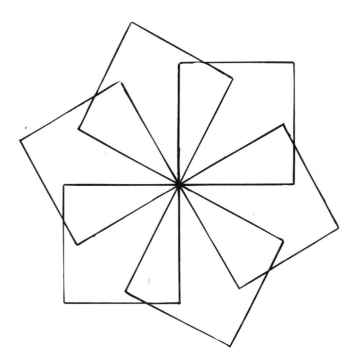

a cardboard template, a drawing pin and a sheet of card and making a repeat pattern. They pin a corner of the card square to a piece of stiff card and draw around it. They then rotate the square by a fixed amount to the left or right (with the square still pinned in the same place to the card). By making a 20° angle wedge out of card they should be able to move their template by the same amount each time. This demonstrates perfectly what the Roamer is doing when the appropriate sequence of commands is entered.

The clever part is to put the sequence of commands into a repeat as shown below. The number of repeats depends on the angle turned through each time. It is better

to keep the number of repeats small. To turn through a complete circle of 360°, we could ask the Roamer to make 10 repeats of 36° or 6 repeats of 60°. The children could experiment with a variety of turns. The commands would look like this:

REPEAT 10 [ P1 R36 ] GO
Where R is the right arrow.

The Roamer will then draw a square, turn through 36° then draw a second square, until 10 squares are drawn. The pattern should complete a circle but often, because of certain factors, there is inaccuracy. Nevertheless, the children will find this a rewarding activity.

### Suggestion(s) for extension

The confident children may like to try a similar pattern but use a different geometrical shape rather than a square. They may also try to put the whole pattern into a second procedure (P2).

### Suggestion(s) for support

The less confident children may require guidance with the entering of commands. The use of Roamer Cards should help them to put the correct sequence together.

INFORMATION TECHNOLOGY

## Assessment opportunities

This activity will allow you to assess how well the children create, test and modify sequences of commands to enable their Roamer to draw a repeat pattern. It will enable you to find out whether they understand the purpose of a procedure.

## Display ideas

The results of the Roamer's pattern drawing will produce an interesting display. Link the appropriate sequences with the pattern, perhaps word processing them on the computer using a large font.

## LETTERS AND NUMBERS

*To use Logo to draw on the screen and to print out the results.*

†† *Pairs.*

🕐 *30 minutes at the computer; 10 minutes discussion/demonstration time.*

## Previous skills/knowledge needed

The children will find it helpful to have some previous experience of a Logo language through using a robot. An understanding of the use of degrees of turn would also be an advantage.

## Key background information

The software allowing the moving of an object and drawing on screen comes under the generic heading of Logo. The screen pointer is often referred to as the 'turtle' and the software used to be termed Turtle Graphics. The screen turtle can be any small object (often chosen from a list of alternative pointers such as frog, a paint brush, an aeroplane, a car and so on) which is moved around by inputting commands at the keyboard. These commands are simple, such as:

> FORWARDS, BACKWARDS, RIGHT, REPEAT, PENUP, HOME, CLEAR.

A command is often followed by a value:

> FORWARD 50
> RIGHT 90
> REPEAT 10

There are close connections between the floor robot and the computer version; both use a Logo syntax, and the children will find it easier to start using Logo if they have had experience with a floor robot first. This will have provided a valuable insight through their physical involvement in planning and pacing out various robot routes, and will have helped them to understand left- and right-hand turns. This can be confusing for children: as they face the screen turtle, the children's right is the turtle's left. If the turtle is coming down the screen from the top, then a left-hand turn will move it to the right of the screen, as seen from the children's viewpoint. However, if the children have played turtle games at floor level using a robot they will have come to terms with this feature.

There are many commands available in Logo software. In this activity, the children enter commands which will make the screen turtle trace out letters of the alphabet and numbers. Not all of these can be produced, however; those with curved outlines are not practical to draw using this software. By carrying out this task, the children will gain confidence in using the simple Logo commands.

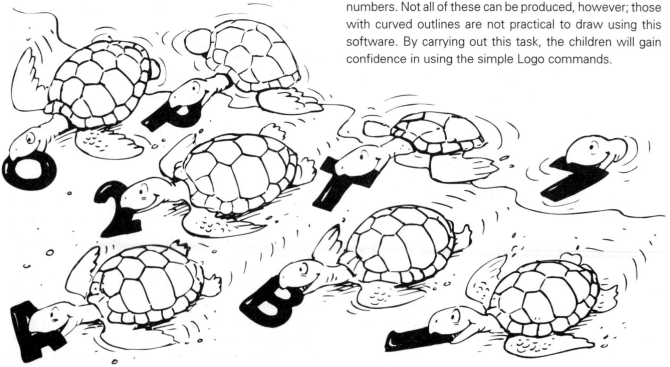

## Preparation

It may be helpful to produce some prompt cards with the shapes of letters and numbers drawn on them and some basic Logo commands. These can be used to support less able children where appropriate.

## Vocabulary

Pointer, screen turtle, commands, values, direction, degree, turn.

## Resources needed

A computer, screen turtle Logo software, a printer, prompt cards (see Preparation), pens, paper.

## What to do

The children will need to be introduced to the basic Logo commands. Some Logo software offers onscreen help in the form of arrows that can be clicked on with the mouse in order to command the direction of movement. Other versions of the software programme the computer's function keys with the most commonly used commands. Whichever way the commands are entered, a sequence can be built up gradually, allowing the children to record their inputs and link these to the turtle's movement.

Choose an alphabet letter and discuss with the children the appropriate Logo sequence to draw it. Ask them to write down the sequences for several more letters and then allow them access to the computer in pairs. Some children may find it helpful to have prompt cards while doing the activity on screen (see Preparation).

The finished product is not the most important aspect of this activity – in fact, printed-out letters produced in Logo are not particularly exciting in visual terms! It is the control process that the children go through when producing their designs which is really important. It is, of course, possible to programme your floor robot to carry out this task on a larger scale if you wish.

## Suggestion(s) for extension

The more confident children may like to use different coloured lines in their letter or number shapes by using the colour command. They could also try creating hollow lettering and filling this with colour by placing the turtle in the appropriate place and entering the colour fill command (usually 'FILL').

## Suggestion(s) for support

For the less confident children, the prompt cards will be an important source of support.

## Assessment opportunities

This activity will allow you to make assessments as to how well your children create, test and modify commands using the turtle graphics software. Look out for a clear understanding of what the commands do and clarity of thought in linking them to form particular sequences. Can the children predict what the outcome will be having produced a particular sequence?

## Display ideas

Use the children's work from this activity to create a class book on Logo activities. You will be collecting a variety of such material over a period of time and, although not immediately aesthetic, it will serve as a useful resource and a record of what the children have achieved.

---

## THROUGH THE MAZE

**To become familiar with Logo commands.**

†† *Pairs.*

🕐 *30 minutes at the computer; 20 minutes discussion/demonstration.*

## Previous skills/knowledge needed

The children should have had a brief introduction to the common Logo commands and be familiar with 90° right-angle turns.

## Key background information

Controlling the screen turtle requires a good deal of estimation. This activity involves moving the screen turtle through a maze and gives the children practice in using the Logo language while also providing feedback with respect to their estimations of distance. The maze is much easier to tackle if all the turns are right-angles, although you could offer the more able children a maze with a variety of angular turns. The task is very straightforward and gives the children a good opportunity to experiment with the Logo commands. There is no correct answer to the task and the children are

INFORMATION
TECHNOLOGY

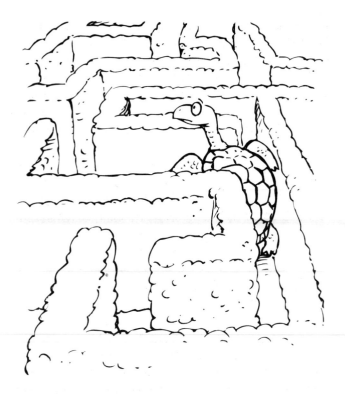

process of interacting with the software and using and understanding the Logo language. Although 30 minutes is recommended for this activity, you could set a challenge and have the children working against the clock.

### Suggestion(s) for extension
The confident children would enjoy a more challenging maze with a variety of different turns, excluding the simpler right-angled turns.

### Suggestion(s) for support
Keep the mazes simple for the less confident children, using only a limited number of right-angled turns. The smaller the mazes, the more quickly they should be completed, as there is less opportunity for errors in their estimations.

### Assessment opportunities
This activity will allow you to assess how well the children create, test and modify the sequences designed to get the turtle through their maze. How able are they in estimating distances on the screen and entering appropriate sequences at the keyboard? Do they have a clear understanding of what the various Logo commands do?

### Display ideas
Mazes make exciting display material. You could display some photographs of real mazes from around the country alongside your own mazes designed for Logo work. Enlargements of printouts of successful routes would add further interest to this.

encouraged to use a process of trial and error. The path through the maze merely provides them with a guideline which they should try to keep to.

### Preparation
Attach a piece of acetate to the computer monitor and carefully trace round the edge of the screen to outline the working area. Also mark the starting point where the turtle will be at the beginning of the journey. Remove the sheet and, using a permanent pen, mark out two lines in a maze pattern then attach the sheet to the screen again. You may prefer to start with 90° turns only, including a variety of angular turns later as the children's confidence develops. You could produce several mazes of varying complexity to provide a more clearly differentiated task.

### Vocabulary
Logo, maze, direction, right, left, forwards, backwards, right-angles.

### Resources needed
A computer, screen turtle Logo software, a printer, acetate sheets, a permanent marker pen.

### What to do
Demonstrate the maze activity to the children, making sure that they are familiar with how to use right-angled turns or other degrees of angle as appropriate. Explain that they must enter commands to move the screen turtle around the maze without going outside the 'walls'. Let them work in pairs at the computer, using a maze which is appropriate to their ability. The outcome is less important than the

---

## LOGO BOOKMARK

***To use Logo to produce a design for a purpose.***

†† *Pairs.*

🕐 *45 minutes at the computer; 15 minutes discussion/demonstration.*

### Previous skills/knowledge needed
The children should be familiar with the common Logo commands and be able to colour fill areas of pattern. However, it is important to bear in mind that interesting results are often obtained by accident when children first start to use the software.

### Key background information
You could consider the use of Logo for any simple design, such as a plate of favourite food, an animal, a spacecraft or a 'tag'-style signature. In this activity, the children use the Logo language to produce a design for a bookmark. Although it could be done more successfully using graphics software, this more prescriptive activity will provide an opportunity for the children to use Logo for a purpose.

Often, the graphics material produced using Logo has a simple charm. This will also awaken the children to the fact that Logo is not totally concerned with routes, directions and journeys, but sequences of commands can also produce some intricate designs which have aesthetic appeal. They will learn that some complex patterns can be built up from the repetition of simple designs, especially when a simple design is twisted or flipped and repeated.

### Preparation
You will need to make sure that a colour printer is available for this activity. Make a copy of photocopiable page 156 for each pair of children.

### Vocabulary
Repeat pattern, rosette, rotate, angle turned, full circle, motif.

### Resources needed
A computer, Logo software, a colour printer (essential), card, a laminator (or sheets of transparent sticky-backed film), adhesive, scissors, coloured wool (for decorating the book marks), a hole punch, photocopiable page 156.

### What to do
Most Logo software has a text function. The idea of this activity is for the children to produce a simple design using Logo, printed with the words 'BOOKMARK', or the name of a person. Give each pair of children a copy of photocopiable page 156. Ask them to look closely at the designs on the sheet and to write down the commands they think would produce these patterns. The sheet is intended to spark their interest and to start them thinking

in Logo language and using simple commands such as FORWARD 20, LEFT 90.

Now tell the children that they are going to choose a pattern to decorate a bookmark, produced by using Logo. While they can use any pattern, a rosette shape is appealing and easy to do using the REPEAT function (see the 'Pattern repeated' activity on page 112. This shows how to use a procedure on the robot to produce a rosette-type pattern). Provide a whole class or large group demonstration, reminding the children what a procedure is and how it is always given a name. Explain that procedures are usually built. The first stage is to build a procedure to draw a square:

```
BUILD SQUARE
REPEAT 4
FORWARD 50
LEFT 90
END
```

Whenever the software is asked to 'DRAW SQUARE', it will now draw a square of sides measuring 50 units. However, to create the rosette pattern, each time a square is drawn it needs to be rotated by 10° before the next one is drawn, and so on until 36 squares are drawn. This sequence can all be placed into another procedure that could be called 'Rose':

```
BUILD ROSE
REPEAT 36
DRAW SQUARE
RIGHT 10
END
```

INFORMATION
TECHNOLOGY

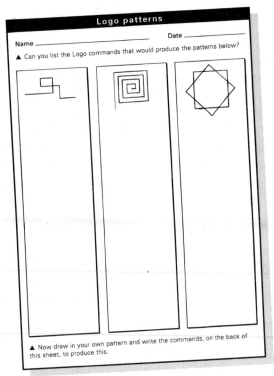

**Logo patterns**

Name _____ Date _____

▲ Can you list the Logo commands that would produce the patterns below?

▲ Now draw in your own pattern and write the commands, on the back of this sheet, to produce this.

Finally, show the children how to use the 'COLOUR' command to colour the background and to make the turtle draw coloured lines.

Allow the children access to the computer in pairs, giving them time to experiment. Ask them to print out their final design and stick this down onto card. Cover it with sticky-backed plastic or use a laminator to give it a longer life. The children could complete their bookmark by punching a hole in the end and threading through strands of coloured wool which they then knot to produce a tassel.

### Suggestion(s) for extension
Ask those children who are able to work confidently and quickly to design motifs for other purposes. Again, this is a laborious way to produce designs but the importance of the activity lies in the thinking involved.

### Suggestion(s) for support
The less confident children could perhaps produce a simple design consisting of filled squares on a coloured background. These designs can still produce attractive results.

### Assessment opportunities
This activity gives you the opportunity to assess how well the children create, test and modify sequences of instructions while designing their Logo bookmark. Those children who are able to use procedures are working at a higher level.

### Display ideas
The results of the children's efforts will create an interesting display if the children wish to produce a second bookmark

for this purpose. Provide an instructional slant by linking the designs with the printouts of the sequences that were used to produce them.

### Reference to photocopiable sheet
Photocopiable page 156 encourages the children to consider the commands necessary to produce a variety of different patterns within Logo. It can be used as a stimulus for the bookmark activity.

## GEOMETRIC SHAPES

*To use Logo procedures to draw a series of specified shapes.*

†† *Pairs.*

🕐 *30 minutes at the computer; 15 minutes discussion/demonstration.*

### Previous skills/knowledge needed
The children should have experience in using Logo and be familiar with the basic commands. They should know that regular polygons have sides of equal length. Depending on their age and ability, knowledge of the external angles of various polygons would also be useful.

### Key background information
The mathematical beauty of regular polygons can be explored easily with Logo. Unlike classroom floor robots, screen turtles are very accurate, drawing with precision. Through the use of Logo, the children may draw simple geometrical shapes, making use of the REPEAT command or the procedure and REPEAT function together.

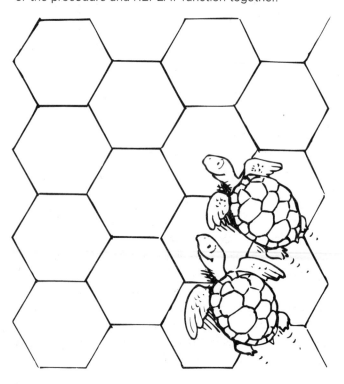

**INFORMATION TECHNOLOGY**

This activity knits together the use of Logo and shape and space in mathematics. The regular polygons have a magic of their own; such shapes occur in the natural world, for example in honeycombs or crystal and rock structures, and in the man-made world, where they are used for constructional and commercial purposes, as in geodome buildings.

## Preparation
Make one copy of photocopiable page 157 for each child.

## Vocabulary
Regular polygon, external angle, side, vertex (the apex of a figure).

## Resources needed
A computer, screen turtle Logo software, a printer, photocopiable page 157.

## What to do
Give each child a copy of photocopiable page 157. This lists a selection of polygon shapes and provides the size of the external angles for each one in degrees, which is essential for the children to know. Allowing the children time to write their commands on paper first will pay dividends when they come to use the computer. Drawing small diagrams to aid their thinking and to provide a visual stimulus is an essential practice to help them create the Logo sequences.

Next, you will need to provide a whole class or large group demonstration of the polygon activity using Logo, but the level to which you do this very much depends on the children's abilities. Remind them that using the REPEAT command will mean making far fewer key presses. (This command has been outlined in previous activities, for example Pattern Repeated on p112 and Logo Bookmark on p116). Details on creating hexagons and setting up a hexagon procedure are included below to guide your demonstration.

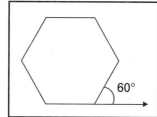

### Creating a hexagon
The hexagon has an external angle of 60°. At each corner, the turtle must turn through 60° before continuing on to create the next side of the hexagon.

The following commands will draw one side and turn the turtle the required amount ready to draw the second side:

```
FORWARD 50
LEFT 60
```

To repeat this the correct number of times using the REPEAT command, enter:

```
REPEAT 6
FORWARD 50
LEFT 60
END
```

### Building a hexagon procedure
To build a procedure named 'HEXAGON,' the following commands are appropriate, but this will depend on your software version of Logo:

```
TO HEXAGON
REPEAT 6
FORWARD 50
LEFT 60
END
```

On the command 'DRAW hexagon', a hexagon should now appear on the screen. An arbitrary side length of 50 units has been used in this example. Frequently, Logo software uses millimetres as a unit of distance but again, this will depend on the version used.

The transition from the children's paper-based sequences to the computer should be as smooth as possible. Encourage a few of them to enter their sequences for a polygon of their choice in front of the whole class or a large group and guide them in this activity to raise their

INFORMATION
TECHNOLOGY

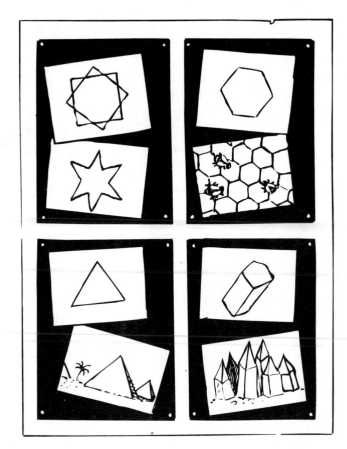

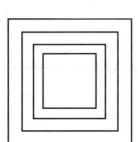

confidence. Finally, allow the rest of the children to try out their use of Logo, in pairs, to create the polygons on screen. The less confident children may not go as far as using the REPEAT command. In this case, limit their shapes up to six-sided hexagons. If they are happy using the REPEAT command, however, they can try out whatever polygon they wish. The more confident children may be able to place their sequences into a procedure such as:

> HEXAGON
> PENTAGON
> OCTAGON

You have complete control over the requirements for this activity, for example asking the children to draw and print out three hexagons, two pentagons and one square all in different colours. The task should match their abilities but also extend them where necessary. Make the tasks challenging and interesting, perhaps including a competitive edge where appropriate.

### Suggestion(s) for extension
This activity lends itself to a wide variation in levels of difficulty. More able children should be able to build procedures, produce filled shapes, and perhaps create other shapes such as regular stars.

A further extension would be for the children to attempt to draw 'nested' shapes, fitting inside one other like a set of Russian dolls. Start with nested squares, by the use of the commands 'PENUP' and 'PENDOWN'. These shapes should not be linked by a line. Can they write a sequence which draws the pattern shown (see below left)?

### Suggestion(s) for support
The tasks set for the less confident should be more straightforward. The children can be expected to draw their shapes without the use of the REPEAT command, and to create those polygons with fewer sides.

### Assessment opportunities
You will be able to assess how well the children create, test and modify their sequences of instructions to draw regular polygon shapes using Logo software. Make a judgement on how confident the children are in understanding the Logo commands and in using Logo to create their shapes.

### Display ideas
Results from this activity will enhance any display on geometrical shapes in your maths corner. Print out the shapes in solid colour for added impact, and accompany them with commercial photographs of regular shapes found in the natural world.

### Reference to photocopiable sheet
Photocopiable page 157 provides a list of regular polygon shapes. The children have to work out the correct sequences to draw these using the 'REPEAT' command.

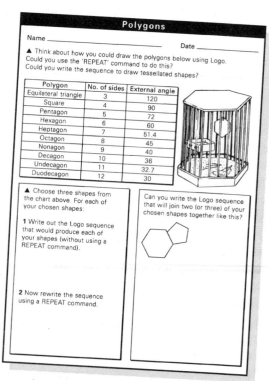

**Polygons**

Name _____    Date _____

▲ Think about how you could draw the polygons below using Logo. Could you use the 'REPEAT' command to do this? Could you write the sequence to draw tessellated shapes?

| Polygon | No. of sides | External angle |
|---|---|---|
| Equilateral triangle | 3 | 120 |
| Square | 4 | 90 |
| Pentagon | 5 | 72 |
| Hexagon | 6 | 60 |
| Heptagon | 7 | 51.4 |
| Octagon | 8 | 45 |
| Nonagon | 9 | 40 |
| Decagon | 10 | 36 |
| Undecagon | 11 | 32.7 |
| Duodecagon | 12 | 30 |

▲ Choose three shapes from the chart above. For each of your chosen shapes:

1 Write out the Logo sequence that would produce each of your shapes (without using a REPEAT command).

2 Now rewrite the sequence using a REPEAT command.

Can you write the Logo sequence that will join two (or three) of your chosen shapes together like this?

**INFORMATION TECHNOLOGY**

# Photocopiables

The pages in this section can be photocopied for use in the classroom or school which has purchased this book, and do not need to be declared in any return in respect of any photocopying licence.

They comprise a varied selection of both pupil and teacher resources, including pupil worksheets, resource material and record sheets to be completed by the teacher or children. All of the photocopiable pages are related to individual activities in the book; the name of the activity is indicated at the top of the sheet, together with a page reference indicating where the lesson plan for that activity can be found.

Individual pages are discussed in detail within each lesson plan, accompanied by ideas for adaptation where appropriate – of course, each sheet can be adapted to suit your own needs and those of your class. Sheets can also be coloured, laminated, mounted on to card, enlarged and so on where appropriate.

Pupil worksheets and record sheets have spaces provided for children's names and for noting the date on which each sheet was used. This means that, if so required, they can be included easily within any pupil assessment portfolio.

Add an adjective, see page 14

# The right adjective

Name _____  Date _____

▲ Look at the sentences below. Some of the words are missing. These words are adjectives.
▲ Complete the sentences by choosing the appropriate words from the list below.

1 The _____ grass had been cut by the farmer and loaded onto his _____ trailer.

2 The parcel was too _____ for me to carry.

3 The sea was _____ the sand was _____ and the day was _____.

4 The boys were _____ in the classroom but _____ when they were outside at play.

5 The _____ wind blew the snow into _____ snow drifts.

6 As I walked up the _____ stairs my _____ footsteps echoed .

7 'Crash!' I turned around quickly to see a _____ pigeon.

8 In the shop window there were loads of _____, _____ toys.

**Adjectives**
Soft, yellow, old, cold, exciting, quiet, dusty, loud, blue, tall, green, expensive, heavy, large, hot

INFORMATION
TECHNOLOGY

Spot the mistakes! see page 15

# Put it right!

Name _____   Date _____

Below are some posters, flyers, leaflets and lists.
You will notice that they contain lots of mistakes.

▲ Can you spot what these mistakes are?
Correct them using a pen or pencil.

Whot you nead too bring:

Parjamas
chang of clotheing
sleeping bag
spunge bag
contining tuth brush
flanel
stronge warking shoos
lunch box
pensil cais

Deer farther christmus

I am riting early to you
becos I no you get

very bizzy and nned lots of
time to mak all

yur toise pleez will you bring
me sum culerd

pens and a torch and
battrise and I wood

Patrick's Pet Shop

we ofera good randge of house
hold pets and there neads
in stok we have kitens, pupys,
hamstas, gerbals, mise, ginnea
pigs, bugrigars, parots, gold
fish, troppical fish, stik insets,
rats, snackes and rabbets.
a variety of diferunt cadges

St Trinian's CE Skool
Sumer Fate

Come and injoy..
Baloon rase ● ice creems
wite elefant stal ● itombola
car bote sail ● cocanut shie
teeny tots gym ● welly wanging
miniture trane rids ● fortune teler
beet the buz ● sekond hand buks
toi stall ● candy flos ● popp cawn
throe the spunge... amd much moor!

Entree 20p
Chilldren free!

INFORMATION TECHNOLOGY

**Editing challenge, see page 16**

# Make it short!

Name _____     Date _____

▲ Can you rewrite the text below in either:
  ▲ Under 40 words?
  ▲ Or between 35 and 50 words?
  ▲ Or in exactly 50 words?

My parents have taught me how to make a cup of tea. At the weekends I get up early and go down to the kitchen to make early morning tea for them. The kettle is the difficult and dangerous bit. By pulling the plug out of the kettle I can lift it to the cold tap to fill it with cold water. Always make sure the electricity is turned off, says my dad. I reconnect the kettle, switch it on and get the milk out of the fridge. As I wait for the water to boil the kettle makes a funny singing noise. Sometimes it sounds like a flock of birds and our cat sits up and looks across to the kettle wondering where the birds are!

**INFORMATION TECHNOLOGY**

Acrostics, see page 18

# Looking at acrostic poems

Name _____     Date _____

Look at these examples of poems. They are called acrostic poems.
▲ For each poem, write down the first letter of the first word in every line.
What do you notice?

Night time creeps up on me
Outside in the darkening woods
Clear evening air all around
Threading my way carefully
Under the leafy branches
Ready to stop quite still and listen to
Nocturnal creatures stirring
All around the wood while
Listening to me.

[   ]

▲ Find another example of a poem
like this and write it in the space
below. What word does it spell out?

[                ]

Splash goes the
Water as
I jump, splash!
Millions of bubbles
Mixing air and water
I swim up to the top
Nearly at the shallow end
Grab the bar – I'm safe.

[   ]

Bring the presents
Into the kitchen
Rustling of wrapping paper
Tearing off the string
Holding the box
Daring to guess – oh no
Another set of pens
Yippee!

[   ]

**Shape poems, see page 19**

## Shaping words

```
Kite
Kite kite
Kite kite kite
Kite kite kite kite fly
                    ing
                        x
                        swoop
                            x
                            ing swirl
                                x
                                ing
please fly up off the ground
```

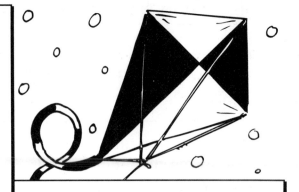

```
            H
            appy
         christmas
      have a very happy
     christmas a very very
   happy christmas such a happy
   happy happy christmas a really
 o o o o o o o h o o o o o o o
               a
               p
              ppp
              yyy
```

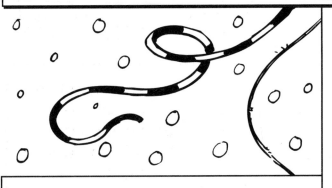

```
            My Snowman

              W
            hy is it that
          at Christmas time
         it never seems to snow
          but all my favourite
           Christmas cards
          clearly clearly show
          lots and lots and lots of
      children pink cheeks all aglow
playing snowballs in the square sledging
          skating everywhere
        up and down the frosty hills
         all those screams and all
        those thrills. Now through
          my window all I see are
      loads of raindrops watching me.
```

```
I sit by the river bank
And watch the water
RIppIIng
Da...nc...ing
Never stopping
M - o - v - i - n - g
The sunshine
S*p*a*r*k*l*i*n*g
T#w#i#n#k#l#i#n#g
So the sun
Dances with the water.
```

**Dear Sir or Madam, see page 21**

# Write a letter

▲ Choose one of the situations below to write a letter about.

'I wish to return the second parrot I bought from your shop. Like the first one I bought from you, it uses very bad language . . .'

'I write to inform you that the community swimming pool has strange creatures swimming about in it . . .'

'On my arrival home yesterday, I found a lorry belonging to your firm in the middle of my lawn ...'

'The photograph of our winning netball team you printed in this week's paper had the incorrect caption . . .'

'Unfortunately your suitcase was sent to the Canary Islands by mistake ... please send a description of the contents of the case to help us in our search ...'

'I am writing to let you know that you have won first prize in our competition. First prize is a bungee jump. You will be jumping next Saturday and you will need to bring ...'

# What is this school like?

...some parents are visiting your school to find out more about it. ...ow are some questions that they need to write down answers to.

Name and address of school

When did the school open?

Names of teaching staff

Names of support staff

How many pupils, girls/boys?

How many classrooms?

How many subjects taught?

Age ranges of pupils

What sports are played?

What clubs are there after school?

How many computers are there in school?

How many pupils are there to one computer on average?

List the software that pupils use in the school

▲ Can you design and lay out a data collection sheet to enable the parents to gather the information below? You will need to think carefully about leaving enough space for them to write in the answers. Consider the type of responses – will they be 'yes/no' or open-ended? What other things will you need to think about carefully?

*Photocopiables*

In the news, see page 26

## Making the headlines

▲ Below is a news story which needs to be redrafted so that it is appropriate for your newspaper's readers. Think carefully about your audience before rewriting this on paper or typing it into the computer for redrafting.

A light aircraft made a forced landing onto a motorway. Traffic swerved to avoid the plane. The plane landed in the direction of the traffic flow. There were two people on board the plane. The plane had flown into a flock of Canada geese and one of them had hit the propeller, breaking it. The plane stopped and pulled into the hard shoulder of the motorway. The pilot's name was Jim Fraser and it was the second time he has made a forced landing. The plane had to be taken apart to get it off the motorway. There was a 24 mile traffic queue while the plane was removed. The passenger in the plane was Mr Fraser's twelve-year-old daughter Catherine. Catherine said it was a great adventure and she wouldn't have missed it for the world.

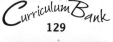

**Designing a poster, see page 29**

# Poster mix-up

The poster on the right is full of mistakes including ambiguous information, impossible times, too many fonts, spelling errors and irrelevant pictures.

*parents join the pta*
*come and spend*
**entrance 50**
an enjoyable
morning

Friday evening

in the school hall
bring a freind
*the* family *bring*
beetle drive

▲ How many mistakes can you spot? Could you design a better poster? What could you do to improve it?

**INFORMATION TECHNOLOGY**

Famous people, see page 33

# Facts on famous people

▲ Choose a member of your family or a friend and pretend that they are famous – you can make up the reason why, perhaps they invented something clever, or showed great bravery at some accident. Use the answers to the questions below to describe your made-up Famous Person.

▲ Produce a storyboard of up to five or six frames illustrating your famous made-up person.

Who are they?

When did they live?

Where did they live?

What did they look like?

Why are they famous?

What followed on from their discovery or achievement?

When did they die?

What are their family details?

▲ Now choose a famous person from history and, using the CD-ROMs you have available, answer the questions above.

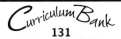
INFORMATION TECHNOLOGY

**Four-colour exercise, see page 37**

# Colour challenge

Name _____     Date _____

▲ Colour in the four pictures below using as few colours as possible.

▲ Make sure that the same colour does not appear on both sides of any line or border in the pictures.

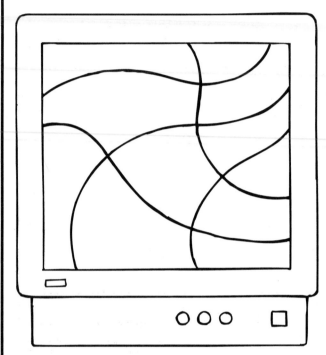
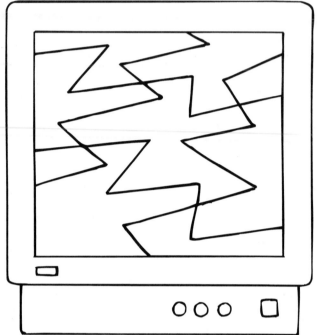
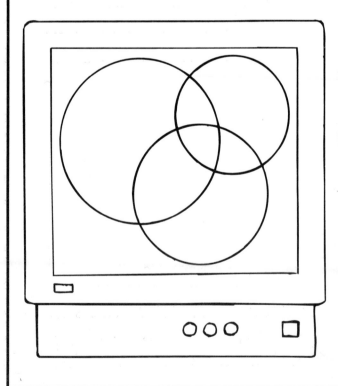
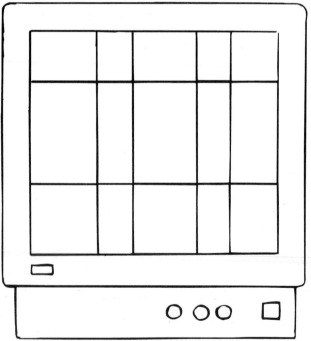

INFORMATION
TECHNOLOGY

**Kandinsky prints, see page 39**

# Create a Cubist print

Name _____     Date _____

Where would you place four circles, four triangles and six rectangles in the screens below to make an interesting pattern?

▲ Try a number of different groupings, varying the size of the shapes and their position in the screens below.

**INFORMATION TECHNOLOGY**

Design a tag, see page 43

## Name tags

Name _____     Date _____

Below are some examples of letters written in 'tag' and other decorative styles.
▲ Choose the style you would like to write your initials in and practise this in the space provided.

ABCDEFGHIJKLM
NOPQRSTUVWXYZ
JACK GURINDER LUCY
GEMMA PETER Rajit

INFORMATION TECHNOLOGY

*Photocopiables*

# Impressions of colour

Name _____  Date _____

▲ Using sharp crayons or fine pointed felt-tipped pens, dot the colour or use very short strokes to produce a series of four small pictures, one for each season of the year.

**Winter** (eg swirly whites, greys and blues)

**Spring** (eg yellows, light green and light browns)

**Summer** (eg darker greens, reds and blues)

**Autumn** (eg browns, reds and oranges)

▲ By mixing the colours can you create an orange by spraying a burst of red onto a burst of yellow? How would you make the following colours: pink, grey, brown, purple, olive and sepia? Use tiny dots of pencil or felt-tipped pens to try these out.

| orange | pink | grey | brown | purple | olive | sepia |

INFORMATION
TECHNOLOGY

7

## Rules and symbols

_____ Date _____

ical school/class rules. The first one is illustrated with a
onvey the message more simply.

1 Don't run in the corridors
2 Single file only/Keep to the right
3 Do not drop litter/Litter in here please
4 Now wash your hands
5 No dogs in the playground
6 Keep quiet in the library
7 Please knock and wait
8 Place lunchboxes here

Running

▲ Now choose a rule from the
list and devise your own symbol
to illustrate it. Draw more than one
symbol if you like.

INFORMATION
TECHNOLOGY

**Sweet wrappers, see page 49**

## A close-up look

Name _____     Date _____

Look at the drawing below. It shows a key.

▲ Focus on a small detail in the drawing and look at this closely, perhaps using a magnifying glass.

▲ Draw this detail, or the whole key, in the space provided, enlarging it as much as possible but still keeping the detail.

MADE IN ENGLAND

QUAY
PIX

**INFORMATION TECHNOLOGY**

**Fashion show, see page 50**

# Focus on colour

Name _____     Date _____

▲ Answer the questions below.

What colours go together?

_____

_____

What colours clash?

_____

_____

What is your favourite colour?

_____

What kind of patterns do you like?

_____

_____

Can you draw one of your favourite patterns?

Where have you seen these patterns before?

_____

_____

_____

▲ Draw yourself wearing your favourite clothes.

**INFORMATION TECHNOLOGY**

Repeat patterns, see page 52

# Miles of tiles

Name _____   Date _____

▲ Draw very simple identical shapes on each of your paper tiles.

▲ Use these tiles to experiment with different tiling patterns. Some examples are shown on the right.

▲ Now draw your own repeat pattern in the space below.

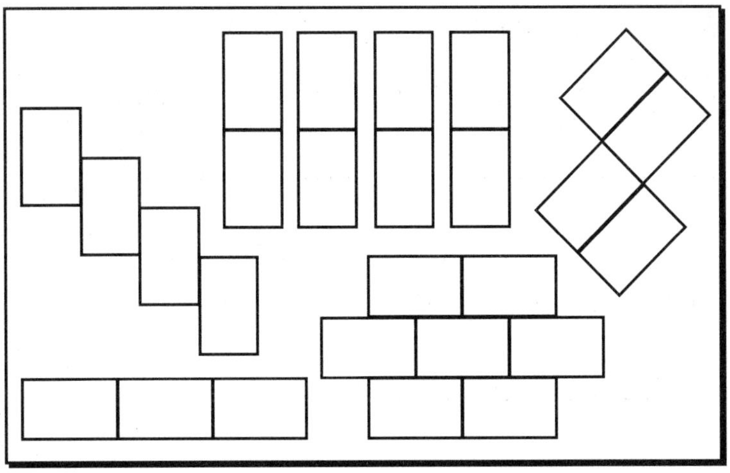

INFORMATION TECHNOLOGY

**Looking at us, see page 66**

# How do you measure up?

Name _____    Date _____

▲ Use this sheet to record your measurements of the attributes listed in the box.

Age and birthday date

_____

_____

Boy/girl _____

Height _____ cm

Weight _____ kg

Foot length _____ cm

Reach _____ cm

Cubit _____ cm

Arm length (hand extended)

_____ cm

Stride _____ cm

Middle finger _____ cm

Span _____ cm

Biceps circumference _____ cm

Chest measurement _____ cm

Standing jump distance _____ cm

Calf circumference _____ cm

Pulse normal _____ beats per minute

Pulse after 50m run _____ beats per minute

Pulse after one minute's rest _____ beats per minute

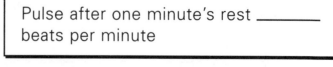

**INFORMATION TECHNOLOGY**

**Watching it grow, see page 69**

# Growth of a hamster graph

Name _____     Date _____

▲ Look at the graph and answer the following questions:

**1** How heavy was Squeaks at the beginning of the measurements?

_____

**2** How heavy was Squeaks by the tenth week?

_____

**3** How much weight had Squeaks gained in that time?

_____

**4** Could you think of a reason for the slowing down in weight gain during weeks 5 and 6?

_____

_____

_____

**5** How do you think the graph might look like between weeks 10 and 20?

_____

_____

_____

_____

**Squeaks our hamster**

grams / weeks

**INFORMATION TECHNOLOGY**

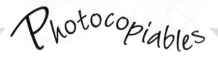

**Whatever the weather, see page 76**

# What kind of weather?

Name _____        Date _____

▲ Describe what the weather is doing from these weather readings.
Cloud cover is measured in octas (eighths of sky covered).

| ◯ | |
|---|---|
| October 23rd | |
| Wind speed on Beaufort scale | 5 |
| Wind direction | SW |
| Cloud cover | 7/8 |
| Minimum temp | 4°C |
| Maximum temp | 10°C |
| Noon temp | 8°C |
| Rainfall | 1mm |

| ◯ | |
|---|---|
| July 3rd | |
| Wind speed on Beaufort scale | 1 |
| Wind direction | S |
| Cloud cover | 0/8 |
| Minimum temp | 12°C |
| Maximum temp | 25°C |
| Noon temp | 23°C |
| Rainfall | 0mm |

| ◯ | |
|---|---|
| June 4th | |
| Wind speed on Beaufort scale | 6 |
| Wind direction | W |
| Cloud cover | 8/8 |
| Minimum temp | 10°C |
| Maximum temp | 14°C |
| Noon temp | 12°C |
| Rainfall | 12mm |

| ◯ | |
|---|---|
| January 3rd | |
| Wind speed on Beaufort scale | 0 |
| Wind direction | |
| Cloud cover | 0/8 |
| Minimum temp | −5°C |
| Maximum temp | 0°C |
| Noon temp | 0°C |
| Rainfall | 0mm |

| ◯ | |
|---|---|
| April 15th | |
| Wind speed on Beaufort scale | 3 |
| Wind direction | W |
| Cloud cover | 4/8 |
| Minimum temp | 7°C |
| Maximum temp | 10°C |
| Noon temp | 8°C |
| Rainfall | 14mm |

| ◯ | |
|---|---|
| March 24th | |
| Wind speed on Beaufort scale | 6 |
| Wind direction | SE |
| Cloud cover | 6/8 |
| Minimum temp | 7°C |
| Maximum temp | 13°C |
| Noon temp | 12°C |
| Rainfall | 0mm |

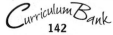

**INFORMATION TECHNOLOGY**

**Finding the facts, see page 78**

# Spreadsheet challenge

Name _____   Date _____

Can you sort out your ANDs from your ORs?

|   | A | B | C | D | E |
|---|------|-------|-------|--------|----------|
| 1 | Name | Eyes | Hair | Pets | Boy/girl |
| 2 | Tom | Blue | Brown | Cat | Boy |
| 3 | Ann | Brown | Brown | Dog | Girl |
| 4 | Susan | Brown | Black | Dog | Girl |
| 5 | Jo | Brown | Black | Fish | Boy |
| 6 | Peter | Blue | Black | Canary | Boy |

▲ Using the data in the spreadsheet, answer the following questions:

**1** Who has blue eyes? _____

**2** Who has blue eyes and a cat? _____

**3** Who has brown eyes? _____

**4** Who has brown eyes or a cat? _____

**5** Who has brown hair or a canary? _____

**6** Is there a girl who has a dog and blue eyes? _____

**7** Is there a boy who has a fish and blue eyes? _____

**8** Who has brown eyes or brown hair? _____

**9** Who has brown eyes and brown hair? _____

**10** Which boys have black hair or blue eyes? _____

_____

**INFORMATION TECHNOLOGY**

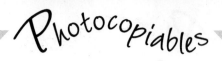

**Looking at spreadsheets, see page 82**

## Spreadsheet challenge

Name _____     Date _____

▲ Look at this spreadsheet example and answer the questions below.

|   | A | B | C | D |
|---|---|---|---|---|
| 1 | pupil | height (cm) | weight (kg) | reach (cm) |
| 2 | Tom | 123 | 34 | 120 |
| 3 | Helen | 137 | 39 | 139 |
| 4 | Sarah | 134 | 32 | 132 |
| 5 | Thomas | 136 | 38 | 135 |
| 6 | Lizzie | 122 | 28 | 122 |
| 7 | Jo | 124 | 29 | 120 |
| 8 | Eleanor | 130 | 35 | 132 |

**1** Can you find the total of the height column – what is the sum of the height column?

_____

**2** What is the average height of the children? _____

**3** How much taller are Helen and Sarah together compared with Tom and Lizzie together?

_____

**4** What is the average reach of the children? Is this similar to their average height?

_____

**5** What is the total weight of the children?_____

**6** What is the average weight of the children?_____

**7** Who is less than the average weight?_____

**8** Who is above the average weight?_____

**9** Who is above the average height?_____

**10** Who is below the average height?_____

**What are we eating? see page 85**

# Eating our breakfast

Name _____ Date _____

▲ Look at the spreadsheet below. It shows the nutritional values of a range of different breakfast cereals.

| | A | B | C | D | E | F | G | H |
|---|---|---|---|---|---|---|---|---|
| **1** | Cereal | Energy (kJ) | Protein (g) | Carbohydrate (g) | Fat (g) | Sodium (g) | Fibre (g) | Cost per 100g (p) |
| **2** | Brantime | 1150 | 15.0 | 45.0 | 3.0 | 1.00 | 24.0 | 16 |
| **3** | Teamsters | 1300 | 9.2 | 65.5 | 2.6 | 0.60 | 17.5 | 20 |
| **4** | Oaties | 1460 | 12.0 | 60.0 | 8.0 | | 14.0 | 8 |
| **5** | Freddies | 1410 | 9.8 | 72.8 | 2.1 | | 10.5 | 17 |
| **6** | Vitalise | 1456 | 9.2 | 72.3 | 2.4 | | 10.5 | 25 |
| **7** | Wheaties | 1510 | 10.5 | 69.8 | 2.7 | 0.30 | 9.4 | 21 |
| **8** | Raisin Bix | 1450 | 9.0 | 71.0 | 2.0 | 0.01 | 9.0 | 28 |
| **9** | Muesli | 1537 | 12.0 | 65.6 | 5.0 | | 8.4 | 18 |
| **10** | Toppers | 1506 | 9.0 | 74.0 | 2.0 | 0.01 | 8.0 | 26 |
| **11** | Sugared Clouds | 1554 | 6.0 | 88.0 | 1.2 | 9.00 | 7.0 | 26 |
| **12** | Starter | 1550 | 8.0 | 77.0 | 2.0 | 0.50 | 6.0 | 29 |
| **13** | Wheeties | 1615 | 6.1 | 78.4 | 4.0 | 0.30 | 6.0 | 23 |
| **14** | Porridge | 1014 | 8.2 | 43.6 | 5.4 | | 3.8 | 7 |
| **15** | Frosted Flakes | 1650 | 5.0 | 89.0 | 0.4 | 0.80 | 2.2 | 23 |
| **16** | Corn Twists | 1600 | 6.4 | 82.2 | 1.4 | 0.80 | 2.2 | 17 |
| **17** | Malted Slims | 1600 | 15.0 | 76.0 | 1.0 | 1.00 | 2.0 | 29 |
| **18** | Cocoa Chips | 1600 | 5.0 | 87.0 | 1.0 | 0.80 | 1.0 | 31 |
| **19** | Sugary Rice | 1650 | 4.0 | 90.0 | 0.5 | 0.80 | 0.4 | 31 |

▲ Now answer these questions on the back of this sheet:

**1** Which cereal contains the most fibre? How much fibre per 100g?
**2** Which cereal contains the least fibre and how much is it per 100g?
**3** Which is the most expensive cereal?
**4** Which is the cheapest cereal?
**5** Which cereal give you the most energy? How much energy is that?
**6** Which cereal gives you the least energy?
**7** Which is the fattiest cereal?
**8** Can you spot any connection between energy and carbohydrate?

*CurriculumBank*
145

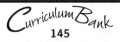

**INFORMATION TECHNOLOGY**

**Business plans, see page 87**

# Chris Chrome's Car Wash

Name _____  Date _____

This spreadsheet shows a month's business figures for a small company.

▲ Enter the data into a computer spreadsheet. Your teacher can help you with this.

|  | A | B | C | D | E |
|---|---|---|---|---|---|
| 1 | Chris Chrome's Car Wash | | | | |
| 2 |  | Week 1 | Week 2 | Week 3 | Week 4 |
| 3 | Cost per wash (£) | 5 | 5 | 10 | 10 |
| 4 | No. of cars | 12 | 24 | 34 | 27 |
| 5 | Total income (£) | 60 | 120 | 340 | 270 |
| 6 | Equipment (£) | 5 | 10 | 20 | 5 |
| 7 | Advertising (£) | 10 | 5 | 10 | 5 |
| 8 | Rent (£) | 10 | 10 | 10 | 10 |
| 9 | Wages (£) | 0 | 0 | 50 | 50 |
| 10 | Total outgoings (£) | 25 | 25 | 90 | 70 |
| 11 | Profit/week (£) | 35 | 95 | 250 | 200 |
| 12 | Profit carried fd. (£) | 35 | 130 | 380 | 580 |

▲ Now answer the questions by using the appropriate formulas in the computer spreadsheet. Use the back of this sheet for your answers.

1 What is the profit after the first week?
2 Why hasn't Chris Chrome paid himself for the first two weeks?
3 How much in wages could Chris have paid himself for the last two weeks?
4 Why has expenditure on equipment gone from £20 to £5 from week 3 to week 4?
5 How might Chris get more cars through his car wash?
6 Is Chris's business succeeding?
7 What is the increase in profit if you double the charge per car?
8 If you can only clean 20 cars per day how can you maximise your profits?
9 If it rains for a whole week and your takings are zero, how does this affect the profits at the end of the month?
10 The rent doubles after two weeks, how does this affect your profit?

**Squares all over, see page 90**

# Practice at procedures

Name _____     Date _____

Procedures consist of a series of steps or instructions that we need to carry out to achieve a certain result. Below are some examples of procedures.

---

### Tea time
▲ Complete this list of instructions to make a cup of tea:

**1** Put water in the kettle.
**2** Heat the water by lighting the gas or switching on the electricity.

**3** _____

**4** _____

**5** _____

---

### Safe crossing!
▲ Complete these instructions for crossing the road:

**1** Stand at the kerb.
**2** Look left.

**3** _____

**4** _____

**5** _____

**6** _____

---

### Square it up!
▲ Now write a list of instructions to draw a square on the computer using Logo software. Use the following letters to list the commands:

    F = forwards, B = backwards,
    R = right, L = left.

▲ Remember to add the distance in cms and the angles in degrees.

**1** _____

**2** _____

**3** _____

**4** _____

What name could you give to this procedure?

_____

---

### Create a procedure
▲ Now create another procedure in Logo, perhaps to draw a different shape, for example. Write the procedure in the space below, listing the necessary commands you would use, and draw or attach a small printout of the result this would produce.

---

**INFORMATION TECHNOLOGY**

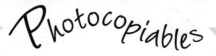

Party time, see page 92

# What would you like to eat?

Name _____     Date _____

▲ Enter what you would like to eat at a class party onto the sheet below. Some examples are already shown. Write the price (if you know it), or an estimate, in the second column.

|  | A | B | C | D |
|---|---|---|---|---|
| 1 | Food | Cost per unit (p) | No. required | Sub total |
| 2 | Crisps | | | |
| 3 | Peanuts | | | |
| 4 | Biscuits | | | |
| 5 | Oranges | | | |
| 6 | Fizzy drink | | | |
| 7 | | | | |
| 8 | | | | |
| 9 | | | | |
| 10 | | | | |
| 11 | | | | |
| 12 | | | | |
| 13 | Total | | | |

▲ Using your completed spreadsheet, write the answers to the following questions on the back of this sheet:

1 What is there in cell A3?
2 What does the number in cell B2 mean?
3 How many oranges are required for the party?
4 How much is one packet of peanuts?
5 How much will all the peanuts cost?
6 What is the subtotal of the fizzy drinks?
7 What subtotal is the greatest?
8 Could you work out the grand total?

# Off and on

Making a single bulb flash on/off at regular intervals, the control sequence may be typically:

> OUTPUT1 ON
> WAIT 10
> OUTPUT1 OFF
> WAIT 10
> OUTPUT1 ON
> WAIT 10
> OUTPUT1 OFF
> WAIT 10
> OUTPUT1 ON
> WAIT 10
> OUTPUT1 OFF
>
> Or use a repeat command,
>
> REPEAT 20
> OUTPUT1 ON
> WAIT 10
> OUTPUT1 OFF
> WAIT10
> END

▲ Try making the bulb flash SOS in Morse code (short, short, short, long, long, long, short, short, short):

> A short flash would be obtained by entering this sequence,
>
> OUTPUT1 ON
> WAIT 50
> OUTPUTOFF1
>
> A long flash would be obtained by entering,
>
> OUTPUTON1
> WAIT 100
> OUTPUTOFF1

Putting these together with an appropriate pause between each flash (WAIT 50 for example) would produce the intended code message.

▲ Try connecting a buzzer to output 1 and making it sound like the rhythm made by a ringing telephone. You might like to try programming the buzzer to sound out SOS. The sequence would be the same as that for the light flashes.

**INFORMATION TECHNOLOGY**

Photocopiables

**Traffic lights, see page 96**

# Stop or go?

Name _____    Date _____

▲ Sit with a friend and write out the sequence for a set of traffic lights, starting with the red light. You may like to speed them up and have the sequence quite short, all within a minute. The sequence has been started for you:

Red on
Wait for 10 seconds
Amber on for 2 seconds . . .

INFORMATION
TECHNOLOGY

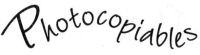
# Switch it on!

Name _____    Date _____

For this computer activity, you will need to connect six bulbs to outputs 1–6 on a control box. You will also need to attach a switch to input 1.

▲ Start by building the running lights procedure below:

```
TO RUNNING
REPEAT 20
SWITCHON 1
WAIT 10
SWITCHON 2
WAIT 10
SWITCHON 3
WAIT 10
SWITCHON 4
WAIT 10
SWITCHON 5
WAIT 10
SWITCHON 6
WAIT 10
SWITCHOFF 1
WAIT 10
SWITCHOFF 2
WAIT 10
SWITCHOFF 3
WAIT 10
SWITCHOFF 4
WAIT 10
SWITCHOFF 5
WAIT 10
SWITCHOFF 6
WAIT 10
END
```

▲ Save this procedure as 'RUNNING'.

▲ Test out this procedure through the control box to see what sequence of lights it produces. You may need to ask your teacher's help to activate the sequence.

▲ Attach a switch to input 1 and write a procedure to that will trigger the RUNNING procedure when the switch is on.

▲ Now write your own procedure to trigger a sequence that uses six or eight lights but switches them on and off in a different 'running' way.

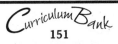

**Jewel security, see page 101**

# Stop those burglars!

Name _____     Date _____

▲ You are responsible for guarding the Crown Jewels. They are on display in the room illustrated below. Note that there are two windows, two doors and a skylight to protect. The jewels are inside the wood and glass cabinet in the centre. Design an alarm system to protect them from being stolen. You may use any kind of switches as alarm triggers, but not infra-red beams!

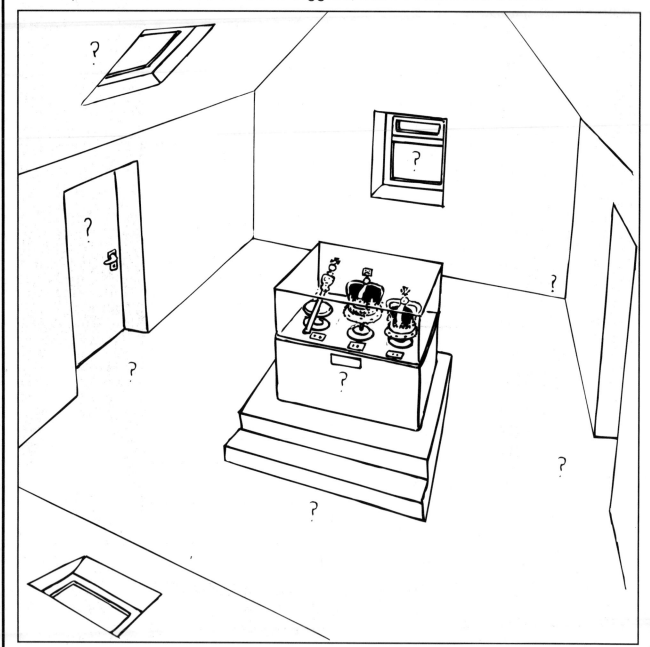

▲ Use the back of this sheet to write down which of the positions labelled **?** may be suitable for an intruder detector and describe what kind of detector would be most appropriate.

**INFORMATION TECHNOLOGY**

Hot spots, see page 103

# How hot?

Name _____ Date _____

Can you find out what temperature each of these are by looking them up in reference books or CD-ROMs? Use degrees Celsius (°C) or Fahrenheit (°F), but remember to show which scale you are using.

| | Temperature |
|---|---|
| The human body (blood temperature) | |
| Boiling water | |
| Ice | |
| Melted 'glue gun' glue | |
| The surface of the sun | |
| The North Pole | |
| Melting lead | |
| Comfortable swimming pool | |
| Outer space | |
| The lowest temperature possible | |
| Molten candle wax | |
| Daytime on the moon | |
| Night-time on the moon | |

**INFORMATION TECHNOLOGY**

24 hours in class, see page 105

# Classroom monitors

Name _____     Date _____

These graphs show some data for temperature, light and sound recorded in a classroom over a 24-hour period.

▲ Can you explain why the graphs look this way?

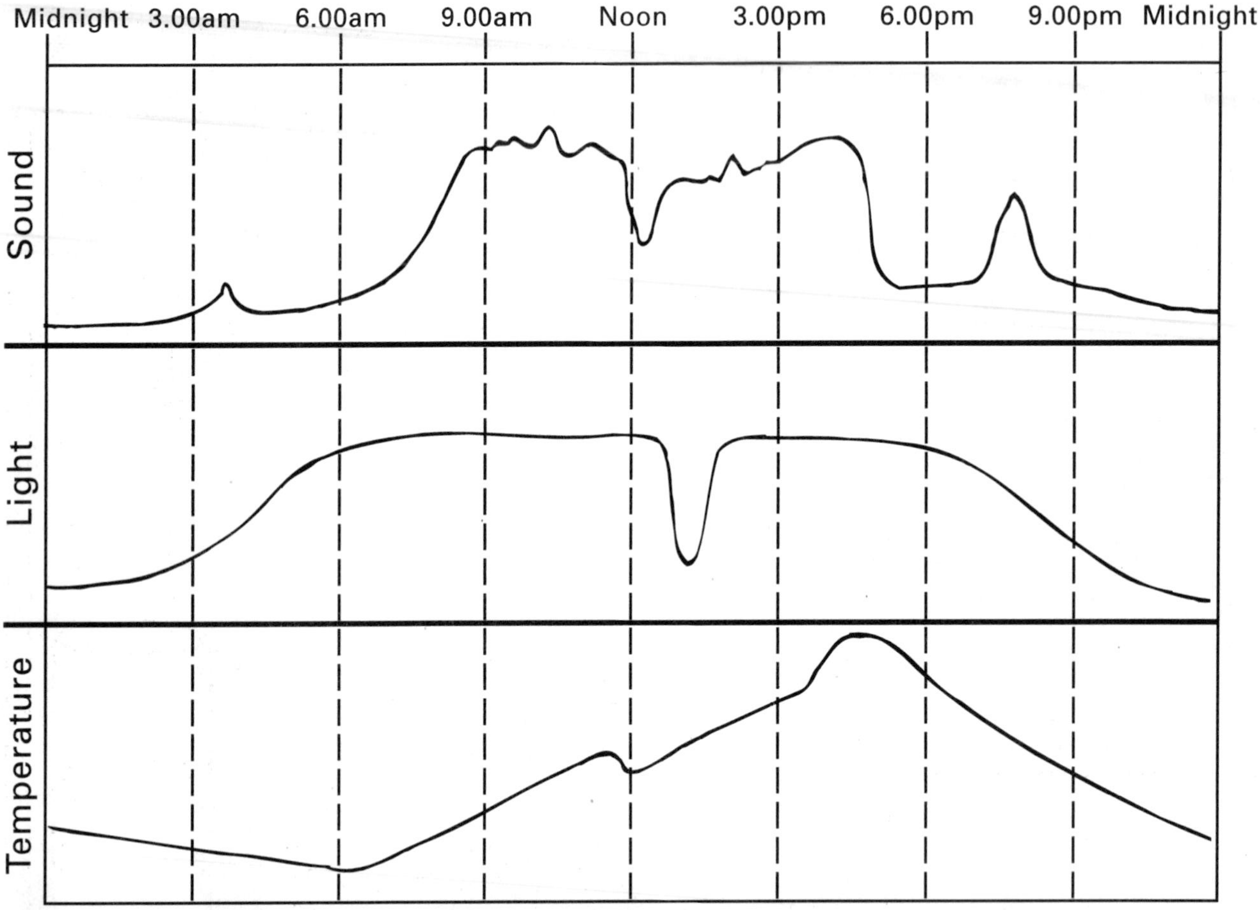

Midnight   3.00am      6.00am      9.00am      Noon      3.00pm      6.00pm      9.00pm   Midnight

Sound

Light

Temperature

INFORMATION
TECHNOLOGY

Hamster watch, see page 107

## What's going on?

Name _____     Date _____

You need to find out what activities the hamster does in this cage overnight, such as sleeping, eating, moving around and so on, and how long it spends doing these things.

▲ Decide which activities you are going to monitor through using IT. You may use as many sensors as you wish. Show where they would be placed in the cage and what information you would obtain from them.

**Logo bookmark, see page 116**

## Logo patterns

Name _____     Date _____

▲ Can you list the Logo commands that would produce the patterns below?

▲ Now draw in your own pattern and write the commands, on the back of this sheet, to produce this.

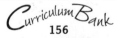
**INFORMATION
TECHNOLOGY**

# Polygons

Name _____    Date _____

▲ Think about how you could draw the polygons below using Logo.
Could you use the 'REPEAT' command to do this?
Could you write the sequence to draw tessellated shapes?

| Polygon | No. of sides | External angle |
|---|---|---|
| Equilateral triangle | 3 | 120 |
| Square | 4 | 90 |
| Pentagon | 5 | 72 |
| Hexagon | 6 | 60 |
| Heptagon | 7 | 51.4 |
| Octagon | 8 | 45 |
| Nonagon | 9 | 40 |
| Decagon | 10 | 36 |
| Undecagon | 11 | 32.7 |
| Duodecagon | 12 | 30 |

▲ Choose three shapes from the chart above. For each of your chosen shapes:

1 Write out the Logo sequence that would produce each of your shapes (without using a REPEAT command).

2 Now rewrite the sequence using a REPEAT command.

Can you write the Logo sequence that will join two (or three) of your chosen shapes together like this?

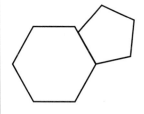

INFORMATION
TECHNOLOGY

# Software

| ACTIVITY | EXAMPLES OF SUITABLE SOFTWARE | |
|---|---|---|
| **CHAPTER 1** | **PC** | **ACORN** |
| Add an adjective | *Talking First Word, Creative Writer, ClickerPlus, Textease, PenDown for Windows, Talking Word for Windows, Talking Write Away* | *Clicker Plus, PenDown/Talking, PenDown, Textease, Phases, TalkWrite* |
| Spot the mistakes! | As for 'Add an adjective' | As for 'Add an adjective' |
| Editing challenge | As for 'Add an adjective' | As for 'Add an adjective' |
| Acrostics | As for 'Add an adjective' | As for 'Add an adjective' |
| Shape poems | As for 'Add an adjective' | As for 'Add an adjective' |
| Dear Sir or Madam | As for 'Add an adjective' | As for 'Add an adjective' |
| My version | As for 'Add an adjective' | As for 'Add an adjective' |
| Making data collection sheets | *Textease, PenDown for Windows, Talking Write Away, Pages* | *Pages, PenDown DTP, PenDown, Junior Impression, Impression Style, Textease* |
| In the news | *Textease, PenDown for Windows, Talking Write Away, Pages, Talking First Word, Create Writer, ClickerPlus* | *Pages, PenDown DTP, PenDown, Junior Impression, Impression Style, Textease, Phases* |
| Pen portraits | As for 'In the news' | As for 'In the news' |
| Our school | *Textease, PenDown for Windows, Talking Write Away, Pages, Word for Windows* | As for 'Add an adjective' |
| Designing a poster | *Textease, Word for Windows, Pages, First Word for Windows* | *PenDown DTP, Junior Impression, Pages, Ovation, Textease* |
| Designing a cover | As for 'Designing a poster' | As for 'Designing a poster' |
| Famous people | *Textease, Word for Windows, Pages, Illuminatus, Multimedia Workshop, Hyperstudio* | *PenDown DTP, Junior Impression, Pages, Ovation, Textease, Multimedia Showcase* |
| The class newspaper | *First Word for Windows, Pages, Talking First Word, Creative Writer, Clicker Plus, Textease, PenDown for Windows, Talking Word for Windows, Talking Write Away* | *PenDown DTP, Junior Impression, Impression Style, Pages, Ovation, Textease, Multimedia Showcase* |
| Four-colour exercise | *Dazzle!, KidPix Studio, PaintSpa Plus, Colour Magic* | *Splosh!, Dazzle!, KidPix, 1ST Paint, Revelation 2* |
| Kandinsky prints | As for 'Four-colour exercise' | *Splosh+, Dazzle!, KidPix, 1ST Paint, Revelation 2* |
| Mood pictures | As for 'Four-colour exercise' | As for 'Kandinsky prints' |
| Monocolour pictures | As for 'Four-colour exercise' | As for 'Kandinsky prints' |
| Design a tag | As for 'Four-colour exercise' | As for 'Kandinsky prints' |
| Impressionist style | As for 'Four-colour exercise' | As for 'Kandinsky prints' |
| Picture the rules | As for 'Four-colour exercise' | As for 'Kandinsky prints' |
| Sweet wrappers | As for 'Four-colour exercise' | As for 'Kandinsky prints' |
| Fashion show | *KidPix Studio, PaintSpa Plus, Colour Magic* | *KidPix, 1ST Paint, Revelation 2* |
| Repeat patterns | *KidPix Studio, Colour Magic* | *KidPix, Revelation 2* |
| Scan a leaf | *KidPix Studio, Picture It!* | *1ST Paint, Revelation 2, Revelation Pro, Big Picture* |
| Growing old gracefully | As for 'Scan a leaf' | *Revelation 2, Revelation Pro, Big Picture* |
| Musical illustration | *Junior Compose* | *Compose World* |
| Let's dance! | *Junior Compose, Music Box, Music Explorer* | *Compose World* |
| Recognise this one? | *Music Explorer* | *Junior Sibelius, Notate* |
| Multimedia music | *Music Explorer* | As for 'Recognise this one?' |

# Software

| ACTIVITY | EXAMPLES OF SUITABLE SOFTWARE | |
|---|---|---|
| **CHAPTER 2** | **PC** | **ACORN** |
| Looking at us | Data Graph, DataPower 2, Information Workshop, Starting Graph, Data Sweet PC | Data Graph, DataPower 2, Data Sweet 2/3, Junior Surveys, Ourselves, Junior Database |
| Watching it grow | Data Sweet PC, Junior Pinpoint, Find It! | Data Sweet 2/3, Graph IT, Junior Pinpoint, Find It!, Junior Database |
| Traffic patterns | Data Sweet PC, Junior Pinpoint, Survey, Data Graph | Data Sweet 2/3, Graph IT, Junior Pinpoint, Junior Database, Data Graph |
| What's on the menu? | Junior Pinpoint, Data Power 2, Survey | Junior Pinpoint, Data Power 2, Junior Surveys |
| Book reviews | Data Sweet PC, Survey | Data Sweet, Junior Surveys |
| Whatever the weather | Weather Watch, Data Power 2, Data Graph, Junior Pinpoint, Sheetwise, Data Sweet PC | Weather Watch, Junior Database, Data Power 2, Data Graph, Data Frame, Junior Pinpoint, Data Sheet 2, Sheetwise, Data Sweet PC |
| Finding the facts | First Workshop, Data Sweet PC, Data Graph, Junior Pinpoint | Junior Database, Data Sweet 2/3, Data Power 2, Data Graph, Junior Pinpoint |
| CD-ROM search | Oxford Children's Encyclopedia, Infopedia, Kingfisher Micropedia, Encarta | Oxford Children's Encyclopedia, Infopedia, Kingfisher Micropedia, Encarta |
| Looking at spreadsheets | Sheetwise, Data Sweet PC, Starting Grid | Data Sweet 2/3, Data Frame, Bearsheet 2, Spreadsheet, Sheetwise, Data Sheet 2 |
| What are we eating? | Sheetwise, Data Sweet PC, Starting Grid, Number Box, The Cruncher | As for 'Looking at spreadsheets' |
| Business plans | As for 'What are we eating?' | As for 'Looking at spreadsheets' |
| **CHAPTER 3** | **PC** | **ACORN** |
| Squares all over | Super Logo – Windows, Start Logo, First Logo | Go Go!, WinLogo, First Logo |
| Party time | Number Box, Data Sweet PC, Sheetwise, The Cruncher | Data Frame, Data Sheet 2, Sheetwise |
| ON/OFF – Controlling outputs | Simple Control, SenSci, CoCo for Windows, Roamer control box | Contract Control, SenSci, CoCo Plus, Roamer control box |
| Traffic lights | As for 'ON/OFF – Controlling outputs' | As for 'ON/OFF – Controlling outputs' |
| Press me and watch! | As for 'ON/OFF – Controlling outputs' | As for 'ON/OFF – Controlling outputs' |
| Jewel security | SenSci, Roamer control box | SenSci, Roamer control box, Contact |
| Hot spots | Smart Box, Logicator, Detector/Excel, Junior Insight, The Discovery Primary Pack | SenSci, Contact, The Discovery Primary Pack |
| 24 hours in class | Junior Insight, The Discovery Primary Pack | SenSci, The Discovery Primary Pack |
| Hamster watch | As for '24 hours in class' | As for '24 hours in class' |
| Letters and numbers | Screen Turtle, WinLogo, SuperLogo – Windows, Start Logo, First Logo | Screen Turtle, WinLogo, Go Go!, First Logo, Tiny Logo |
| Through the maze | As for 'Letters and numbers' | As for 'Letters and numbers' |
| Logo bookmark | Screen Turtle, WinLogo, Go Go!, First Logo, Tiny Logo | As for 'Letters and numbers' |
| Geometric shapes | As for 'LOGO bookmark' | As for 'Letters and numbers' |

INFORMATION TECHNOLOGY

## SOFTWARE RESOURCES

This page lists the sources of the software programs referred to in this book.

**1stPaint**, Resource, Exeter Road, off Coventry Grove, Doncaster DN2 4PY.

**Bearsheet 2 Spreadsheet**, Eric, Papabera, Findon Road, Findon, West Sussex BN14 0RD.

**Big Picture**, Logotron, 124 Cambridge Science Park, Milton Road, Cambridge CB4 4ZS.

**Clicker Plus**, Crick Software Ltd, The Avenue, Spinney Hill, Northampton NN3 6BA.

**CoCo for Windows Commotion**, Unit 11, Tannery Road, Tonbridge, Kent TN9 1RF.

**CoCo Plus**, Commotion, as above.

**Colour Magic**, Research Machines plc, New Mill House, 183 Milton Park, Abingdon, Oxfordshire OX14 4SE.

*Complete Animator,* Iota, Wellington Court, Cambridge CB1 1HZ.

**Compose World**, ESP, A2 Dominion Way, Rustington, West Sussex BN16 3HQ.

**Contact**, Data Harvest, Woburn Lodge, Waterloo Road, Linslade, Leighton Buzzard, Bedfordshire LU2 7NR.

**Creative Writer**, Microsoft, Microsoft Campus, Thames Valley Park, Reading RG6 1WJ.

**Data Graph**, Topologica, Islington Wharf, Penryn, Cornwall TR10 8AT.

**Data Sweet PC**, Kudlian Soft, 8a Nunhold Business Centre, Dark Lane, Hatton, Warwickshire CV35 8XB.

**DataPower 2**, Iota, as above.

**Datasheet 11**, Kudlian Soft, as above.

**DataSweet 3**, Kudlian Soft, as above.

**Dazzle!** SEMERC, 1 Broadbent Road, Watersheddings, Oldham OL1 4LB.

**Detector/Excel**, Research Machines plc, as above.

**Encarta**, Microsoft, as above.

**Find it!** Appian Way, Old Co-operative Buildings, Langley Park, Durham DH7 9XE.

**First Logo**, Logotron, as above.

**Full Phase**, SEMERC, as above.

**Graph IT**, Sherston, Angel House, Sherston, Malmsbury, Wiltshire SN16 0LH.

**Impression Style**, Computer Concepts, Gaddesten Place, Hemel Hemstead, Hertfordshire HP2 6EX.

**Infopedia**, Learning Company, Soft Key, Heritage House, 21 Inner Park Road, Wimbledon SW19 6ED.

**Information Workshops**, Research Machines plc, as above.

**Junior Compose**, ESP, as above.

**Junior Database**, Iota, as above.

**Junior Impression**, Computer Concepts, as above.

**Junior Insight**, Logotron, as above.

**Junior Sibelius**, Sibelius, 75 Burleigh Street, Cambridge CB1 1DJ.

**Junior Surveys**, Soft Teach, Sturgess Farmhouse, Long Bridge, Deverill, Warminster, Wiltshire BA12 9YB.

**Kidpix**, Broderbund, Allen House, Station Road, Egham, Surrey TW20 9NT.

**Kidpix Studio**, Broderbund, as above.

**Kingfisher Micropedia**, ESM, Duke Street, Wisbech, Cambridgeshire PE13 2AE.

**Logicator**, Economatics, Epic House, Darnall Road, Attercliffe, Sheffield S9 5AA.

**Multimedia Showcase**, CSH (Cambridge Software House), PO Box 163, Huntingdon, Cambridgeshire PE17 3UR.

**Music Box**, Topologica, as above.

**Music Explorer**, Research Machines plc, as above.

**Notate**, Logotron, as above.

**Number Box**, Black Cat, Lion House, Bethel Square, Brecon LD3 7JP.

**Ourselves**, ESM, as above.

**Ovation**, Beebug, 117 Hatfield Road, St Albans, Hertfordshire AL1 4JS.

**Oxford Children's Encyclopedia**, OUP, Great Clarendon Street, Oxford OX2 5DP.

**Pages**, SEMERC, as above.

**PaintSpa Plus**, SPA, PO Box 59, New House, Longdon, Tewkesbury, Gloucestershire GL20 6AB.

**Pendown**, Logotron, as above.

**Pendown DTP**, Logotron, as above.

**Pendown for Windows**, AVP Computing, School Hill Centre, Chepstow, Monmouthshire NP6 5PH.

**Pictogram**, Kudlian Soft, as above.

**Picture It!**, Microsoft, as above.

**Picturepoint**, Logotron, as above.

**Revelation Pro**, Logotron, as above.

**Revelation 2**, Logotron, as above.

**Roamer Control Box**, Valiant, 3 Grange Mills, Weir Road, London SW12 0NE.

**Roamer World**, Research Machines plc, as above.

**Screen Turtle**, Topologica, as above.

**SenSci**, Valiant, as above.

**Sheetwise**, SEMERC, as above.

**Simple Control**, Camboard, PO Box 416, Cambridgeshire CB3 7YS.

**Smart Box**, Economatics, as above.

**Splosh**, Kudlian Soft, as above.

**Start Logo**, Camboard, as above.

**Starting Graph**, Research Machines plc, as above.

**Strating Grid**, Research Machines plc, as above.

**Super Logo Windows**, Logotron, as above.

**Talking First Word**, Research Machines plc, as above.

**Talking Write Away**, Black Cat, as above.

**TalkWrite**, Resource, as above.

**Textease**, Softease Ltd, The Old Courthouse, St Peter's Church Yard, Derby DE1 1NN.

**The Cruncher**, Davidson, Ablac, South Devon House, Newton Abbot, Devon TQ12 2BP.

**The Discovery Primary Pack**, Economatics, as above.

**Tiny Logo**, Topologica, as above.

**Weather Watch**, Soft Teach, as above.

**WinLogo**, Logotron, as above.

**INFORMATION TECHNOLOGY**